DESCENDANTS OF
Daniel and Margaret (Keane) Keane
OF COUNTY CLARE, IRELAND

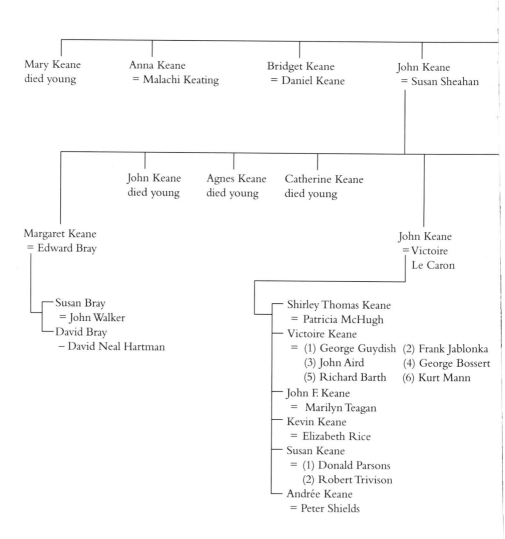

Mary Keane
died young

Anna Keane
= Malachi Keating

Bridget Keane
= Daniel Keane

John Keane
= Susan Sheahan

John Keane
died young

Agnes Keane
died young

Catherine Keane
died young

Margaret Keane
= Edward Bray

John Keane
= Victoire
Le Caron

Susan Bray
= John Walker
David Bray
– David Neal Hartman

Shirley Thomas Keane
= Patricia McHugh
Victoire Keane
= (1) George Guydish (2) Frank Jablonka
(3) John Aird (4) George Bossert
(5) Richard Barth (6) Kurt Mann
John F. Keane
= Marilyn Teagan
Kevin Keane
= Elizabeth Rice
Susan Keane
= (1) Donald Parsons
(2) Robert Trivison
Andrée Keane
= Peter Shields

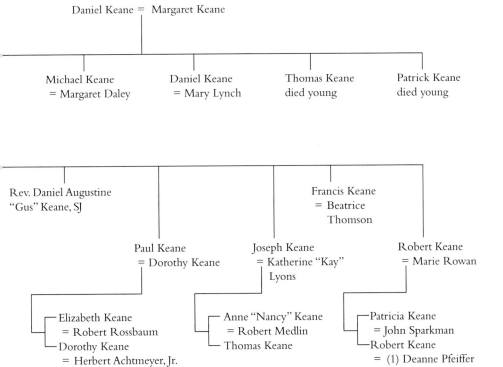

Daniel Keane = Margaret Keane

Michael Keane
= Margaret Daley

Daniel Keane
= Mary Lynch

Thomas Keane
died young

Patrick Keane
died young

Rev. Daniel Augustine
"Gus" Keane, SJ

Paul Keane
= Dorothy Keane

Joseph Keane
= Katherine "Kay"
Lyons

Francis Keane
= Beatrice
Thomson

Robert Keane
= Marie Rowan

Elizabeth Keane
= Robert Rossbaum
Dorothy Keane
= Herbert Achtmeyer, Jr.

Anne "Nancy" Keane
= Robert Medlin
Thomas Keane

Patricia Keane
= John Sparkman
Robert Keane
= (1) Deanne Pfeiffer
(2) Christina Carlo

The Keane
and Sheahan Families
of BRIDGEPORT, CONNECTICUT

The Keane
and Sheahan Families

of BRIDGEPORT, CONNECTICUT

Compiled by
D. JOSHUA TAYLOR

2013

ISBN-13: 978-0-88082-293-0
Library of Congress Control Number: 2012956480
Printed by IBT/Hamilton, Castleton, New York

NEWBURY STREET PRESS
imprint of New England Historic Genealogical Society
Boston, Massachusetts
AmericanAncestors.org

CONTENTS

PREFACE

THE PROCESS OF COMPLETING a genealogical study of a family often begins with a thorough search of key record types. While the content and coverage of records varies greatly from locality to locality, researchers frequently refer to census records, which dutifully enumerate the entire population of a country, and vital records, which note the births, marriages, and deaths of a particular region. These two sources form a considerable foundation for further genealogical research. Newspapers, land records, oral interviews, and other sources continue to supplement and expand our knowledge of a family. Genealogists depend upon the accuracy of documents and their own careful analysis when conducting research.

For those researching families within the United States, federal census records, collected every ten years, are available from 1790 on. Vital records, though not kept at a national level, can offer more detailed information about a family, including names, dates, and locations essential for filling out one's family tree. In addition, many American families can connect their own family to work conducted by other genealogists, and after careful verification and documentation can potentially trace their families to the earliest settlers, to their overseas origins, or even further.

Tracing a family of Irish descent, however, can often be very difficult, owing in part to the commonality of first and last names, but largely to the widespread destruction of records. Many researchers spend years — and even lifetimes — attempting to determine an exact county or parish in Ireland where a family originated.

While the United States is missing only one entire census (1890), nearly all of Ireland's censuses before 1901, with a few small exceptions, are lost. In 1886, civil servants in Dublin destroyed the country's original 1861 and 1871 enumerations for confidentiality reasons. The 1881 and 1891 census records were pulped during World War I in an effort to overcome Ireland's paper shortage. During the Battle of Dublin, which marked the beginning of the Irish War of Independence, the accidental detonation of an explosive device on 19 June 1922 destroyed the Irish

Public Record Office. Its many holdings included the nation's 1821, 1831, 1841, and 1851 census enumerations as well as countless other probate documents, including wills and estate records and a number of Church of Ireland parish registers.

A few census fragments and scraps of these documents did survive the explosion, though the pattern of record destruction created a barrier for many who would later wish to trace their roots in Ireland. The country did not begin a nationwide system of recording birth, marriage, and death records until 1864, by which time countless Irish families had left the country due to the Great Famine. With the late start of civil registration and the history of struggles between Catholic and Protestant Irishmen, researchers are greatly limited in documenting births, marriages, and deaths before 1864. Though church records do exist for a wide variety of areas in Ireland, they are often incomplete and cover only limited time periods.

Despite these circumstances, those tracing Irish families can still have a successful search. Some Irish immigrants to America left their own clues in the records they created in the United States, naming their Irish townland on tombstones or in church and vital records.[1] Other records, such as Griffith's Valuation (1847–1864) — a land valuation that references approximately 1 million residents of Ireland — serve as a substitute for the destroyed census schedules and provide important clues to a family's origin. Court records, directories, newspapers, and other surviving Irish records all offer important resources for tracing Irish families.

In the case of the John Francis Keane family, careful research and analysis of surviving Irish church records and clues left by the clan's first American immigrant have led to the discovery of the family's exact townland and parish of origin. Records clearly document Daniel Keane's departure from Kilcloher, a small townland in County Clare that likely served as the home of the Keane family for many previous generations. As with all genealogical research, there are undoubtedly further records that will be discovered to expand upon what has already been found. Additions, corrections, and other notes will continue to enhance the family history of the Keane family for many future generations.

---

[1] In his book *Richard Griffith and His Valuations of Ireland,* James Reilly gives an excellent definition: "A townland is a small area of land such as a family farm or group of farms. It is the smallest of the administrative divisions. Townlands frequently take their name from physical characteristics of the area, from ruins of churches or forts, and from clan names." (Baltimore: Clearfield Co., 2000), page 73.

ACKNOWLEDGMENTS

DOCUMENTING THE LIFE of an Irish American family is not an easy task, and one that takes many minds and talents. I am grateful to D. Brenton Simons and Thomas R. Wilcox, Jr., of NEHGS, who saw such promise in the initial research conducted on the Keane family that they approached the topic of creating a book documenting the family's story.

NEHGS archivist Judy Lucey's skills as an Irish researcher are nearly impossible to put into words. It was with her guidance that the details regarding the Keane family buried in Griffiths Primary and Revised Valuations were unearthed. Her patience, communication skills, and clear understanding of Irish records were essential to putting together the many pieces of the Keane family in Newtown, Connecticut, and County Clare, Ireland. It was a privilege and an honor to work alongside Judy as we explored the Keane family together.

Other genealogists at the New England Historic Genealogical Society — including Christopher C. Child, Marie Daly, Mary Blauss Edwards, Henry B. Hoff, and Rhonda R. McClure — applied their skills to this project, gathering records and assisting in interpreting records related to the Keane family.

Many others were also instrumental in gathering relevant documentation and providing information, including Angela Craft at the Connecticut Department of Health; Jason B. Harrison of the Family History Library in Salt Lake City; genealogist Harlan Jessup, an expert on the Irish community of Newtown, Connecticut; Richard G. Roberts, who located the records of Susan E. Sheahan at the Connecticut State Library; and Jane Seymour-Ford, Research Librarian at the Perkins School for the Blind.

Maureen Taylor's unmatched interview skills provided tremendous depth to the Keane family's story, and the countless hours she spent talking with members of the family are evident in the detailed transcriptions now preserved at NEHGS and excerpted in this book.

Many members of the Keane family contributed to this volume by completing questionnaires, sending photos and documents, and emailing information about the family. They are acknowledged in the endnotes and in the photo credits; sincere apologies to anyone I have inadvertently failed to mention.

The process of compiling numerous genealogical notes and thoughts into a cohesive manuscript is not an easy task. Members of the Newbury Street Press staff — including Ginevra Morse, Penny Stratton, and Scott C. Steward — brought their expert skills as organizers and editors to the project. In particular, Penny's kind encouragement and incredible skills as an editor are deeply appreciated. Thanks also to a number of freelancers who helped bring the book to fruition: transcriptionist Linda Skinner Austin, copyeditor Shannon Hunt, proofreader Anne Rebecca Starr, layout artist Anne Lenihan Rolland, and indexer Steve Csipke.

Finally, I am grateful to John Francis Keane III (now known as John Keane, Sr.), who allowed me the privilege of researching his ancestors. Mr. Keane's kindness and respect for his past provided the greatest encouragement in tracing the family. There are undoubtedly still many discoveries to make; Mr. Keane has provided this essential starting point for future researchers.

D.J. T.

About the Format of This Book

Beginning in Part III of this book, the reader will encounter a genealogical format that traces ancestry from forebears to the present day.

In this format, the earliest head of each family is given the number 1. Each child is represented by a roman numeral. Sequential arabic numbers are given to each individual who is given his or her own "sketch" within the book. A superscript number refers to the person's generation. For example, the earliest ancestor of the Keane family treated is Daniel Keane, who carries both the number 1 and the generational number 1:

1. **Daniel**[1] **Keane** was born in County Clare, Ireland, about 1832. He died at Sandy Hook in Newtown, Fairfield County, Connecticut, 19 March 1886, and was buried at St. Rose Cemetery in Newtown. He married, likely in County Clare, about 1854, **Margaret Keane**, who was born in County Clare in January 1828, daughter of Michael and Mary (Lynch) Keane. . . .

Each notable family group is treated this way, with a "person number" and a generational number, and all data presented in one or more paragraphs.

Children of that family group are listed in a roman-numeraled list. Any children who will become the subject of their own sketches, and will be treated in more detail, are assigned arabic numbers also. (It is conventional to "carry someone forward" to his or her own sketch only if he or she has children, but we have made some exceptions, such as with Father Gus Keane, who deserved significant and lengthy treatment.)

In the list of Daniel and Margaret's children, you can see that the first child, Mary, carries the generational number. The second child,

Anna, and four others are assigned arabic numbers and will be treated at more length in coverage of the subsequent generation.

Children of Daniel and Margaret (Keane) Keane:

    i.   Mary² Keane, b. Kilcloher April 1855; d. in the U.S. prob. bef. 1870.

2   ii.   Anna "Annie" [Hannah] Keane, b. County Clare Feb. 1857; m. Newtown 18 Oct. 1883 Malachi Keating.

3   iii.   Bridget Keane, b. Ireland Feb. 1860; m. Newtown 25 May 1889 Daniel G. Keane.

4   iv.   John Francis Keane, b. Kilcloher Sept. 1861; m. Red Creek, Wayne County, N.Y., 19 Aug. 1891 Susan Elizabeth Sheahan.

5   v.   Michael Joseph Keane, b. prob. Newtown Jan. 1865; m. New Haven 16 Oct. 1893 Margaret B. Daley.

6   vi.   Daniel P. Keane, b. Newtown 1 Feb. 1867; m. Newtown 25 June 1905 Mary F. Lynch.

    vii.   Thomas Keane, b. Newtown 3 June 1870; d. Newtown 26 Aug. 1870.

    viii.   Patrick Keane, b. Newtown 24 March 1872; d. Newtown 14 Feb. 1876.

In generations after the first, a generational line is given in parentheses after the subject's name. For instance, in the third generation, we see person number 10:

10. John Francis³ Keane, Jr. *(John Francis², Daniel¹)*

This notation indicates the direct line of descent: John Francis is the third generation; his father, also John Francis, is the second; and his grandfather, Daniel, is the first.

The reader will notice several other conventions: Unknown names are denoted by blank lines. Maiden names are inserted within parentheses once a woman is married. The order of information given is always birth, then death, then marriage(s). Although the numbering and conventions may seem confusing at first, the reader will quickly appreciate that they are helpful ways of organizing large quantities of information.

When family names are spelled variously — e.g., Keane/Kean/Kane, Sheahan/Sheehan — we have used the spelling that we have found most prevalent in the records.

PART I

The Keane Family in Ireland

CHAPTER ONE

ON THE COAST OF IRELAND

The Keane Family of Kilcloher,
Kilballyowen Parish, County Clare

AMONG THE MANY markers scattered in St. Rose Cemetery in Sandy
Hook, Connecticut, rests the tombstone of Daniel Keane, progenitor of
the John Francis Keane family of Bridgeport. Inscribed on the stone is
a reference to "Kilclagher," the ancestral homeland of the Keane family.
Kilclagher, or Kilcloher (as it is known in Ireland), is in the southwestern
portion of County Clare's southern peninsula, sitting just a few miles
from the Atlantic Ocean. Situated in the civil parish of Kilballyowen,
the small townland of Kilcloher was home to only twenty-two families
when John Francis Keane, Sr., was born there in 1861. He left in 1863,
when he was just two years old. Owing to the coastal location, many
of the townlands and parishes of County Clare have a strong maritime
connection, though some — like Kilcloher — have been home to
farmers for many generations.

A popular destination for tourists, County Clare is perhaps most
famous for the Cliffs of Moher. In his 1780 publication, *A Short Tour in
the County of Clare,* John Lloyd remarks, "From its agreeable situation,
the climate is remarkably wholesome, the air clear and temperate, and
the prospect pure and delightful."[1] Though the Keane family would
begin their migration to the United States by 1863, they undoubtedly
spent many generations before in Kilcloher and surrounding areas. To
begin an exploration of the Keane family in Ireland, it is fitting to
explore the rich cultural heritage of County Clare and its many parishes.

Before the Norman Conquest in the eleventh century, the area
now known as County Clare was the home of the O'Brien family, who

ruled the territory during the eighth and ninth centuries. After gaining control of the Irish lands in 1171, the Normans named the territory Thomond, granting control to Thomas de Clare. Unable to maintain control of the territory, de Clare succumbed to the O'Briens, who were in turn named the Earls of Thomond and ruled the territory for many generations thereafter. While some traditions suggest that the county is named for Thomas de Clare, others claim that "Clare" was derived from the Irish word *clár*, meaning board or plank. It is said that a plank was placed across the river Fergus outside Ennis (now a major city in County Clare) to allow access to the land. After many years of territorial wars, the area formally joined the Kingdom of Ireland as a county in 1543, but it was not until 1565 that the English administration defined its present boundaries.[2]

Kilballyowen, the Keane family's civil parish, is one of many civil parishes in County Clare and also includes the Keane family's Catholic parish of the same name. Kilballyowen is located in the barony of Moyarta; its many villages include Cross, Kilbaha, Kiltrellig, Ross, and Tullig. Kilballyowen is also the home of Loop Head, a peninsula that derives its name from the story of Cúchullain, chief of the Red Branch Knights of Ulster. According to legend, Cúchullain wanted to leave his mistress, and ran from her in the middle of the night. As she followed, he jumped to the tiny headland (nearly 52 feet) to escape. Thereafter known as Leam Cúchullain in Irish, it was anglicized to Leap Head, which gradually became Loop Head. The area is the site of many ancient ruins, including Cloghansavan Castle in Ross, known as the "Church of the Nine Saints," and a friary. An 1834 count of Protestants and Catholics found just 18 Protestants and 3,950 Catholics. In 1831 (Daniel Keane was likely born in 1832), the parish had a population of 3,695; by 1841, it had increased to 4,346. The rural areas surrounding the parish, including the Keanes' townland of Kilcloher, had just 2,740 people in 1841 and included only 440 houses.[3]

While the patron saint of Kilballyowen has not been identified, the parish is the site of a *tobar*, or holy well, Tobar Senán, which lies in Kilcloher. The well dedicated to St. Senán is still the site of a few devotions or prayers each year. It is probable that the Keane family would have visited this well. Kilcloher is also home to one of the parish's two graveyards, making it a likely burial location for members of the Keane family — though family tombstones have not been located.

Within Kilballyowen Parish, and indeed throughout Ireland, a small number of individuals controlled the rights and ownership to the land. These landlords and agents, many of whom did not live on — or near — the land they owned, collected rent and taxes from their tenants on a frequent basis. At the time of his son John Francis's birth in 1861, Daniel Keane was a tenant on 41 acres of the land of Marcus Keane, a Protestant who owned the entire townland of Kilcloher in the 1850s.[4] Keane was a common surname in County Clare, and there is no evidence that Marcus Keane and Daniel Keane were related.

Conflicts between Protestant and Catholic Followers

The history of County Clare and its parish of Kilballyowen during the seventeenth and eighteenth centuries, and thus the history of the Keane family, was marked by conflicts between Catholic and Protestant settlers. The familial landscape of County Clare was greatly altered by the Irish Rebellion of 1641, during which Ireland's Catholic leaders and other prominent citizens rose against an impending invasion by anti-Catholic forces. In 1642, clergy and other high-ranking citizens formed the Catholic Confederation, which served as a makeshift government for Ireland until their defeat by Oliver Cromwell's forces in the 1650s. In response, many of the lands of County Clare were set aside as the home of "delinquent proprietors" — landowners who did not proactively oppose the rebellion of the Confederacy. County Clare, now with an influx of defeated Catholic rebels, and the rest of Ireland remained part of the United Kingdom.[5]

Distrust of the Catholic clergy continued throughout Ireland. At the close of the seventeenth century, a series of penal codes were enacted that prevented members of the clergy from purchasing land, teaching in schools, or holding office. The Registration Act, passed in 1704, required all Catholic priests to register with the authorities. Only forty-five priests from County Clare registered; the majority refused to comply with what was deemed to be discriminatory legislation. Many of these priests went into hiding, assisted by the Irish peasants in Clare's countryside.

By 1710 every priest save two in County Clare had been declared outlawed, after many refused to sign the Oath of Abjuration (1709), which favored the line of English Protestants over the Catholic Stuarts as heirs to the English throne. Many of County Clare's farmers began to rebel, and violence broke out in 1711. William Butler, who served as Clare High Sheriff, was ordered to arrest all of Clare's Catholic priests. Twenty-four priests gave themselves up, but the rest remained in hiding, despite an intensive search of the forests surrounding the county. By 1728, Catholic priests had been stripped of their voting rights, yet they still fought to carry out their responsibilities to their parishioners in Clare. Eventually the move to eliminate Catholicism was abandoned, and County Clare's Catholic stronghold quickly recovered. The presence of the Protestant churches in County Clare decreased significantly. By 1763, sixty-two of Clare's seventy-six parishes had no Protestant church; most of the other fourteen parishes had only a remote, rather than a residential, rector. It was not until 1828, a hundred years after their voting rights were removed, that the last of the Penal Laws were fully repealed. Even so, religious persecution continued.[6]

County Clare and the Irish Rebellion of 1798

Amid constant religious struggles, political and social conflict also found its way to County Clare and Kilballyowen Parish. The late eighteenth-century revolutions in France and the American colonies created an atmosphere that seemed to promote open rebellion. Even in the seemingly isolated coastal environment of County Clare, the Keane family was undoubtedly affected by the Irish Rebellion of 1798, which saw an attempt to regain parliamentary control and establish a free Irish Republic. Led by the United Irishmen, the unsuccessful movement demonstrated the strength of the Irish people — despite their religious differences — to gather in support of their homeland.

Founded in 1791 by a group of Protestants in Belfast, the United Irishmen also included Catholics, Methodists, Presbyterians, and followers of other denominations in its ranks. It openly called for cooperation between Irishmen of different faiths, with the aim of ending Catholic oppression and gaining autonomy from England. The movement gained strength when the leader of the United Irishmen, Theobald Wolfe Tone, journeyed to France to seek assistance from the newly established French government. With the support of the French secured, the movement looked toward their fellow Irishmen, particularly those in County Clare. It is estimated that by 1797 nearly

200,000 men had joined the resistance movement, including a large number of Catholic farmers (also known as the "Defenders").

In 1797, members of the United Irishmen began traveling through County Clare looking for additional recruits. Owing to its prominent location, County Clare was prime for French invasion. Its accessibility to the River Shannon would make it easy to reach Dublin, the center of Irish government. While the Keane family is not mentioned in the records of the United Irishmen, the military presence in their county would have made them very much aware of the growing rebellion in their homeland. In response to the growing numbers of rebels, the Irish government established the Yeomanry, a voluntary military corps charged with searching for members of the United Irishmen and sympathizers of the cause for Irish autonomy. Headquartered in Ennis and Clarecastle — less than 7 miles from Kilcloher — the Yeomanry exacted punishments of death and expulsion, passing from townland to townland in an attempt to quell the rebellion.

By the first days of January 1799, the western area of County Clare was in open rebellion. Residents began to retaliate against their landlords, many of whom were withholding more and more precious resources from their tenants. As cattle, property, and other goods were damaged, landlords began to offer large rewards for information leading to the capture of the rebels. Members of the United Irishmen attacked the homes of landlords and stole military supplies from the Yeomanry. Tenants, especially women and children, were sent to Ennis, whose town square had been converted into military barracks.

On Saturday, January 12, an estimated 4,000 rebels paraded through the nearby town of Ennistymon, armed with French muskets. By the following morning, rumors that the army was nearby caused many to prepare themselves for conflict — yet they dispersed when the army did not materialize by the afternoon. By that evening, members of the army stationed at Ennis had arrived in Ennistymon, bringing an immediate end to the protests in the area. Though County Clare was declared to be "in a state of disturbance" a few days later, by the end of January 1799 the rebellion had weakened. The army implemented curfews and other regulations to regain control of the local population. By the spring of 1799 the majority of County Clare's residents had returned to their normal lives. Many members of the United Irishmen were put on trial; those found guilty were sentenced to transportation to a penal colony or, in some cases, to death.[7]

The Great Famine and
Marcus Keane, the Unpopular Landlord

As if the destruction and unrest from religious and political conflicts were not enough, County Clare's tenant farmers soon found themselves facing an almost unbeatable enemy. With their food supply and economy largely dependent upon the potato crop, the spread of potato blight in the mid-1840s led to one of the greatest disasters in Ireland's history. The resulting Great Famine led to massive poverty and hunger — and unrest — throughout the country.

Under Ireland's traditional landlord and tenant policies, rents, taxes, and other expenses continued to grow — despite the shrinking wages for farmers and tenants. Unrest, poverty, disease, hunger, fever, and rising living costs created a climate wherein millions of Irish left their homeland to seek a new life in the United States, Canada, or Australia. By the mid-1850s, death and migration had reduced the population of Ireland by nearly 25 percent.

The Great Famine deeply affected all of County Clare. The county saw a massive decline in population, with more than 50,000 deaths between 1845 and 1850 alone. Between the mortality rate and emigration, the county's population, which was 286,000 in 1841, dropped to 212,000 in 1851.[8]

In the midst of the famine's devastation, Daniel Keane started his own family, marrying Margaret Keane around 1854, likely in Kilbally-owen. He began renting property from Marcus Keane, a prominent landowner in County Clare, by 1857.[9] Perhaps the only commonality between landowner and tenant was their surname, for the two families had many differences. Marcus Keane's family was Protestant, while Daniel Keane's was Catholic. Marcus Keane was a wealthy landowner who used his lands and money to force his tenants to convert to Protestantism, while Daniel Keane was a tenant farmer who struggled to support his growing family.

Marcus Keane had amassed nearly 5,000 acres of land by 1880, including a large house near Beech Park, which remained in the family into the twentieth century. He is said to have carried out multiple evictions on his estates, leading him to become a very unpopular — and feared — landlord.[10]

Marcus Keane's staunch Protestant beliefs permeated his dealings with his tenants and other residents. In attempts to promote the Protestant faith in the Loop Head area, he built schools that provided food in exchange for allegiance to the Protestant faith. Further, he threatened tenants with eviction if they did not convert to Protestantism.[11]

In the 1850s the celebration of Catholic Mass was prohibited in the area, and in much of Ireland. The Catholic priest in the Loop Head area, Father Michael Meehan, struggled against that prohibition and against Marcus Keane's pro-Protestant efforts. He built schools for Catholic children and he unsuccess

fully tried to find a site for a church. He attempted to construct a canvas shelter for worship, but it wasn't suitable. He then commissioned a local carpenter, Owen Collins, to build a portable box on wheels, which became known as the "Little Ark." Between 1852 and 1856, "ark" was the site of Mass on the shore of Kilbaha. In 1858, the first stone was laid for the church that would eventually be built on the same site and would incorporate the Little Ark.[12] That church still stands today, and the Little Ark is remembered by locals with the following verses:[13]

THE LITTLE ARK

On a stormy shore of our western isle,
Stood a movable home at rest for a while,
It gave hidden light in times that were dark,
And salvation for all dwelt in that little ark.

Not floating serenely, on waters wide,
But on shifting sands from a restless tide,
Loving service was given when danger was high,
For him, for whose sake, they would readily die.

Now happier days have come to Clare's shore,
A memento is kept of those days of yore,
The little ark rests in its rightful place,
In the hallowed ground of the author of grace.

And blessings will come to the people of Clare,
In which all our land will surely share,
What we do for him, we have been told,
It will be repaid one hundredfold.

We do not know where Daniel Keane's family worshipped, but it is possible that — aware of the conflicts between their landlord and the

Catholic clergy — they traveled the few miles to Kilbaha. As Marcus Keane did not own the land rented by Daniel and Margaret Keane until 1857, several years after the famine, he would not have been a specific threat to Daniel and Margaret Keane until then. Even so, Daniel and Margaret would have been aware of widespread efforts to discourage Catholicism. They remained faithful followers of the Catholic Church, however, baptizing their children in the parish of Cross/Carrigaholt. Their daughter Mary, likely the couple's first child, was baptized there on 20 April 1855, sponsored by Martin Keane and Bridget Keane. Another daughter, Hannah (who often appears in U.S. records as Anna) was baptized 24 February 1857, sponsored by Tom Gibson and Bridget Keane. Their first son, John Francis, was baptized there in 1861, sponsored by John and Eliza Keane.[14] (Unfortunately, we do not have sufficient information to determine how the sponsors were related to the family, if at all.)

Religious persecution by Marcus Keane and other landlords was not the only hardship facing Daniel and Margaret Keane and other tenants in County Clare. The extreme conditions resulting from the Great Famine were only made worse by the numerous tenant evictions, many at the hands of Marcus Keane. In fact, County Clare had the highest number of landlord-forced evictions during the Famine (some estimate that evictions included nearly 10 percent of its total population). Among the evictions in County Clare, the largest number took place within Kilrush Poor Law Union, which encompassed Marcus Keane's land.[15] Marcus Keane's reputation for being a "stringent and successful collector of rents" was well known throughout County Clare. One newspaper, the *Limerick Reporter,* noted that he was "unhappy when not exterminating"; in fact, Marcus Keane became known as the Exterminator General of Clare.[16]

Many of County Clare's residents were forced into workhouses in order to survive. Short on food, water, and other supplies, the workhouses provided little comfort to evictees. One worker noted, "I was so maddened by the sights of hunger and misery . . . that I [wanted] to take the gun from behind my door and shoot the first landlord I met."[17] The first public monument in Ireland dedicated to the victims of the famine, specifically the children, is located in Ennistymon, just 15 miles from the birthplace of John Francis Keane. The site marks the mass grave of nearly 20,000 residents of a local workhouse who died during the famine.

It was under these circumstances that, in 1863, Daniel and Margaret Keane and their young children — now including daughter Bridget —

left their home in County Clare for America. Lacking any written letters or diaries stating exactly why the family emigrated, we can only speculate. Certainly it was a time of massive Irish emigration to America, and we do know that many families left for a better life, away from poverty, Famine-engendered disease, and religious persecution. While research has been conducted in various arrival records in major ports, such as Boston and New York, a definitive record of the entire family's arrival into the United States has not been located. It is possible that some members of the family traveled separately from one another.

County Clare Today

Today, Kilcloher and County Clare, like most of Ireland, are still largely rural. The 41 acres occupied by Daniel Keane in the 1850s has not changed much since his family's departure in 1863. The holy well in Kilcloher, dedicated to St. Senán, is still thought to be the source of many miracles, and is referenced in local folklore to the present day. In addition, the symbol of Catholic faith, the "Little Ark," still stands as part of the church where the Keane family likely baptized some of their children.

As a whole, County Clare continued to experience a decline in its population throughout the twentieth century, as its communities struggled to reestablish themselves after the massive migration from the area during and after the Famine. In 1861, just two years before Daniel Keane and his family left the area, County Clare's population was 166,305, down 25 percent from what it had been in 1851. The population had fallen another 11 percent only ten years later in 1871, and by 1901 was listed at just 112,334 — just under 40 percent of the 1841 population of 286,394.[18] The majority of its residents remained farmers, working the land they had known for many generations. Clare's population reached a low of 73,500 in 1966; it was not until the 1970s that the population began to increase.[19] As of 2011, the population was reported as 116,885, slightly higher than its reported population in 1901.[20]

By 1901, the townland of Kilcloher included nineteen families, comprising fewer than 120 individuals. Of the nineteen, nine bore the Keane surname, including the oldest resident of the townland, Bridget Keane, who at the age of 96 was living with her son Michael Keane. Also living in the town was John Keane, aged 86 (born about 1815), with his wife Margaret.[21] Both would have been living there at the same time as Daniel and his family.

The year of the next census, 1911, found the population of Kilcloher reduced, with just eighty-five inhabitants in seventeen families, two fewer than in 1901. Bridget Keane's son Michael, now 76, was still living. The townland's oldest inhabitant was John Keane, now listing his age as 98 and living with his wife, Margaret. Listing his birthplace as County Clare, John could not read or write but was recorded as a member of the Catholic faith. Possibly considered the patriarch of the Keane family in Kilcloher, John was the father of nine children, six of whom were living as of 1911.[22] (The subsequent Irish census, taken in 1926, has not yet been publicly released.)

It is probable that relatives of the Daniel Keane family still reside in Kilcloher, and that they might have access to written and/or oral sources tracing the Keanes on Ireland's west coast. Unfortunately, existing records cannot prove or disprove relationships.

CHAPTER TWO

Tracing the Keane Family in Ireland

Gleanings of the Family's Origins and Ancestry

Origins of the Keane Surname

THE ORIGINS OF the Keane surname in Ireland can be traced to the Clan O'Catháin (anglicized to O'Cahan), which had its origins in the early ninth century near the river Bann, where they lived for many generations. Catháin, the first recognized member of the O'Catháin family, descended from Fergal Mac Mael Duin, King of Tara, who died in 772. Others have claimed that the clan itself can be traced to legendary Irish king Niall of the Nine Hostages through his son Owen (known today as the father of Clan Owen).

At least one branch of the O'Catháin clan played a prominent role in Ulster by the twelfth century, when the family first appears in the *Annals of Ulster*. For the next several centuries the clan was the appointed subclan of the O'Neills, kings of Ulster. The families ruled Ulster until the seventeenth century, when many of Ireland's leaders fled Northern Ireland for England over a nine-year span known as the Flight of the Earls.[23]

Descendants of the O'Catháin clan include Sir Richard Kane (1666–1736), a distinguished soldier in the British army and military writer; Echlin O'Kane of Ulster (1720–1790), a harpist who performed in several European courts; and the prominent scientist Sir Robert John Kane (1809–1890), author of *The Industrial Resources of Ireland* and *Elements of Chemistry*. Other families bearing the Keane surname claim descent from the Thomond O'Cahans or O'Keanes. The Thomond

O'Cahans are likely related, albeit distantly, to the O'Cathāin clan of Ulster, though no complete pedigree of the family is known to have survived. Members of the Thomond O'Keane family fought in the French and Spanish armies during the eighteenth century. Eugene O'Keane, one of fourteen brothers, was killed in action in Italy in 1693.[24]

The O'Cahan clan appeared in western Clare during the thirteenth and fourteenth centuries. The family, which at times wrote its name as MacCahan, is thought by many to have been ancestral of the County Clare families bearing the names O'Keane, Keane, and Kane. Unlike the Ulster-based Clan O'Cathāin, the O'Cahans served as *coarbs* of St. Senān church in western Clare — that is, they served as the keepers and guardians of the church, occupying its lands and overseeing its estate. The last member of the O'Cahan clan to hold the office was Calvagh O'Keane, the son of Siacus O'Keane. Calvagh had openly opposed decisions made by the Crown regarding the church's governance. When he died in 1581, the role of the coarb was discontinued, yet the family retained title to the bell shrine of the church until 1730, when it was passed by marriage to Robert Cahane of Ballyvoe, a descendant of the O'Cathāin clan. Robert Cahane's descendants, including Marcus Keane, kept possession of the church's bell shrine, later making it available for public display and study. Members of the original O'Cahan clan continued to play a prominent role in County Clare: Nicholas O'Cahane served as coroner of County Clare in 1588, and Brian Cahane was noted to be "one of the chief gentry and ablest persons" in Kilrush, County Clare, in 1690.[25]

The Keanes of County Clare

It is difficult to connect the O'Keane and O'Cahane families of the seventeenth century directly to Daniel Keane and his family, as no specific records exist to provide those linkages. Further, according to the Clare Heritage Centre, the Keane surname was "relatively strong" in the county in the nineteenth century; the Centre's Master Index of Baptisms records more than 1,080 families with that name.[26]

Tithe Applotment Books, kept during the 1820s, do provide some clues to Daniel's parentage, however. These books record the tithes paid on all agricultural land in a specific region. The tithe, originally a tenth of the total land production for the year, was paid by all tenants, regardless of their religious denomination, for the maintenance and upkeep of the established church, the (Protestant) Church of Ireland. Information recorded in the Tithe Applotment Books varied from parish to parish, though usually the books provide the name of the tithe payer, the number of acres, and the total amount paid.

The earliest Tithe Applotment Books for Kilballyowen, the civil parish where Daniel Keane and his family lived, date from 1826. In that year, eight Keane families occupied titheable land in the townland of Kilcloher:

John Keane & son	*leasing 35 acres of land*
James Keane	*leasing 11 acres, 30 perches of land*[27]
Thomas Keane	*leasing 11 acres, 3 roods (quarter acres), and 10 perches of land*
Anthony Keane	*leasing 19 acres, 30 perches of land*
Edward Keane & John Magner	*leasing 19 acres, 20 perches of land*
Michael Keane	*leasing 9 acres, 2 roods, and 10 perches of land*
Patrick Keane	*leasing 11 acres, 30 perches of land*
Thomas Keane	*leasing 11 acres, 30 perches of land*

It is possible that one of the men named above was the father or even the grandfather of Daniel Keane, who left Ireland for the United States in 1863. It is Irish custom for a father to name his eldest son after his own father. As Daniel Keane named his eldest son John Francis, it is possible that Daniel's father might have been the John Keane who was renting 35 acres of land. Daniel Keane's wife, Margaret, also bore the surname of Keane. According to the record of her death in Connecticut, her father was Michael Keane — possibly the Michael Keane who was leasing 9 acres, 2 roods, and 10 perches of land.[28]

Kilcloher in Griffith's Valuation

Genealogists rely on censuses, vital records, and church records to help reconstruct the stories of families. As mentioned in the introduction, many of these standard sources are not available to researchers of Irish families. Irish genealogists thus often turn to other records. One key record set is Griffith's Valuation, land-valuation records constructed by Richard Griffith between 1847 and 1864. Used alone, Griffith's is simply a nineteenth-century tax valuation of the land, its occupiers, and their landlords. But the clues found in these records allow family historians to develop research strategies and utilize other records such as church, civil registration, estate, and so on. Used in this way, Griffith's Primary Valuation serves as the gateway to Irish research, helping the genealogist overcome the loss of the records.[29]

Although Griffith's Valuation does not often directly identify any familial relationships, ages, occupations, birthplaces, or other data important for genealogical research, it is helpful because records mention each individual leasing a piece of property, the name of the lessor, and a description of that property. Also, to distinguish between individuals with the same given name, a record sometime appends the name of an individual's father within parentheses; in the case of a widow, the Valuation will often include the name of her deceased husband in parentheses. Known as *agnomens,* these clues can help the family historian develop hypotheses about possible relationships.

The Valuation was created in the spirit of reform, part of an attempt to standardize taxation throughout Ireland that began in the 1820s. Richard Griffith, an English geologist, was appointed Commissioner of Valuation and charged with surveying every household in Ireland. First, however, the whole of Ireland needed to be surveyed geographically in order to provide a guide for Griffith and his team. The team of engineers began their work in 1824 and by 1846 had completed mapping all of Ireland. The Ordnance Survey maps were published in 1846.

The Primary Valuation of Tenements began in 1847 and was completed in 1864. It is organized by county; within each county, it is arranged by Poor Law Union. (A Poor Law Union was a geographic area delineated for administering relief to the poor.) The printing dates of each Poor Law Union began once each area was completed, beginning in 1847 and continuing through 1864. Revisions to the valuations were also issued. The various versions provide key information about people and where they lived—but an in-depth study of the revised valuations of an entire townland demonstrate changes in a community over an extended period, and in some cases they document the departure of an individual or a family from Ireland.[30]

The official printed Valuation of Kilballyowen Parish was printed on 20 August 1855, as part of the Valuation of the Poor Law Union of

Kilrush; see the image of the records for the townland of Kilcloher, on the following page.[31] As can be seen there, the Valuation record includes the following headings:

Reference to Map	*The reference number printed on the Ordnance Survey Map*
Names — Townlands and Occupiers	*The name of the townland; the name(s) of the individual(s) renting or leasing the property (and responsible for payment of rent and taxes)*
Names — Immediate Lessors	*The name of the individual(s) receiving rent from the occupier*
Description of Tenement	*Brief description of the property and its structures (e.g., houses, gardens, offices)*
Acres	*Number of acres as surveyed*
Rateable Annual Valuation — Land	*Taxable value of the land*
Rateable Annual Valuation — Buildings	*Taxable value of the buildings*
Rateable Annual Valuation — Total	*Total taxable value of land and buildings*
Observations	*Notes and other information recorded by the valuator*

Many members of the Kane/Keane families appear on this page, Daniel not among them. The Tenement Valuation of County Clare occurred between 1854 and 1856. At the time it commenced, Daniel Keane was a young man, recently married and starting a family. He most certainly was living in a Kilcloher household but was not yet the person responsible for the payment of rent and taxes.

Daniel does appear in the first revision to the printed Valuation, which was issued in April 1857. He is listed as the occupier of house, offices, and land on lot number 6. But note that an important thing has happened between the first Valuation and this revision: the immediate lessor changed from William Armstrong to Marcus Keane, the previously mentioned landlord. William Armstrong had inherited his uncle John MacDonnell's landholdings in 1850 — but he had also inherited his uncle's debts, which were sizable. Armstrong probably found the debt

VALUATION OF TENEMENTS.

PARISH OF KILBALLYOWEN.

No. and Letters of Reference to Map.		Townlands and Occupiers.	Immediate Lessors.	Description of Tenement.	Area. A. R. P.	Land. £ s. d.	Buildings. £ s. d.	Total Annual Valuation of Rateable Property. £ s. d.
		KILBALLYOWEN—*continued.*						
—	i	Patrick M'Grath,	Nicholas Westby,	House and land,	1 0 35	0 15 0	0 5 0	1 0 0
—	j	John M'Grath,	Same,	House and garden,	0 0 6	0 1 0	0 5 0	0 6 0
—	k	John Jordan,	Same,	House,		—	0 5 0	0 5 0
—	l	Honoria Curtin,	Same,	House and garden,	0 0 25	0 3 0	0 5 0	0 8 0
—	m	John Roberts,	Same,	House,		—	0 5 0	0 5 0
—	n	Patrick Kelly,	Same,	House, office, and land,	3 3 25	2 12 0	0 8 0	3 0 0
—	o	John Carmody,	Same,	House, offices, & garden,	0 2 35	0 10 0	2 0 0	2 10 0
—	p	Thomas Curtin,	Same,	House and garden,	0 2 35	0 10 0	0 10 0	1 0 0
—	q	John Clohane,	Same,	House and land,	2 3 0	1 15 0	0 10 0	2 5 0
—	r	Mary Curtin,	Same,	House,		—	0 5 0	0 5 0
—	s	Anne Griffin,	Same,	House and garden,	0 1 0	0 5 0	0 15 0	1 0 0
		Michael Roche,	Same,	Land,	1 2 20	1 5 0	—	1 5 0
—	t	Thomas Roberts,	Same,	House,		—	0 10 0	0 10 0
—	u	Catherine Carmody,	Same,	House,		—	0 5 0	0 5 0
—	v	Honoria Cahill,	Same,	House,		—	0 5 0	0 5 0
—	w	Thomas Darry,	Same,	House and garden,	0 2 30	0 10 0	0 5 0	0 15 0
—	x	Thomas Blake,	Same,	House,		—	0 5 0	0 5 0
—	y	John Galvin,	Same,	House,		—	0 3 0	0 3 0
—	z	Michael Curtin,	Same,	House,		—	0 3 0	0 3 0
—		. . .	. . .	Waste,	1 2 32	—		
				Total,	1012 2 14	355 6 0	36 0 0	371 6 0
		KILCLOHER. (Ord. Ss. 71 & 72.)						
1	a	Mary Kane,	William Armstrong,	House, offices, and land,	32 1 0	10 0 0	0 10 0	10 10 0
2	a	Margaret Kane,	Same,	House, offices, and land,	4 1 34	1 10 0	1 5 0	2 15 0
3		Jeremiah Lynch (*Mart.*)	Same,	Land,	31 0 20	12 10 0	—	12 10 0
4		Jeremiah Lynch (*Mart'n*)	Same,	Land,	13 2 0	7 0 0	—	10 0 0
5			Same,		13 2 0	3 0 0	—	
6		Jeremh. Lynch (*Anthony*)	Same,	Land,	13 1 25	6 0 0	—	9 0 0
7			Same,		13 2 0	3 0 0	—	
8	a	John Lynch,	Same,	House, office, & land,	51 0 30	5 0 0	0 10 0	5 10 0
		Patrick Lynch,		Land,		7 10 0		7 10 0
9	a	Peter Lynch,	Same,	House, office, and land,	12 3 20	4 5 0	0 10 0	4 15 0
—	b	Patrick Kane (Tom).	Same,	House and office,			0 10 0	0 10 0
10	a	Martin Lynch,	Same,	House, offices, & land,	18 3 10	8 0 0	0 15 0	20 15 0
11					34 3 0	12 0 0		
12					32 1 20	11 0 0	—	
13	a	Bridget Lynch,	Same,	House, offices, & land,	20 3 20	5 0 0	—	16 0 0
14					18 0 20	10 5 0	0 15 0	
15	a				9 0 10	3 10 0	0 16 0	
16		Honoria Lynch, John Lynch,	Same,	House, offices, & land,				7 15 0
								7 15 0
17					39 2 23	11 10 0	—	
18		Patrick Kane (Tom),	Same,	Land,	11 3 5	6 0 0	—	10 0 0
19	a	James Kane (Tom).	Same,	House, offices, and land,	13 0 0	4 0 0	—	8 0 0
20		James Kane (Tom).	Same,	Land,	14 0 20	7 8 0	0 12 0	5 0 0
	a	John Kane,	Same,	House, offices, & land,	49 0 13	5 0 0	0 10 0	10 10 0
21		James Kane (*Edward*),	Same,	Land,	24 1 37	6 0 0	—	6 0 0
22					12 2 0	3 0 0	—	
23	a	Connor Houan,	Same,	House, offices, & land,	17 0 10	6 5 0	0 10 0	9 15 0
—	b	Jeremiah Kane,	Same,	House,		—	0 5 0	0 5 0
24	a	Thomas Roach,	Same,	House, office, and land	26 3 0	10 0 0	0 10 0	10 10 0
—	b	Jerh. Lynch (*Donald*),	Same,	House,		—	0 6 0	0 6 0
—	c	Jeremiah Lynch (*Mich.*)	Same,	House,		—	0 6 0	0 6 0
—	d	Jerh. Lynch (*Anthony*).	Same,	House,		—	0 6 0	0 6 0
25	a	Michael Kane,	Same,	House, office, and land.	64 1 39	26 5 0	0 15 0	27 0 0
26	a	Jeremiah Kane,	Same,	House and land,	33 0 0	12 2 0	0 8 0	15 10 0
27					13 3 0	3 0 0	—	
28	a	William O'Donnell,	Same,	House, offices, and land,	26 1 0	14 5 0	0 15 0	15 0 0
—	b	Patrick Lynch,	Same,	House,		—	0 5 0	0 5 0
29		John Keniery,	Same,	Land,	13 0 7	4 0 0	—	4 0 0
				Total,	678 3 3	238 5 0	10 13 0	248 18 0

The primary valuation (above) of 1855 shows Lot 25 occupied by Michael Kane, leasing land from William Armstrong. After this, William Armstrong sold the land to Marcus Keane, who apparently reapportioned the lots of Kilcloher. (See map on facing page.) Lot 25 was divided into three new lots, numbered 6, 7, and 8. Daniel Keane lived on lot number 6.

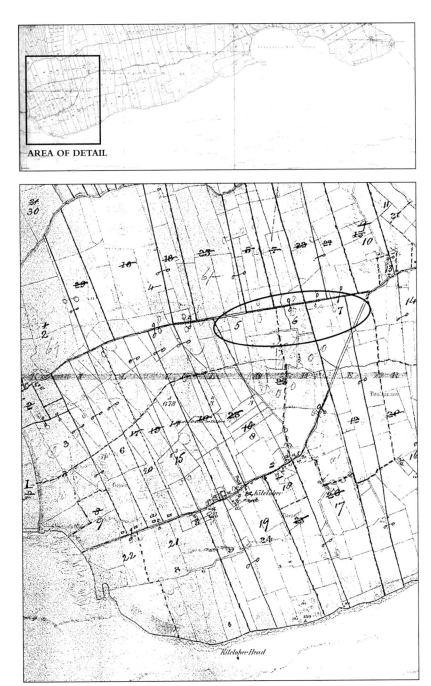

Detail of Ordnance Survey map of Kilcloher with annotations by Valuation Office surveyors, showing lot 25 being subdivided and relabeled 5, 6, and 7. The map is difficult to read; see the circled area.

burdensome and sold the land through the Encumbered Estates Court, which auctioned it to Marcus Keane. Marcus Keane then redrew all the lots. He eliminated lot numbers 23–29 and renumbered nearly all the lots.

In the handwritten revision, the eliminated lots are crossed out and marked as "cancelled." The corresponding map shows that what was once lot 25, occupied by Michael Keane, is now lots 5, 6, and 7. Daniel Keane appears as occupier of lot 6, which also consists of land formerly on the original lot 7. Nearby are Mary, Margaret, John, and Thomas Keane.

Valued by itself, the land of lot 6 was worth 15 pounds, 15 shillings; the house was worth 15 shillings, making it one of the five most valuable houses in Kilcloher. It appears that this house was from the original lot 25; there was no house on the former lot 7, and no houses would have been built in the time between the primary valuation and the 1857 revision.

At the time of the 1861 revision, Daniel Keane is still listed as occupier of house, office, and land at No. 6. Daniel also appears in the 1865 revision, but with a significant annotation that signals his emigration. His name is crossed out as occupier at No. 6 and John McGuire is added. We see a "63" in the "Observations" column, referring to the year 1863: this tells us that Daniel left Kilcloher that year. The property was taken over by John McGuire by April 1865.

Jumping ahead 120 years, the 1985 and 1986 electoral registers list just thirty households in the small townland of Kilcloher, including a McGuire family. It is possible they are descendants of that same John McGuire and occupants of the land once held by Daniel Keane. Keanes still abound in County Clare: of the thirty households listed, nine of Kilcloher's households, nearly one-third, bear that surname.[32] Perhaps these possible distant cousins of the John Francis Keane family have more clues to the story of the Keanes who left and those who stayed behind.

The 1861 Revision of Griffith's, showing Daniel Keane occupying lot number 6. His son John Francis Keane was born that year.

Detail of the 1865 Revision, with Daniel Keane crossed out—marking his emigration to the United States.

PART II

The Keane Family
in the United States

CHAPTER THREE

Settling at Sandy Hook

The Keane Family of Sandy Hook in Newtown,
Fairfield County, Connecticut

BY THE TIME DANIEL KEANE and his family left Kilcloher and
emigrated to the United States sometime before 1865, several families of
Irish immigrants, many from County Clare, had already made their way
to the small community of Sandy Hook nestled among the Pootatuck
River. The families of John, Thomas, and Michael Keane, all from Clare
and possibly relatives, had settled in Newtown by 1860. Other possible
relatives who had already made their homes at Sandy Hook included
branches of Keating family, many of whom likely trace their origins to
or near the townland of Kilcloher. Records show that Daniel and his
family settled in Sandy Hook by 1865.

Families leaving County Clare often would purchase tickets through
an agency in their town before heading to a seaport for departure. The
time between the ticket purchase and the actual departure could be
quite lengthy, sometimes forcing families to live in or near seaports
before boarding the ships to America. Many would have left from the
port of Liverpool, England, arriving in New York City fifty to seventy
days later. The journey was usually less difficult in April or May. High
winds — leading to a longer journey — often kept emigrants from
leaving during July and August.[1]

We know that Daniel, Margaret, and their children left Kilcloher
in 1863 and arrived in Sandy Hook by 1865. Research indicates that
they may have sailed on the *Kangaroo*, which left Liverpool, bound for
New York City, on 11 July 1863. According to the ship's manifest, the
passengers included Daniel Keane, age 30, a laborer from Ireland, his

wife, Margaret, also age 30, and two children: Mary, age 7, and John, age 1.[2] While this record does not account for daughters Anne/Anna and Bridget, it does support an anecdote passed down in Keane family oral tradition: that John Francis Keane learned to walk on the ship crossing the Atlantic Ocean. Family members did sometimes travel separately, and ages were often approximated on immigration records (Mary would have been 8 years old in 1863).

The Irish Come to Newtown

Founded in 1705 and incorporated a few years thereafter, Newtown was established by people from the existing communities of Milford and Stratford, who plotted Newtown's boundaries in 1709. Along the Pootatuck River, they created the settlement of Sandy Hook, which quickly became the home of sawmills and gristmills that supported Newtown and its neighbors. At the outbreak of the Revolution, the town was used as a British stronghold, with many residents supporting the Tory cause. Following the Revolution, the water wheels from the mills built near Sandy Hook quickly expanded Newtown's economy, making it into a center of small industries that manufactured buttons, combs, and other materials.[3]

Genealogist Harlan R. Jessup, who has extensively studied the Irish of Newtown, points out:

> The first evidence of Irish in Newtown is the death of a farm laborer, "Robert Morris, said to be a native of Ireland, a transient person," recorded in the town books on December 15, 1798. Two or three other deaths of apparently single Irish farm workers are found in Newtown records in the very early nineteenth century. Then, in 1846, the first Irish property owners appear on the tax rolls, brothers-in-law Daniel Quinlivin and Patrick Madigan, both from County Clare. These were followed by about a dozen more in the next five years, many of them also from County Clare. These first settlers had small farms, but a great many more Irish soon began coming to work in the rubber factory [described below]. From a reading of place names on their tombstones, it is estimated that by 1900 fully half of the large Irish

population of Newtown was from County Clare, most from the small Loop Head peninsula on that county's west coast.[4]

It was not until the outbreak of Ireland's Great Famine that Newtown experienced a dynamic shift in the composition of its residents and local economy. The influx of hundreds of Irish immigrants, many of whom made their homes at Sandy Hook, provided a labor source for the community's manufacturing companies — particularly the newly completed factory of the New York Belting and Packing Company, which employed a large percentage of Irish immigrants. Between 1860 and 1900, Newtown's Irish population grew from 5.6 percent to 44.2 percent, most of whom worked in the rubber factory or as domestic laborers.[5]

While Daniel Keane and his family settled in a predominantly Irish area, they were not met with complete acceptance by all of Newtown's residents. According to Newtown's town historian, Daniel Cruson, "The Irish were very polarizing socially, religiously, and politically in town."[6] They had their own newspaper from 1880–1882, the *Newtown Chronicle*, which often ran articles reporting news from Ireland. The Catholic Church soon became a leading force in the community, due almost solely to the rise in the Irish population.

The Keane family attended St. Rose Church, the first Catholic Church established in Newtown. The church, rebuilt in the mid-1900s, first opened in 1859, becoming one of the few Catholic churches in the area. As the Irish population grew in Newtown, additional parishes were formed, making St. Rose the "Mother Church" of those parishes surrounding Sandy Hook. At the time of the Keane family's arrival, the parish was under the care of Rev. James Daly, who stayed through 1868; he was succeeded by Rev. John Rogers, who remained until 1873. Rev. James McCarten was in charge of the parish from 1873 until his death in 1889.[7] The church's cemetery is the final resting place of Daniel and Margaret Keane, as well as of their sons Thomas and Patrick.

The New York Belting and Packing Company

By 1870, the Irish-American population of Newtown had grown tremendously, with many Irishmen working in the rubber factory of Sandy Hook. The New York Belting and Packing Company was one of the nation's largest manufacturers of India rubber. According to a profile of the company published in 1860, the factory produced fire hoses and common household items such as carpets, sinks, door springs, bedsprings, and clothes wringers. The company's patents and technologies would "produce a revolution in many workshops" with innovative techniques. The primary manufacturing headquarters was a four-story Italianate brick building, consisting of just over 70,000 square feet. Newtown Pond was a source of hydroelectric power.

New York Belting and Packing took over buildings abandoned by the Goodyear Rubber Packing Company, which had gone bankrupt by 1856. In that same year, fire destroyed one of the mills, which was replaced by the factory building where Daniel Keane likely spent most of his work time. According to historic records, the factory's buildings included the first circular knives to cut rubber into slabs, making the rubber easier to manipulate and process into other products. The factory continued to be used until 1901, when it was leased to the Fabric Fire Hose Company; in 1977, the site was permanently closed. Throughout its history, the factory's buildings employed thousands of immigrants from across the world.[8]

The Keanes: A Growing Family

We know the Keane family had arrived in Connecticut by at least 1865 because their son Michael Joseph reported in the 1900 census that he was born in January 1865 in Connecticut.[9] Another son, Daniel P. Keane was born in Newtown in February 1867.[10] Thus, by the time of the 1870 Census, the first federal record that enumerated the Keane ("Kane") household in its entirety, the family included Daniel, Margaret, "Hannah" (Anna), Bridget, John, Michael, and Daniel. (See next chapter for additional details.) They were living in the same house as Patrick Haugh and George Malee [Malley], both Irish and likely from County Clare, and both rubber factory workers.[11]

In 1870 Daniel and Margaret had another son, Thomas, who died two months later.[12] Another son, Patrick, was born in 1872 and died of scarlet fever in 1876.[13]

The year 1880 found Daniel and Margaret living at Sandy Hook with their two youngest surviving children, Daniel and Michael.[14] Their eldest daughter, Anna, was working as a domestic servant in the household of Dennis and Olive Gately.[15] Their son John Francis and daughter Bridget were working as clerks in the store of Henry Sanford.[16] It is possible that it was from Henry Sanford that John Francis Keane learned the skills he would use to build John F. Keane & Company in Bridgeport, Connecticut.

After Daniel died of pneumonia in 1886, his tombstone was engraved with the name of his birthplace, Kilcloher, commemorating the family's Irish origins for future generations.[17]

Upon leaving Kilcloher in 1863, it would have been impossible for Daniel and Margaret Keane to envision the progress descendants would make, and the impact they would have, within a few short generations. The family would flourish beyond their humble beginnings at Sandy Hook, with many of Daniel and Margaret's grandchildren attending some of the nation's most prestigious universities, and others pursuing active and successful careers in the U.S. military.

Within a hundred years of the Keane family's arrival in the United States, members would be living in Connecticut, Texas, California, New York, and Florida. Daniel and Margaret's descendants would become entrepreneurs and global travelers, opening successful business ventures and studying around the world. The family's strong work ethic and drive to succeed would leave a positive and lasting impact on the communities they touched for generations to come.

Part III of this book, beginning on page 53, details the genealogy of the family.

CHAPTER FOUR

BEGINNINGS IN BRIDGEPORT

*John F. Keane & Co. and
the John Francis Keane, Sr., Family*

JOHN FRANCIS KEANE, born and baptized in September 1861 in Kilcloher, County Clare, was still an infant when he left Ireland with his parents. According to family lore, John learned to walk while on board the ship that took the family to America, around 1863. (See previous chapter.)

At Sandy Hook, in the town of Newtown, Fairfield County, Connecticut, John was among a multitude of cousins and other relatives, many of whom had traveled from County Clare and found work at the factories in and around Newtown. By 1880 he was working as a clerk in the store of Henry Sanford in Newtown. Sanford was noted to be an "enterprising prosperous business man," and likely provided John with a great deal of experience in managing a business.[18]

By 1887, John had moved to Bridgeport in Fairfield County, where he became the junior partner in Jones, Keane, and Co., a local clothing and furnishings store. Located on Main Street, at the corner of John Street (the former site of Burroughs Library), the store had originally been established by William S. Jones and would be a centerpiece of Bridgeport's Main Street for nearly forty years.[19]

In the late nineteenth century, Bridgeport was in the midst of a vast transition. Originally part of the town of Stratford, Bridgeport at first was a center for farming and fishing. During the American Revolution, however, it became known for piracy and privateering, its Black Rock Harbor serving as the resting point for loads of captured goods and other cargo.

It was not until 1836 that Bridgeport received an official charter as a city, though it had been incorporated as a borough in 1800 and a township in 1821. The city's growth continued when, in 1840, it was connected by railway to New Milford; by 1849, it was connected to Waterbury, New Haven, and New York City. In March 1860, Abraham Lincoln stopped in Bridgeport during his tour of the eastern United States to speak at Washington Hall (located at the corner of State and Broad Streets). According to tradition, it was in Bridgeport that Lincoln first tried New England fried oysters. Showman P. T. Barnum built multiple homes in the area — and even served as mayor of Bridgeport for one year, in 1875. (He is buried in the city's Mountain Grove Cemetery.)

Following the Civil War, Bridgeport became a center of manufacturing, producing carriages, sewing machines, and ammunition. During this time multiple corporations were established in Bridgeport, including several corset manufacturing companies, such as Warner Brothers Manufacturers, Thomson, Langdon & Company, and H. W. Lyon, who made the first "crown" corset around 1885. In 1868, E. R. Ives and Cornelius Blakeslee founded Ives, Blakeslee and Company, which manufactured toys and other novelty goods. In 1877, E. L. White and others started the Bridgeport Paper Box Company. Other businesses that established themselves in Bridgeport before 1890 included the Bridgeport Knife Company, carpet makers David M. Read and Company, and Glover Sanford and Sons, a hat manufacturer.[20]

John Francis Keane's first documented appearance in the city is in the 1887 Bridgeport City Directory: as a co-owner, with William S. Jones, of Jones, Keane, and Co. The directory features a large advertisement for the company on its front cover.

The company grew to become one of the city's "oldest and best known clothing firms." By 1890, John's youngest brother, Daniel P., had joined him in Bridgeport as the store's clerk.[21] A year later his other brother, M. Joseph, also became a clerk in the store. The three brothers lived together that year, boarding at 191 Fairfield Avenue.[22] Joseph's time in Bridgeport was short, as he left for New Haven in 1892, though Daniel continued to room at 191 Fairfield Avenue.[23]

A New Family

Sometime around 1891, possibly on a trip to New York, John met the young Susan Elizabeth Sheahan, who had been living with her aunt, Susan Platt, in Fair Haven, New York. The two were married 19 August 1891 in the nearby St. Thomas Church.

As a young girl, Susan had been struck in the eye with a snowball containing rocks, rendering her partially blind. In 1878 her mother, Margaret, and others petitioned the State of Connecticut and Governor Richard D. Hubbard for support in enrolling Susan at the Perkins School for the Blind in South Boston, Massachusetts. A few of the letters, preserved in the Governor's Official Letter Book at the Connecticut State Library, illustrate Susan's condition and outline the steps taken to secure funding for Susan to attend Perkins.[24]

On 3 September 1878, Margaret C. Sheahan wrote Governor Hubbard a follow-up letter to her initial request:

> Bridgeport, CT, Sept 3rd 1878
> Gov. Hubbard
>
> Honorable Sir,
>
> About three weeks ago I sent you a few lines in reply to yours received, containing a certificate from my physician here, Dr. Robert Hubbard stating that my daughter was a fit subject for the Perkins institute, asking for your permission that she be admitted. I have received no reply. Shall you kindly do me the favor of the same has been received to answer at your earliest convenience.
>
> > Yours very respectfully,
> > Mrs. M. C. Sheahan

It appears the governor contacted Dr. Robert Hubbard of Bridgeport to inquire about Susan and her mother. Dr. Hubbard's response followed on 9 September:

> Bridgeport, CT. Sept 9th, 1878
> Hon R. D. Hubbard
>
> Dear Sir
>
> Your letter inquiring about Mrs. M. C. Sheahan and her daughter is before me. As I am not personally

acquainted with the family or their character and circumstances I may take a day or two to make the investigation which I can do with no trouble. Will write promptly when I have investigated. In haste with great esteem.

Yours truly
R. Hubbard

During this time, Dr. Hubbard was able to locate Margaret and Susan living with the Hawley family. On 16 September 1878 Mrs. Thomas Hawley wrote to the governor in support of Susan. Enclosed with the letter was a note from Dr. Robert Hubbard, noting that Mrs. Hawley was "one of our most respectable and valued citizens [of Bridgeport]." Mrs. Hawley's letter notes that Margaret and Susan were living with the family during the summer of 1878:

Bridgeport Sept. 16th, 1878

Mrs. Sheahan and her daughter Susan have been living in our family the past three months. So far as I know they are very worthy respectable people, but poor. Susan the girl who has applied for admission to the Perkins Institute is blind in one eye, and partially with the other, so much so that at times she can hardly find her way about. She is quiet, and well behaved, and in some respects her abilities are more than ordinary —

Mrs. Thos Hawley

Dr. Hubbard made his report to the governor the following day, stating that Susan was an excellent candidate for admittance to Perkins:

Bridgeport, Ct. Sept. 17th, 1878

Hon. & dear friend:
Susan Elizabeth Sheahan is nearly absolutely blind and unable in my opinion to pursue any profession or occupation which is self supporting.
I have made all verifiable effort to ascertain the condition of the family in respect of <u>capabilities</u> and am

satisfied that they are deserving and doing all in their power for independence and support.

I think she is a proper subject for treatment in an institution for the blind and deserving of state aid. In Haste,

Yours with esteem
Robt. Hubbard

Dr. Hubbard reported again on the Sheahan family the next day:

Bridgeport, Sept. 19 [18]78
Hon and dear friend,

I have discovered Mrs. Sheahan and find that her daughter is absolutely blind with one eye and Dr. Agnew says the other will follow and in spite of any resistance from our poor art.

She has been a resident of this state many years — is a respectable industrious woman and I think worthy of consideration on the part of the state. The mother is a servant in one of our best families and barely earns a living.

I am not certain as to the birth place of the mother, but the girl I think was born in Connecticut.

Mrs. Hawley who employs the mother is a perfectly reliable person and any statement made by her or her daughter Miss Mary Hawley is in my opinion properly reliable. — In haste

Yours truly,
R. Hubbard

The letters of Mrs. Hawley, Dr. Hubbard, and Margaret C. Sheahan successfully persuaded Governor Hubbard to support Susan's attendance at the Perkins Institute. According to the school's records, Susan was admitted at the age of 18 on 23 September 1878 and was discharged seven years later, on 26 September 1885.[25] Her treatment successful, by 1886 she was living with her mother in Waterbury, Connecticut, where she worked as a music teacher.[26] She moved with her mother to Fair Haven, New York, in 1888.[27]

Shortly after Susan and John were married, John returned to Bridgeport to prepare for his new wife's arrival. On 1 September 1891, he wrote his first letter to his "darling wife," from Adams House at 443 Washington Street in Boston, detailing his travel plans. Preserved by the Keane family, the letter reveals the deep love John and Susan felt for one another, the energy John brought to the store, and his excitement about settling himself and his new bride in Bridgeport.[28]

My Darling Wife:

For the first time I write to you under the above endearing caption and I feel a thrill of pride course through my mind as I write. I arrived in Bridgeport safely Monday at 12:30 p.m. and everything appeared strange for a few hours but gradually became as familiar as formerly. To walk about the streets as a young married man was a novelty to me and I do not doubt but it was the same to the observers who knew me. I arrived in Boston at 11 oclock last night feeling tired but happy in the contemplation of my possessions. I must confess that I missed you when I retired and did not before realize how very essential to comfort and contentment a wife's presence is. I am trying to arrange to get to Bridgeport Wednesday night and if I can everything will be ready for you to come Friday. I ordered the furniture for sleeping rooms & dining room & kitchen to be put in today also what dishes, &c that will be necessary to begin with. The other things we will finish when you come here. We will be prepared to eat & sleep at home but will not be able to entertain callers for a few days. You don't realize how much I miss you and I cannot describe the longing to see you. It's greater and more ardent than at any former time. I will write you soon again and until then please accept the kiss of your husband in the loving spirit which prompts it. Kindly remember me to your Aunt and Uncle Platt, Cousins Fannie & Kittie, and Mr. Chaperaw. With the most ardent love consistent with the capacity of a young husband I am for the first time to subscribe myself as.

Your Loving Husband
John

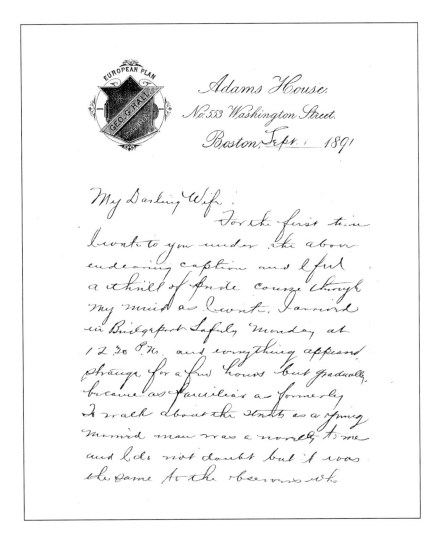

Within a year, John and his wife purchased property on West Liberty Street in Bridgeport through a mortgage of $25 from Samuel Curtis, released on 9 July 1892.[29] Later, John expanded his original purchase on West Liberty Street, completing his mortgage payment for the property on 2 January 1900 for $2,100.[30] The home remained in the Keane family for nearly thirty years before being purchased by the Hennessey Funeral Home. The large home included a magnificent library, full of books for the family who were all "avid readers."[31]

Soon after John's marriage, his business partner, William S. Jones, decided to move to Waterbury, Connecticut, to start Jones, Morgan

Company. He sold his equity in the company to John, and from that point forward, the store would bear the name John F. Keane & Co. Clothing and Furnishings for Men and Boys [32]

A New Generation

John and Susan's first child was born in 1892, a girl they named Margaret. Their second child was born in 1894, a son named John Francis Keane, Jr., but the child grew gravely ill and died shortly after his birth. Two other daughters, Agnes and Catherine, joined the family in 1895 and 1896 respectively. The family was hard hit by the diphtheria epidemic sweeping through Bridgeport; when their two youngest daughters became afflicted, they agreed to separate for a brief time in order to protect Margaret. John went to Newtown; Susan moved to Waterbury. While the move prevented the epidemic from spreading further into the family, Agnes and Catherine died within eleven days of one another in 1898. [33]

That same year, still in the midst of the epidemic, Susan gave birth to her second son, also named John Francis Keane, Jr. The couple's next child, another son, Augustine ("Gus"), was born in 1899. This boy was actually baptized as Daniel Keane, much to the displeasure of his mother. According to family oral history, when John took the baby to be baptized, Susan—having just given birth and unable to accompany him—pleaded with him not to name the baby Daniel, as there were so many other Daniel Keanes in the family. When John arrived at the church, however, he couldn't remember any other name *except* Daniel. But when he returned home, he told Susan that he had named the baby Augustine, after St. Augustine's Church, site of the baptism. [34]

In 1900 fraternal twin boys, Joseph and Paul, joined the family. The twins were raised in the same bed, were kept in the same playpen, and were "always together," a bond that followed them "through their lives." [35] Joe and Paul learned the benefits of looking alike. One summer, one of the twins had a job delivering prescriptions for the local drugstore. While he was out on deliveries, the other twin came into the drug store. The owner, mistaking the second twin for the first, offered him an ice cream soda for his hard work. When the first twin returned ten minutes later, covered in sweat from the deliveries, his brother was just finishing the ice cream soda.

Another fondly remembered story of the twins took place when they were much younger, and it shows Susan's strong sense of morality and honesty. Joe and Paul accompanied their mother to the pharmacy, which was located next to a penny-candy store. Susan gave them a penny to put into the gumball machine, and it became stuck. The twins told the store owner, who put another penny in the machine. The next time the twins visited the pharmacy, they asked Susan for a penny, but she said, "No, not today." Not to be deterred, they still went to the penny-candy store, and — remembering their last experience — told the store owner that the machine was stuck again. Again he gave them a penny. Later Susan discovered what her boys had done. She hitched up the horse and buggy and made them return to the store to return the penny.[36]

Two more boys were born to John and Susan: Francis B. "Frank" Keane in 1904 and Robert Joseph "Bob" Keane in 1905. According to tradition, one Thanksgiving, when Susan directed her family to say what they were thankful for, young Bob noted that he was thankful "for mashed potatoes."[37]

The family regularly participated in mass at St. Vincent's Hospital, where Paul and Joseph served Mass from the age of seven onwards. The twin brothers spoke their parts entirely in Latin, making a lasting impression on their siblings.[38]

John's business in Bridgeport continued to flourish. When not busy with his store, he served as a member of the Philip Sheridan Assembly, the Park City Council of the Knights of Columbus, the Weatogue Country Club, and the Bridgeport Chamber of Commerce.[39]

The success of the family business gave the Keanes enough disposable income for Susan to get a glass eye. She was fitted for it at St. Vincent's Hospital, where her niece Martina (Daniel's daughter) had studied to be a nurse. Susan died on 15 June 1921 at the age of 59, of complications of a gallbladder infection. Her grandchildren and children remembered her as a "stoic and upstanding mother" who was very nurturing. Her death was difficult on the children, particularly for Frank and Bob, who were only 16 and 18.[40]

John F. Keane passed away only months after Susan's death, on 29 September 1922, of pernicious anemia. His obituary notes that he was "man of great ability, of very pleasing personal quality, generous, without being lavish, and one of the best salesman in the clothing business."[41] It continues:

> He established a profitable trade upon expert skill in the business, his fair dealing and his purpose to give the very best to his friends.

He was a man who would have succeeded in public life. He was well informed over a large range, took a keen interest in affairs, and was a tr[e]nchant, keen, and pleasant debater. He was one of a limited number of persons with whom conversation was an art. In talking with his friends, he gave them the benefit of much thought and experience.

He was essentially a family man. He believed that one of the most essential duties of a good man is to be a good father, and leave to the world a property in young men and women, to take his place and carry on his work. He prospered in every way, leaving behind him an established business, a comfortable estate and a splendid family.

After John's death, his sons Paul and Joe Keane continued to operate the store on Main Street until December 1926. The *Bridgeport Telegram* reported the closure:[42]

KEANE CLOTHING CO, 38 YEARS IN BUSINESS, TO CLOSE DOORS

John F. Keane and company, Inc. one of the oldest and best known clothing firms in the city announced today that they will retire from business Dec. 15. Lease conditions and the inability to secure a satisfactory location are accountable for the retirement although it is possible that if a suitable site is secure the firm may re-enter the clothing business here within the next few years.

ESTABLISHED IN 1888

The company has been 38 years in its present location, the old Burroughs library site at Main and John Streets. This building will be torn down early in 1927 to make room for a new home of the City national bank, a five story or perhaps taller building.

The John F. Keane company was established in March 1888 as Jones, Keane and company by the late John F. Keane and W. S. Jones. The latter is now associated with Jones, Morgan company in Waterbury. Mr. Keane purchased control and as John E. [F.] and company the firm continued under his active direction until his death in September 1922. The company was then purchased by his sons Paul A. and Joseph A. Keane. The present officers are President Paul A. Keane; vice president, George H. French; treasurer and secretary, Joseph A. Keane.

MAY START AGAIN

Joseph A. Keane said today: "While we regret exceedingly to sever the business relations we have enjoyed with the people of Bridgeport and vicinity, many of them dating back a quarter of a century and more, and with our host of new friends who have made possible the large increase in business since my brother and I took control four years ago, still we feel that in view of the rapidly shifting business district we cannot see, at the present time, the advisability of signing a long lease. It is entirely possible that should a suitable location develop whose stability is assured we may re-enter the clothing field in Bridgeport within the next two or three years. We are not ready as yet to disclose our personal plans but expect to do so in the near future."

The closure of John F. Keane & Co. greatly affected the business community of Bridgeport, with the move being called "extraordinary" as the city adjusted to changes in the late 1920s:[43]

NEW BUSINESS DISTRICTS

That a long-established and successful retail firm should close its doors because its lease has expired and it cannot see its way clear to make a lease in another location in view of shifting business districts seems extraordinary. Yet such is the reason given by Joseph F. Keane in behalf of the firm of John F. Keane and company and there is no reason to doubt it.

We take it from this that the owners of one of Bridgeport's well established Main street stores cannot make up their mind whether to stay on Main street or move elsewhere. A lease in the retail district, to be satisfactory, must be for long term. The Keane firm prefers the rather startling alternative of closing, to taking a chance and possibly guessing wrong.

Bridgeport has been famed as a "one street town," but it is no longer. Ten years ago, or even five years ago there would have been no hesitation. A firm looking for a business lease would have taken Main street or nothing. But today it is different and on the whole, healthier. Other business districts are developing fast. Whether to stay or to move, and in the latter case, which way, is a question of judgment. But business is only a succession of such judgments, and there is no reason of fearing the issue.

While the decision to close the business might have been called "a startling alternative," it proved to be a strong decision. Less than three years later, in October 1929, the stock market crashed, plunging America into the Great Depression. Over the next few years hundreds of America's Main Street stores — including many in Bridgeport — went bankrupt and were forced to close their doors.

CHAPTER FIVE

THE LAMP OF LEARNING

The Keane Family's Work Ethic and Tradition of Education

FEW FAMILY ATTRIBUTES are as precious to the Keane family as their tremendous work ethic and "the lamp of learning" — the tradition of educational excellence passed down to the present day. It is evident that the principles of frugality, hard work, and education can be traced to the family's experiences in County Clare. It is likely that Daniel's own education was greatly threatened by his landlord, Marcus Keane, whose work to infiltrate the traditional Catholic upbringing of his tenants permeated life in Kilcloher and surrounding areas. It is not known if Daniel and Margaret Keane spent any time in school, as they would have been steered toward Protestant schools instead of those grounded in their Catholic faith. Upon arriving in the United States, the family worked hard to establish itself under "the lamp of learning," nearly all graduating from high school and many attending some of the world's most prestigious colleges and universities.

Smith College (Northampton, Massachusetts)
Columbia University (New York City)

Margaret Keane was the first of John Francis and Susan (Sheahan) Keane's children to attend college. She received a bachelor's degree from Smith College approximately forty years after the college was founded by Sophia Smith "for the higher education of young women, with the design to furnish for my own sex means and facilities for education equal to those which are afforded now in our colleges to young men." One of the "seven sisters" colleges, Smith counts among many notable women among its alumnae, including Barbara Bush, Betty Friedan,

Julia Child, and Sylvia Plath. Margaret's connections to Smith remained strong throughout her life, and she was an active member of the Smith College Club of Bridgeport, at one point serving as its president.

Margaret then received a master's degree from Columbia University's Teachers College, the nation's oldest and largest graduate school of education. With an interest in teaching foreign languages, she embarked on a trip abroad and received certificates from the Alliance Française and the University of Paris. Before she married Edward Bray, she taught both French and Spanish in public schools.

St. Vincent's School of Nursing (Bridgeport, Connecticut)

One of the first members of the Keane family to attend college was Martina Keane, daughter of Daniel and Bridget (Keane) Keane. Martina was an early graduate of St. Vincent's School of Nursing, founded in 1905 by the Daughters of Charity of St. Vincent de Paul and recognized as a leading educational institution for nursing and medicine. Martina's nursing degree enabled her to become a prominent local health official, passing along the tradition of health and education to thousands of Bridgeport's school children.[44] She also frequently visited incoming seamen to check them for tuberculosis before allowing them to enter the city.[45]

Martina became the nursing supervisor for the Bridgeport City Health Department. During her tenure, she organized and oversaw physical checks for Bridgeport's school children. An article from *The Bridgeport Post,* dated 6 October 1957, outlines a series of upcoming physical checks and illustrates the significant role Martina played in educating the public about the process and the role of school nurses. The article includes her personal thoughts on the process: "A lot of children like to go to the nurse. They sometimes feel a need for that kind of attention and there is often a personality attraction."[46]

Yale University (New Haven, Connecticut)

Other members of the Keane family attended Yale University in New Haven, Connecticut. Founded in 1701, the institution was the first school in the United States to award the Ph.D. (in 1861) and was a founding member of the Association of American Universities. Graduates from Yale University have included some of the world's most influential citizens, including U.S. Presidents William Howard Taft, Gerald Ford, George H. W. Bush, and George W. Bush. Noah Webster, Samuel F. B. Morse, and Eli Whitney also attended Yale.[47]

The first members of the Keane family to attend Yale were James Louis and Daniel Joseph Keane, both children of Michael Joseph and Margaret (Daley) Keane; they graduated in 1916. Prescott Bush, father of U.S. President George H. W. Bush and a 1917 graduate, was likely in some of the Keanes' classes. According to the official statistics of Yale's Class of 1916, 324 students graduated in 1916, only 20 of them Catholics. As a group, the graduates' favorite subject was history, and their most valued individual in history was President Abraham Lincoln. While at school, Daniel Joseph Keane was a member of the debating club and James Louis Keane attended the Sheffield Scientific School.[48]

Sylvester John Keane, third son of Michael Joseph Keane, received a master's degree in engineering from Yale in 1940 after performing military service. Both James and Sylvester pursued engineering and were likely part of the Yale Engineering Association, which was founded in 1914 "under the direction of some of Yale's most prominent graduates." By 1916, it had become the institution's largest alumni association, tasked with working in conjunction with one of the university's departments.[49]

College of the Holy Cross (Worcester, Massachusetts)

John Francis Keane, Sr., and his wife, Susan, worked to instill the principle of the lamp of learning and a strong work ethic in their own family, sending three sons — Francis, Paul, and Joseph — to the College of the Holy Cross. Their son Daniel Augustine ("Gus") also spent a year there before pursuing the priesthood. A private Catholic college, Holy Cross was founded in 1843. By the time Paul, Joe, and Gus attended, it was the largest Catholic undergraduate college in the United States; its curriculum emphasized classics and philosophy. Anthony J. Kuzniewski, author of a history of the college, refers to the time period 1911–1927 as the "halcyon years."[50]

John and Susan Keane kept in regular touch with their college-student sons; fortunately, the letters survive. For example, on 25 September 1919 John Keane wrote to tell the twins that he was sending furnishings for their rooms:[51]

> Dear Paul & Joe
> I am sending the things which we think will meet your needs in room decorations. We send one pair of curtains as it is the conclusion that your room has but one window. Will send the others if you need them. The couch covers and pillow and center table covers should give

your room a luxurious complexion and we all hope our
selection will please you and harmonize with the interior
embellishments of your room. I am very glad that your
food is more likeable than we imagined it to be and met
[with] the addition of 5¾ lbs to Pauls figure the efficacy
of the food cannot be doubted. It is a great advantage to
you to be in the strong spirit of good fellowship for your
associates and all the other students and I hope you will
maintain this spirit throughout your college course. I am
pleased to know that Gus is so favourably regarded by his
class that they remember him even after so long time has
passed. John had a very short vacation this time and it's too
bad he had no more time to rest after a hard years work.

In the same letter John also conveyed news of their brother, John
Francis, who had crashed the family car while at Harvard College in
Cambridge, Massachusetts:

John wrote that he sideswiped the white fence on the road
and smashed his car to the extent of about $100.00. I do
not know whether it was between Worcester and Boston

or west of Worcester. Did you know about it? I think John Grancy went to Boston with John and he probably told you all about it. Francis has taken charge of the car and this is doing quite well. We had the fences put in shape and will take up the stack in the gear box and fix the wheel and then I think the car will be in good shape for the season. We expect to use the car every day while it is pleasant and I feel sure that Francis and Robert can and will care for it properly and drive safely after a week's driving experience.

Though John encouraged his children to leave home for their education, it is clear that he was missing his sons, as he continued:

We are a very quiet family now, with no noise or disturbances so that it looks as though peace and quiet will be with us till you return. Margaret has changed things around so that the spaces are large and the rooms not so pokey looking. The leather set is in Margaret's room and looks good there. The other rooms are relieved [*sic*] of the furniture that so crowded them so that we feel that the change is an improvement for now at least. The new man at the store . . . takes hold good. He's quite familiar with cars and he is quite a help to Francis when he goes out with him. I hope you will get the package I send by parcel post and that you will find your needs supplied for the present. Let us hear from you quite often as we are anxious to [know] how you get along without ills of the mind or body. We all send our best wishes for your Freshman start and await the glowing reports from our latest contribution to the world uplift. Lovingly your
Father

John sent Paul and Joe money both to cover their tuition bills and to give them some spending money. He wrote to them on 9 October 1919:[52]

I enclose a check for $475. This is to pay the college bill for the first semester and the 28.00 for personal needs until it is gone. We all would like to have you come home over the holiday but if you think John could entertain you better why go there and see Harvard and Boston. You must pay all the expense so that John will only spend time while you are there. I enclose [a] request to Father

Wheeler asking for permission for you to go to see John during your coming Holidays. It pleases all of us to know we sent you the things you needed and that you have your equipment complete respecting your room & also that one of my Birthday cakes Made by Mother was so surprisingly good. . . .

> With best wishes from all of us I am
> Your Loving Father

While at Holy Cross, Paul became ill with appendicitis and had to schedule an appendectomy. His father made preparations for his immediate departure from school on 4 November 1921:[53]

Your letter received and I am enclosing $10.00 to pay your expenses home at once. Don't delay coming home. We will have everything ready for your care at St. Vincent's Hospital and whosoever you would prefer to operate. Among the Bridgeport surgeons there are a good number who are very efficient and I will select one or you may do so if you have a preference for any individual doctor.

We all concluded that you better come home and we will be in a position to help you and we would feel better about your care if you are with us instead of being 200 miles away. Telegraph when you leave Worcester and we will meet you at the station when the train arrives home.

If you can come alone do so. If you think it would be better for Joe to come with you have him come.

Keep on a light diet and I think you will get through the trip in good shape and while you are here we will tone you up and get you in good trim for the operation.

Cheer up and try to beat the old appendix which has had your attention for some time.

We all are awaiting your coming and send you, Joe & Francis our best love.

> Affectionately
> Your Father

Paul and Joe proved to be exceptional students. On 18 November 19[20], their mother wrote to celebrate their academic accomplishments:[54]

> My Dear boys,
>
> We were all very much pleased with the letter Father brought home last night and I wish you could have seen your father when he told of the splendid marks you had received. He was so proud of them. We are all well and Pa is fine and everything seems to be going on all right — John is coming home for the Yale Harvard game but will not be here Thanksgiving vacation. His Graylock vacation must have done him good but it is a family secret, don't give it away....
>
> We are all anxious to see you both....
>
> > Your loving mother.

In letters to Paul and Joe, Susan emphasized the importance of continuing their education. Even though their younger brothers and father had been ill, she wrote on 9 February 192[1], the twins were not needed at home enough to "give up college":[55]

> It is so good of you to write me again and to remember that I would worry about you and Joe at this time and as one good turn deserves another I am going to let everything go this morning and answer it. First we are all well now thank God. Robert and Francis were both laid up a week at different times with colds but are better now and both out at school.... Father was not very well last week but he got out through all the storms and would not even hail for a taxi which we tried to get the first day. So far I do not see much change in his general condition and while he is able to do business it is better for him to go on as he is and don't worry about any thing at home because if I thought you were needed here enough to give up college I would send for you at once so leave that to me, but be sure to offer your Communion for him and don't leave the Chapel at night without saying a prayer for us both. Whenever we feel that you can do more than that I will let you know....
>
> > Your loving mother —

Susan died only a few months later, in June 1921, and John died fifteen months after that. After their father's death, Paul and Joe Keane returned to Bridgeport permanently, tasked with running the successful business their father had established more than thirty years earlier. Undoubtedly, the time they spent at Holy Cross proved invaluable. According to Bridgeport newspapers, they continued to increase their family's business before it closed in December 1926.

Harvard University (Cambridge, Massachusetts)

The oldest college in the United States, Harvard was founded in 1636 and has been the alma mater of many of the world's most prominent individuals. U.S. Presidents John Adams, Theodore Roosevelt, and John F. Kennedy graduated from Harvard, as did founding fathers John Hancock and Samuel Adams. Intellectuals W. E. B. Du Bois and Ralph Waldo Emerson, businessmen David Rockefeller and John Loeb, and other innovators all attended Harvard and became leaders in their fields.[56]

The first members of the Keane family to enroll at Harvard University were two sons of John Francis and Susan (Sheahan) Keane: Francis, who earned his MBA there after attending Holy Cross for undergraduate school, and John Francis, Jr., who entered Harvard as an undergraduate in 1917, having already received some college credit owing his academic achievements at Bridgeport High School.[57] He graduated *cum laude* in 1921 and received an MBA in 1922.

On the occasion of his tenth-year report to Harvard's Class of 1921, published in 1931, John wrote that he "decided in 1925 to get some practical experience in corporate financing. Got it. Now busily engaged in attempting to pay tuition fee. Former employer: Guaranty Company. Now investment banker on my own account."[58]

At the time of his twenty-fifth reunion, John was living with his family at Manorville on Long Island in New York, while working for Delafield and Delafield, 14 Wall Street, New York City. In his own words, he described his life after graduation, including his difficulties in facing the stock market troubles of the 1930s. He noted:[59]

> The past twenty-five years have been full to the point of being crowded. They contain great success and great failures. I have acquired some wisdom and a great deal of knowledge. I am still shoveling away the debris of 1932, perhaps to build a better structure in its place.
>
> My wife is too special to put into print. My children are good physical specimens, well behaved, and with high I.Q.'s. My business is absorbing and satisfying. My hobbies are farming, hunting, and speculation.
>
> My Harvard graduation seems four or five years ago rather than twenty-five. What I drew from that font of learning has proved invaluable.

A Continued Tradition

After the stock market crash, John moved his family to a farm on Long Island. The children grew up doing jobs around the farm, handling chickens, goats, cows, pigs, and other animals, learning the value of work as part of their education — and also earning money to pay for their later college education. Each Saturday their father roused them from bed with a simple, "Up John, up Kevin, up Susan, up Andrée." "We were like indentured servants," laughingly recalled sons John and Kevin. Andrée, the youngest child, was sent into the crawlspace under the house to work on the plumbing. The children helped build cesspools and pigpens and burned stumps to clear land. Work came before play; the children could not play baseball or participate in other sports until their chores were done.[60]

John worked at a vinery; Kevin grew hybrid flowers. The children worked together to raise asparagus plants, devoting nearly an acre and a half of their land to the crop. They rose early each morning to cut the asparagus and deliver it to the store for sale. As a result, the children were often five or ten minutes late to school. Their principal, a man by the name of Halleck Wood, would constantly berate John and Kevin for their tardiness, threatening them that they would never make it into college and "were doomed" if they "didn't straighten out."

John made arrangements on his own to pick potatoes for a neighbor, working alongside migrant workers and earning four cents per bushel. He could pick about 40 bushels per day. When he received his first check, for $18, he raced home to show his father. His father told him to take one-third of the check to give to his mother "for the family." Another third, he was told, should be put away for college. The final third he was allowed to keep for himself. "I was absolutely crushed," John relates, and "in tears and so forth," but he followed his father's instructions. "It was a very subtle way of inculcating work, frugality: we had to save for the future."

All of John and Buddy's children were required to save one-third of their income for college, which proved to be essential as each child left the home to pursue an education. After receiving an MBA from Harvard in 1954, John started one of the nation's leading IT firms and developed a systematic project management technique, later published as *Productivity Management*. In 1999, John F. Keane, the boy who was "doomed" for arriving a few minutes late each day to school, was awarded the Alumni Achievement Award from Harvard Business School, the school's highest award. Kim B. Clark, then Dean of Harvard Business School, remarked, "John Keane has been a terrific leader and an outstanding professional example throughout his career. . . . His personal dedication to ethical leadership and his ability to lead others with an entrepreneurial spirit represent some of the most important qualities we are working to develop in our students today."[61]

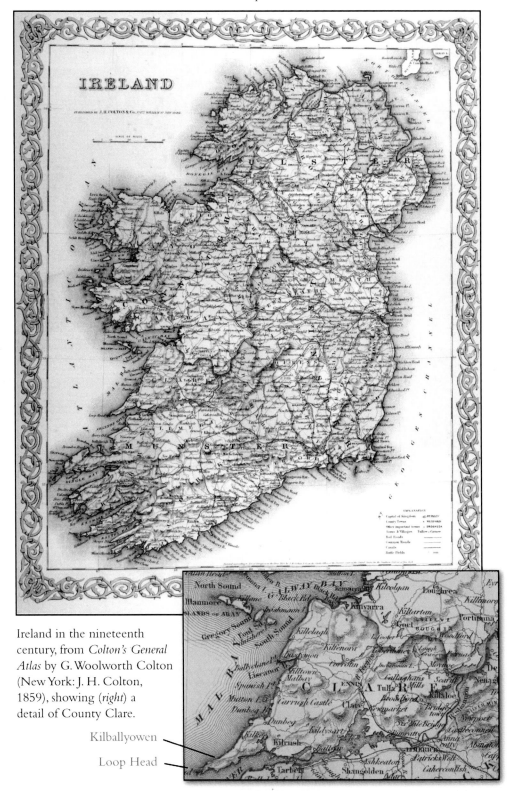

Ireland in the nineteenth century, from *Colton's General Atlas* by G. Woolworth Colton (New York: J. H. Colton, 1859), showing (*right*) a detail of County Clare.

Kilballyowen

Loop Head

The "Little Ark of Kilbaha," in a nineteenth-century engraving of the ark at the time of a mass.

The Little Ark today, inside Our Lady Star of the Sea in Moneen, where it was placed in the 1850s.

"Miss Kennedy distributing clothing at Kilrush," depicting a seven-year-old child, daughter of the Poor Law Inspector of the Kilrush Union. Miss Kennedy gave clothing — some of it her own — to children made destitute by the famine. A writer for the *Illustrated London News* reported that she "was very much affected by the misery of the poor children she saw; and so completely did it occupy her thoughts that, with the consent of her parents, she gave up her time and her own little means to relieve them." From "Conditions in Ireland — Illustrations of the New Poor-Law," *Illustrated London News,* 22 December 1849.

The dramatic Loop Head peninsula.

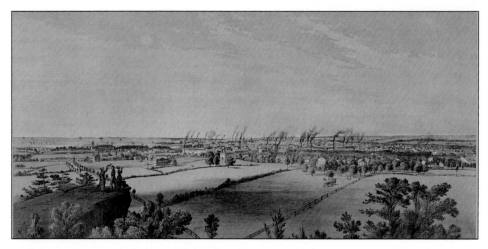

Bridgeport, Connecticut, from "Old Mill Hill" in 1882, shortly before the Keanes arrived from Ireland.

Bird's-eye view of Bridgeport in 1875.

Sepia stereograph of Perkins School for the Blind, South Boston (Dorchester Heights), Massachusetts, ca. 1878, about the time Susan Sheahan entered as a student.

John F. Keane,

Susanna E. Sheahan.

Married at St. Thomas' Church,

Red Creek, New York,

Wednesday, August nineteenth, eighteen

hundred and ninety-one, at 10:30 a. m.

At Home

72 West Liberty Street,

Bridgeport, Connecticut,

after October first.

John and Susan (Sheahan) Keane's wedding invitation and at-home card, 1891.

Above left: Gus Keane, born in 1899. *Right:* Twins Paul and Joe Keane, born in 1900.

Tintype of John F. Keane, *center*, with his daughter Margaret, *rear*, and twins Joe and Paul.

Keane family homestead, North Main Street, Bridgeport, Connecticut.

You Know How It Is When You Buy Clothing

Regardless of what you are paying, there are times when you feel better satisfied when the purchase is made than you have felt in making previous purchases at a similar price. The average man knows when he gets his money's worth. He KNOWS when he is doubtful as to the wisdom of a purchase he has made, but be perfectly sure that no purchase you make here will ever seem other than a thorough bargain—and by "bargain" WE mean exceptional value for the price.

$15 Suits

A suit purchased here for $15 is a bargain in every sense. If we marked the price ticket "$15, reduced from $25," you'd believe it, for the quality is there. However, not a suit in this $15 line is a markdown—and everyone possesses full measure of summer quality, style and tailoring.

John F. Keane & Co.
Main St. at John

Top: John F. Keane & Co. letterhead. *Left:* An ad for the store. *Above:* the store in 1920, advertising a "gigantic supersale."

The family of John and Susan (Sheahan) Keane, at the baptism of Robert Keane, 1905: *Left to right:* Gus, Susan, Robert, Joe, John, Paul, Frank, Margaret, John.

John F. Keane, Sr., with his sons. *Front, left to right:* Robert, John Sr., John, Jr. *Back, left to right:* Paul, Joe, Frank, Gus.

John F. Keane, Jr., during World War I (above) and (right), riding at Camp Zachary Taylor, Kentucky, 1918.

DESCRIPTION OF APPLICANT.

Age: **29** years.		Mouth: **Medium**	
Stature: **5** feet. **5** inches, Eng.		Chin: **Round**	
Forehead: **High**		Hair: **Auburn**	
Eyes: **Brown**		Complexion **Fair**	
Nose: **Straight**		Face: **Round**	
Distinguishing marks **None**			

Miss Margaret Keane,
92 Sanford Place,
Bridgeport, Conn.

A signed duplicate of the photograph to be attached hereto must be sent to the Department with the application, to be affixed to the passport with an impression of the Department's seal.

Margaret Keane (*above*) and her passport application (*right*).

Ordination of "Father Gus," 1931. *Front row:* Margaret (Keating) Burns, Margaret (Keane) Bray, Father Gus, Joe Keane, cousin Martina Keane. *Back row:* Rena Reardon (family friend), Edward Bray, Frank Keane, Dorothy (Keane) Keane, Paul Keane, Marie (Rowan) Keane, Bob Keane.

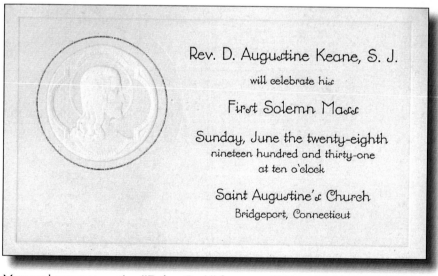

Rev. D. Augustine Keane, S. J.

will celebrate his

First Solemn Mass

Sunday, June the twenty-eighth
nineteen hundred and thirty-one
at ten o'clock

Saint Augustine's Church
Bridgeport, Connecticut

Mass card commemorating "Father Gus's" first mass, 1931.

"Father Gus" Keane, Headmaster of the Cranwell School, at his desk.

Above left: Paul Keane. *Above right:* His wife,
Dorothy (Enola) Keane. *Right:* Bob Keane.

Top left: Victoire "Buddy" (Le Caron) Keane with her children: *front,* John, Kevin; *middle,* Shirley Thomas, Susan, Victoire. *Top right:* Shirley Thomas and young Victoire.

Shirley Thomas, Victoire, Kevin, and John Keane.

John F. Keane, Jr. and "Buddy" Keane, Easter Sunday, Manorville, New York, ca. 1952, in a photo taken by their daughter Andrée.

In another photo by Andrée, the Keane family home in Manorville.

The family of John and "Buddy" Keane, 1950. *Back row:* Susan, Buddy, John, Jr., Victoire, John III, Kevin. *Front row:* George Guydish (son of Victoire), Andrée.

Above Patricia and Robert Keane, Jr.
Right: Bob and Marie (Rowan)
Keane with young Bob and Pat.

Edward and Margaret (Keane) Bray with their children, Susan and David.

Surviving children of John F. and Susan (Sheahan) Keane, 1958. *First row, left to right:* Rev. D. Augustine "Gus" Keane, S. J.; Margaret (Keane) Bray; Robert Keane. *Second row, left to right:* John F. Keane, Jr.; Paul Keane; Frank Keane; Joe Keane.

Keanes at the wedding of Pat Keane and Jack Sparkman. *Left to right:* Bob and Marie Keane, Edward and Margaret Bray, John and Victoire "Buddy" Keane, Frank and Beatrice "Trixie" Keane, Martina Keane, Father Gus, Kay Keane, Paul and Dorothy Keane, Joe Keane.

Keanes in the Keane/Sparkman wedding party: Dorothy Keane (later Achtmeyer), *second from left*; Patricia Keane and Jack Sparkman, *center*; Betty Keane (later Rossbaum), next to Jack; Bob Keane, next to Betty; Susan Bray (later Walker), *far right*.

DESCENDANTS OF

Daniel and Margaret (Keane) Keane

First Generation

1. **Daniel[1] Keane** was born in County Clare, Ireland, about 1832.[1] He died at Sandy Hook in Newtown, Fairfield County, Connecticut, 19 March 1886, and was buried at St. Rose Cemetery in Newtown.[2] He married, likely in County Clare, about 1854, **Margaret Keane**,[3] who was born in County Clare in January 1828, daughter of Michael and Mary (Lynch) Keane. She died, likely in Bridgeport, Fairfield County, on 18 August 1906, though her death is recorded in the vital records of Newtown.[4] She was buried at St. Rose Cemetery.[5]

From April 1857 until 1863, Daniel leased just over 41 acres in the townland of Kilcloher, County Clare, from Marcus Keane, valued at 15 pounds, 15 shillings.[6] Sometime in 1863, Daniel, Margaret, and at least two of their children left Kilcloher for the United States. The family had settled at Sandy Hook by January 1865.[7] Daniel worked for the New York Belting and Packing Company in Newtown.

At the time of the 1870 U.S. Census, the family included Daniel, 38, who was working in a rubber factory; Margaret 40, who was keeping house; and Hannah [Anna], 13, Bridget, 10, John, 7, Michael, 5, and Daniel, 2. The youngest two children were recorded as having been born in Connecticut; all others were born in Ireland. Daniel and his family were living in the same house as Patrick Haugh and George Malee [Malley], both Irish and likely from County Clare, and both rubber factory workers.[8]

In 1880, Daniel and Margaret were still living at Sandy Hook with their two youngest children, Daniel and Michael.[9]

In 1900, fourteen years after Daniel's death from pneumonia, Margaret was living in Newtown with her daughter Anna (Keane) Keating.[10] In 1902 she was living with her son Daniel, boarding at 582 Myrtle Avenue in Bridgeport. She lived there until her death in 1906 from cirrhosis of the liver.[11]

Children of Daniel and Margaret (Keane) Keane:[12]

-     i.   MARY[2] KEANE, b. Kilcloher April 1855;[13] d. prob. in the U.S. bef. 1870.[14]
- 2   ii.   ANNA "ANNIE" [HANNAH] KEANE, b. County Clare Feb. 1857;[15] m. Newtown 18 Oct. 1883 MALACHI KEATING.[16]
- 3   iii.   BRIDGET KEANE, b. Ireland Feb. 1860;[17] m. Newtown 25 May 1889 DANIEL G. KEANE.[18]
- 4   iv.   JOHN FRANCIS KEANE, b. Kilcloher Sept. 1861;[19] m. Red Creek, Wayne County, N.Y., 19 Aug. 1891 SUSAN ELIZABETH SHEAHAN.[20]
- 5   v.   MICHAEL JOSEPH KEANE, b. prob. Newtown Jan. 1865;[21] m. New Haven 16 Oct. 1893 MARGARET B. DALEY.[22]
- 6   vi.   DANIEL P. KEANE, b. Newtown 1 Feb. 1867;[23] m. Newtown 25 June 1905 MARY F. LYNCH.[24]
-     vii.   THOMAS KEANE, b. Newtown 3 June 1870;[25] d. Newtown 26 Aug. 1870.[26]
-     viii.   PATRICK KEANE, b. Newtown 24 March 1872;[27] d. Newtown 14 Feb. 1876.[28]

SECOND GENERATION

    2. ANNA[2] "ANNIE" [HANNAH] KEANE (*Daniel*[1]) was born in Kilcloher, County Clare, Ireland, in February 1857 and was baptized 24 February 1857 at Carrigaholt Catholic Church, County Clare.[29] Her baptism was sponsored by Thomas Gibson and Bridget Keane, likely her relatives. She died in Bridgeport, Fairfield County, Connecticut, 3 March 1927, and was buried at St. Rose Cemetery, Newtown, Fairfield County.[30] She married in Newtown, 18 October 1883, MALACHI KEATING.[31] He died, likely in Newtown, between 1892 and 1900.[32]

    Like his father-in-law Daniel Keane, and like his brother-in-law Daniel G. Keane, Malachi Keating worked at the New York Belting and Packing Company in Newtown until his death. Following his death, Annie moved her family to Bridgeport, where her brother John Francis had moved in 1892, and purchased a home at 582 Maple Avenue. Her mother, Margaret (Keane) Keane, lived with Annie from 1900 until sometime around 1903.

    In 1909, Annie moved to 194 West Liberty, closer to John Francis and to the shop where her daughter Alicia worked as a dressmaker. In 1916, she moved with her daughters Alicia and Josephine to a home at 694 Laurel Avenue, where was joined by her nephew Daniel Vincent Keane in 1920. Soon after she moved to 772 North Avenue, where she lived until her death in 1927.

    Children of Malachi and Anna (Keane) Keating:

      i. MARY M.[3] KEATING, b. Newtown 29 June 1884;[33] d. Bridgeport 12 April 1967;[34] unmarried.

          A resident of Bridgeport for most of her life, Mary worked for many years at the Bridgeport City Welfare Department. She was a member of the Rosary Confraternity of St. Patrick's Church and the Council of Catholic Women. She is buried next to her parents at St. Rose Cemetery in Newtown.[35]

ii. MARGARET KEATING, b. Newtown 15 Nov. 1886;[36] d. Fairfield
Co. 19 July 1984;[37] m. Fairfield Co. abt. 1917 GEORGE BURNS,[38]
b. Bridgeport 6 October 1889 and d. there 30 Oct. 1918, son of
George and Josephine (Baltes) Burns.[39]

Margaret's husband, George, was the son of George Burns,
Sr., who founded Burns Company in Bridgeport. The *Bridgeport
Telegram* of 31 Oct. 1918 reported the death of George Burns, Jr.,
the previous day, a victim of the influenza epidemic that struck the
United States and the world in 1918 and 1919. Nearly 180,000
cases were reported in Connecticut, and many of the state's doctors
were called to Boston due to the outbreak there. George, who was
only 29 years old, was reported to have caught a cold a week before.
As with many other victims of the flu epidemic, the cold quickly
turned into pneumonia.

After the sudden death of her husband, Margaret continued to
work for Burns Company, serving as both treasurer and secretary.
She lived at 32 Parrott Ave. in Bridgeport until her death in 1984.

7   iii. ALICIA KEATING, b. Newtown 12 March 1888;[40] m. prob. Conn. abt.
1916/1917 WILLIAM J. CASEY.[41]

iv. JOHANNA "JOSEPHINE" KEATING, b. Newtown 15 Oct. 1889;[42] d.
Bridgeport 7 April 1964;[43] m. Conn. bef. 1930[44] FRANK M. DAVEY,
b. Ireland 18 March 1893,[45] d. Bridgeport 29 Nov. 1975.[46]

Before her marriage, in 1916, Josephine worked as a school nurse
for the Bridgeport Board of Health. The 1930 census records her
as living with her husband Frank and her two sisters, Margaret
(Keating) Burns and Mary Keating, at 32 Parrott Ave. Frank worked
as a superintendent at a local grocery store in Bridgeport.

The couple lived in Bridgeport for most of their lives, where
Josephine was a member of the Rosary Confraternity of St.
Patrick's Church and the Council of Catholic Women, and was the
chairman of the St. Vincent's Unit of Grey Ladies. She was buried
at St. Rose Cemetery.[47]

8   v. SUSAN KEATING, b. Conn. June 1892;[48] m. Bridgeport 4 April 1923
OTTO WILLIAM HEISE.[49]

3. BRIDGET[2] **KEANE** (*Daniel*[1]) was born, likely in County Clare,
Ireland, in February 1860.[50] She died, possibly in New Jersey or
Connecticut, before 1910.[51] She married in Newtown, Fairfield County,
Connecticut, 25 May 1889, **DANIEL G. KEANE,**[52] who was born in
Ireland in May 1860.[53] He likely died in Essex County, New Jersey,

between 1910 and 1917.[54] According to the Newtown Vital Records, the Reverend P. Donohue, possibly of St. Mary's Catholic Church at Sandy Hook in Newtown, conducted their marriage.

Bridget immigrated to the United States as a young child with her parents, around 1863; Daniel immigrated sometime around 1879, as a teenager. He settled in Newtown. He worked in a rubber factory, possibly New York Belting and Packing Company, the same company that employed his father-in-law. According to census records, Daniel became a naturalized citizen sometime before 1910.[55]

In 1900, Daniel G. Keane and his family — Bridget and their two living children, Martina and Daniel Vincent — were living in Newtown, next door to Dennis H. Keane (possibly Daniel's brother).[56]

After Bridget's death, Daniel moved with his two children to Bloomfield, Essex County, New Jersey, where he is listed as a widower in the 1910 federal census with Martina and Daniel Vincent.[57] After Daniel's death, the children returned to Connecticut to live with their uncle and aunt, John F. and Susan E. (Sheahan) Keane. John and Susan's daughter Margaret was close to her age.

Children of Daniel G. and Bridget (Keane) Keane:

i. MARTINA[3] KEANE, b. Newtown 4 May 1891;[58] d. Bridgeport 16 Oct. 1961;[59] unmarried. Following the death of her father and mother sometime after 1910, Martina moved from New Jersey to Bridgeport, Connecticut, where she lived with her uncle, John Francis Keane, Sr., and his family. Martina quickly became an integral part of the household, becoming godmother to several of his children. Her cousin Paul's daughter, Dorothy (Keane) Achtmeyer, recalls that Martina "was absolutely the warmest, most loving, most beautiful person one would ever like to meet. She was delightful."[60] On 24 Sept. 1923, Martina Keane arrived at the port of New York aboard the *Fort St. George,* having visited Hamilton, Bermuda.[61] Martina maintained close ties to her cousins in Bridgeport and was the maid of honor at the wedding of her cousin Margaret M. Keane to Edward E. Bray on 20 Oct. 1926.[62]

After attending St. Vincent's College in Bridgeport, Martina became a registered nurse and worked for over forty-three years for the Bridgeport City Health Department, eventually rising to become the supervisor of the department's nurses.

In late 1960, to celebrate her retirement, her colleagues, friends and other guests honored Martina with a dinner at the Fairfield

Inn. She died in Bridgeport less than a year later, on 16 Oct. 1961, and was buried alongside other members of her family at St. Rose Cemetery in Newtown.[63]

ii. MARY MARGARET KEANE, b. Newtown 23 April 1893;[64] d. Newtown 4 Sept. 1897.[65]

iii. DANIEL VINCENT KEANE, b. Newtown 11 Sept. 1896;[66] d. Bridgeport 8 Dec. 1973;[67] m. likely Conn. bet. 1925 and 1930 ANN A. REBER,[68] b. Conn. 13 Jan. 1899,[69] d. prob. Fairfield, Fairfield Co., Conn., 30 May 2000.[70]

Sometime after 1910, Daniel Vincent, who appears in most official records as "D. Vincent" or "Vincent," moved from New Jersey to Bridgeport, Conn., to live with his Keating cousins. He completed his World War I draft registration card there in 1917, naming his sister Martina as his nearest relative.[71] In 1920, Vincent was living in Bridgeport with his aunt Annie (Keane) Keating and working as a dental assistant.[72] Between 1920 and 1930, he met Ann Reber, whose parents were born in Bohemia. The two married and made their home at 61 5th Street in Bridgeport. By 1930, D. Vincent was working as an optician and Ann was employed as a stenographer at a local insurance company.[73] He submitted a draft registration for World War II, in which he noted that his nearest relative was his wife "Anne" Keane, and that he was employed by Ray Mason Leonard Inc., of Bridgeport, Conn.[74] Sometime after 1945, Vincent and Ann moved to 213 Wade Street in Bridgeport; they were living there at the time of his death in 1973.[75]

Connecticut Governor James C. Shannon appointed Daniel to the Selective Service Local Board 14 in 1948. This board included the east side of Bridgeport and the entire town of Stratford. Daniel served as vice-chairman until 1967, when he was appointed its chairman.[76] He retired from the board in 1972, shortly before his death in December 1973.[77] He was buried at St. Rose Cemetery in Newtown, the final resting place of his grandfather and other members of the Keane family.[78] Ann remained in Bridgeport until her death in 2000 at the age of 101.[79]

4. JOHN FRANCIS[2] KEANE, SR. (*Daniel[1]*) was born in the townland of Kilcloher, County Clare, Ireland, in September 1861. He was baptized at Carrigaholt Parish 9 September 1861.[80] He died in Bridgeport, Fairfield County, Connecticut, 29 September 1922.[81] He married at St.

Thomas Church in Red Creek, Wayne County, New York, 19 August 1891, **Susan Elizabeth Sheahan**,[82] daughter of Daniel and Margaret C. (Geary) Sheahan. John's brother, Michael Joseph, was a witness at the marriage. Susan was born in Massachusetts in September 1861[83] and died in Bridgeport 15 June 1921.[84]

For more information about John Francis Keane, Sr., and Susan Elizabeth (Sheahan) Keane, see Chapters 4 and 5.

Children of John Francis and Susan Elizabeth (Sheahan) Keane:

9   i.   Margaret M.[3] Keane, b. Bridgeport 1 July 1892;[85] m. Bridgeport 20 Oct. 1926 Edward Emmett Bray.[86]

       ii.   John Francis Keane, Jr., b. Bridgeport 7 Feb. 1894;[87] d. Bridgeport 4 Aug. 1894.[88]

      iii.   Agnes Honora Keane, b. Bridgeport 3 April 1895;[89] d. Newtown 28 April 1898.[90]

      iv.   Catherine Elizabeth Keane, b. Bridgeport 5 Nov. 1896;[91] d. Bridgeport 17 April 1898.[92]

10   v.   John Francis Keane, Jr., b. Bridgeport 27 June 1898;[93] m. Braidwood, Ill., 16 March 1927, Victoire Shaw (Le Caron) Kelley.[94]

11   vi.   Daniel Augustine "Gus" Keane, b. Bridgeport 30 Oct. 1899.[95]

12   vii.   Paul Anthony Keane (twin), b. Bridgeport 21 Dec. 1900;[96] m. Bridgeport 28 June 1928 Dorothy Enola Keane.[97]

13   viii.   Joseph Aloysius "Joe" Keane (twin), b. Bridgeport 21 Dec. 1900;[98] m. abt. 1940 Katherine "Kay" Lyons.[99]

      ix.   Francis Bernard "Frank" Keane, b. Bridgeport 1 Sept. 1903;[100] d. New Haven, Conn., 24 July 1967;[101] m. New Haven 14 June 1947 Beatrice (Thomson) Turner, b. Woodbury, Conn. 15 Aug. 1896,[102] dau. of Frank H. and Ida (Judson) Thomson, d. New Haven 13 Aug. 1978.[103]

            Frank graduated from Holy Cross and Harvard Business School and worked as a self-employed sales consultant in New Haven.[104] His niece, Dorothy (Keane) Achtmeyer, remembered Frank has an "absolutely delightful person." He was known to be very educated, an excellent piano player, and a scratch golfer. He had no children but was the stepfather to Norman Turner of Oxford, Conn.

14   x.   Robert Joseph "Bob" Keane, b. Bridgeport 6 Feb. 1905;[105] m. 1928 Marie Rowan.

5. MICHAEL JOSEPH[2] **KEANE** (*Daniel*[1]) was born, probably in Newtown, Fairfield County, Connecticut, in January 1865.[106] He died, likely in New Haven, New Haven County, Connecticut, in 1926 or 1927.[107] He married at St. Mary's Church in New Haven, 16 October 1893, **MARGARET B. DALEY**,[108] who was born in New Haven in February 1867.[109] She died in Waterbury, New Haven County, 28 January 1949.[110]

Michael Joseph (who is often recorded as "M. Joseph") moved from his family's home at Sandy Hook to Bridgeport, where he was working as a clerk in his brother John Francis's furniture store in 1891. By 1892 he had moved again, this time to New Haven, where he would meet his future wife, Margaret, and start a family.[111]

By 1919, Joseph was working as a druggist from his home at 43 Putnam Avenue in New Haven and also at Country Club Pharmacy, located at 1339 Whitney Avenue.[112]

Following her husband's death, Margaret moved to 28 Walden Street in New Haven. By the 1930 census, she had moved to Hamden in New Haven County.[113]

Children of Michael Joseph and Margaret B. (Daley) Keane:

15   i.   DANIEL JOSEPH[3] KEANE, b. New Haven, New Haven Co., Conn., 3 Feb. 1895,[114] m. Conn. bet. 1920 and 1928 CORINA YOUNG.[115]

16   ii.   JAMES LOUIS KEANE, b. Bridgeport 9 Jan. 1896;[116] m. Conn. abt. 1930/1931 NANCY VERONICA O'CONNELL.[117]

        iii.   CHRISTINA M. KEANE, b. Conn. Sept. 1897;[118] d. Hamden, New Haven Co., 26 Nov. 1978;[119] unmarried.

            By 1922 Christina was working as a public school teacher, eventually teaching physical education to elementary students in New Haven, where according to one student, her "specialty was dodge ball."[120] In 1930, she was living with her widowed mother at 120 Carleton Ave. in Hamden.[121] Christina attended the Univ. of Bridgeport, graduating in 1935; she received an alumni award in 1974.[122]

17   iv.   SYLVESTER JOHN KEANE, b. New Haven 31 Dec. 1900;[123] m. San Antonio, Bexar Co., Texas, 17 Dec. 1938 GRACE WILMA BECK.[124]

        v.   JOSEPH KEANE, b. in Connecticut abt. 1906.[125] *No further record.*

        vi.   MARGARET KEANE, b. in Connecticut abt. 1910; d. 1981.[126] In 1930 she was living with her mother and sister "Christine" at 120 Carleton Avenue in Hamden.[127] A stellar student and athlete, she received a bachelor's degree from Arnold College and MA and PhD degrees in classics from Catholic University, Washington, D.C.

In 1937 Margaret entered the order of the Sisters of St. Joseph of Chambery. Known as Sister Marie Michael, she taught English and foreign languages, directed plays, and coached track at various schools and various grade levels. A collection of her poems, *Love Like This,* was published posthumously. According to the website of the publisher, Antrim House, "Always central to her existence was the God who was the inspiration for her life and her poetry."

6. **DANIEL P.**[2] **KEANE** (*Daniel*[1]) was born in Newtown, Fairfield County, Connecticut, 1 February 1867.[128] He died, likely in Connecticut, after 1940, when he was listed in a city directory.[129] He married in Newtown, 25 June 1905, **MARY F. LYNCH,**[130] who was born in Newtown about 1867,[131] the daughter of Patrick and Honora (Finnell) Lynch. She died in Newtown 6 October 1915 and was buried there at St. Rose Cemetery.[132]

Daniel worked as a clerk in his brother John Francis's furniture store. In the 1900 city directory, he is listed as a tailor at 43 John Street, while rooming at 294 South Avenue.[133] In 1902, he founded Readfield and Keane,[134] and in 1904 he established Daniel P. Keane and John Meredith, clothiers, furnishers, and tailors, at 923 Main Street.[135]

By 1906, Daniel had become the manager at Bridgeport's Auction and Salvage Company, located at 944 Iranistan Avenue.[136] In 1910, Daniel and Mary lived on Washington Street in Bridgeport, where Mary was working as a bookkeeper in a local bank and Daniel had established himself as an auctioneer.[137] By 1912 he was working as an auctioneer of second-hand furniture at 1287 Stratford Avenue and 129 State Street, while residing at 551 Washington Avenue.[138]

His yearly advertisements in the Bridgeport City Directories note that he was a "reliable auctioneer and appraiser" for real estate, furniture, merchandise, stock, fixtures, antiques, and other collectibles.

By 1930 the business had relocated to 46 Kossuth Street and included stove repairs, hammered brass, and copper novelties. The business relocated again in 1940, this time to 419 E. Main Street, not far from where his brother's furniture store stood nearly twenty years before.[139]

Third Generation

7. Alicia[3] Keating (*Anna[2] Keane, Daniel[1]*) was born in Newtown, Fairfield County, Connecticut, 12 March 1888.[140] She died in Stamford, Fairfield County, 29 April 1976.[141] She married, likely in Connecticut, about 1916 or 1917, **William J. Casey**,[142] who was born in Connecticut 23 June 1887.[143] He died in Stamford 3 January 1968.[144]

Before her marriage, Alicia worked as a dressmaker. In 1916 she was the director of the Hat and Gown Shop, located at 45 Washington Avenue in Bridgeport.[145] After her marriage, she and her husband rented an apartment at 87 Clinton Avenue in Stamford, where William worked as a factory manager in 1920.[146]

By 1930 William and Alicia had purchased a home at 89 Clovelly Road in Stamford, valued at $18,000, and William was working as a foreman in a local paper box-manufacturing company.[147]

Children of William J. and Alicia (Keating) Casey:

  i. **William F.[4] Casey**, b. Bridgeport 3 April 1920;[148] d. Stamford 13 June 1992;[149] unmarried.

     At age 21 William enlisted at Fort Devens, Mass., for service in the U.S. Army. Having completed two years of college, he was working as an accountant at the time. His enlistment papers describe him as being 6'5" tall and weighing just 128 pounds.

     William lived at the family home, 89 Clovelly Rd., until his death in 1992.[150]

  ii. **Margaret M. Casey**, b. Conn. 13 Sept. 1923;[151] m. **Arthur J. McDonald**, b. 11 Jan. 1921.[152]

     Arthur enlisted in the United States Air Force at Fort Devens, Mass., 29 Nov. 1943. Before enlisting, Arthur had completed a postgraduate degree and was working as a toolmaker.[153]

8. S<small>USAN</small>[3] K<small>EATING</small> (*Anna[2] Keane, Daniel[1]*) was born, likely in Newtown, Fairfield County, Connecticut, in June 1892, though a record of her birth has not been found in Newtown.[154] She died in Bridgeport 5 June 1973.[155] She married at St. Patrick's Church in Bridgeport, 4 April 1923, O<small>TTO</small> W<small>ILLIAM</small> H<small>EISE</small>; the Reverend John C. Lynch officiated.[156] Otto was born in Jersey City, New Jersey, 16 September 1894,[157] and died in Danbury, Connecticut, 17 May 1972.[158]

Susan lived with her mother, Annie, before her marriage to Otto. According to his World War I draft registration card, completed in 1917, Otto was tall and slender, with gray eyes and light hair. At that time, he was a gauge maker at Ashcroft Manufacturing Company in Bridgeport and lived at 318 Goddard Avenue in Bridgeport.[159]

Otto was the owner and founder of the Heise-Bourdon Tube Company, and was known as an industrialist and philanthropist during his lifetime. Before starting the company, he worked for Manning, Maxwell, and Moore as a development engineer from 1918 to 1923. In 1923 he went to Philadelphia to design pressure gauges and equip planes for their manufacture for the Nelson Valve Company. When the company was sold, he moved to the Taylor Instrument Company in Rochester, New York, where he worked as a development engineer. He specialized in designing equipment for the production of Bourdon tubes, used in the construction of pressure indicators and recorders as well as thermometers and controls.

By 1925, Heise had returned to Manning, Maxwell, and Moore, where he assisted in building the first electric steel safety valves. During his time with the firm, he was granted more than thirty patents, most of which were assigned directly to the company. Heise organized the Heise-Bourdon Tube Company in a one-room loft in Bridgeport in 1930. The company specialized in the high-accuracy gauge, which measures gas or liquid pressure to an accuracy of one-tenth of one percent. The company relocated to Newtown around 1941 on Brook Road in the Palatine district. In 1961, the company built a new plant on South Main Street.

As a philanthropist, Otto was dedicated to the Museum of Art, Science, and Industry in Bridgeport and donated funds to build the pool at the Newtown high school (which was subsequently named after him, along with several other pools in area elementary schools).

He established the Otto W. Heise scholarship fund for graduating students with an interest in science at the University of Bridgeport. Today the award is known as the Otto W. Heise Science Award and is "awarded annually to a junior or senior majoring in science," usually to a student residing in Newtown or Fairfield County.

Otto served as director of the Connecticut National Bank and was an honorary director at the time of his death. He was a chairman of the advisory board of the Newtown branch of CNB and a member of the American Society of Mechanical Engineers, the World War II War Price Board, and the Manhattan Project. In addition, Otto was a member of the Algonquian Club and a justice of the peace in Newtown.[160]

Otto and Susan divorced in 1938, after which Otto married second in Virginia City, Nevada, 6 November 1938, MARY JANE "MOLLY" TRECARTIN.[161] Otto and Molly divorced and he married third, 24 October 1954, NANCY HAWLEY. Otto and Nancy later divorced as well.[162]

After 1942, Susan worked as an employee of Jenkins Brothers and was a member of the Assumption Guild of Assumption Church and the Council of Catholic Women.[163]

Child of Otto William and Susan (Keating) Heise:

    i. JOAN[4] HEISE, b. Conn. 11 July 1924;[164] m. 1949 THOMAS F. CUMMINGS, JR., who d. Palm Coast, Fla., 12 May 2012.[165]

    Children of Thomas F. Cummings, Jr. and Joan (Heise) Cummings:[166]

    1. *Thomas F.[5] Cummings III*, m. Newtown 12 Sept. 1981 *Linda A. Ruffles*.
    2. *Peggie Cummings.*
    3. *Jim Cummings.*

9. MARGARET M.[3] KEANE (*John Francis[2], Daniel[1]*) was born in Bridgeport, Fairfield County, Connecticut, 1 July 1892.[167] She died in Bridgeport 29 July 1973.[168] She married in Bridgeport, 20 October 1926, **EDWARD EMMETT BRAY,**[169] who was born in Bridgeport 20 February 1897, son of Patrick and Delia (_____) Bray.[170]

Margaret received a bachelor's degree from Smith College in Northampton, Massachusetts. She then attended Columbia University, where she received a master's degree in education.[171] On 31 May 1922, she applied for a U.S. passport for study abroad in France, Switzerland, Austria, Spain, Belgium, Italy, and Germany. That year she received a teaching certificate of proficiency in the French language from the Alliance Française. She received a certificate of aptitude in the French language from the University of Paris.[172]

After her parents died, Margaret quickly assumed the duties as leader of her family, as she had a few younger siblings still at home. Before she was married, she taught Spanish and French in both the Bridgeport and

Fairfield, Connecticut, public education systems. While a young teacher in Bridgeport, she was frequently called to the principal's office to hear of the latest hijinks of her younger brother.[173]

Margaret was a member of the Honorary Council of the Girl Scouts of America, served on the Women's Executive Committee for the Children's Ward of Bridgeport Hospital, and was a founding member of the College Club of Bridgeport. She also served as president of the Bridgeport Smith College Club and was a member of the Bridgeport Garden Club, Assumption Guild, the National Council of Catholic Women, the Algonquin Club, the Fairfield Beach Club, and the Brooklawn County Club.[174] Her husband was president of the building and engineering firm Edward E. Bray Company.

Margaret was always close to her brother Gus, who often spent holidays with her family when his school and priestly duties would allow.

Children of Edward Emmett and Margaret M. (Keane) Bray:

18   i.   SUSAN KEANE[4] BRAY, b. Bridgeport 21 Jan. 1930; m. Fairfield 4 Jan. 1958 JOHN DAVID WALKER.[175]

     ii.   DAVID E. BRAY [adopted], b. 20 Nov. 1935, New York City, New York Co., N.Y.

       David attended Cranwell Preparatory School during the time Father Gus was rector of the school; he graduated in 1955. He was a member of the class of 1959 at Georgetown Univ. He served in the U.S. Army for two years. He worked in the advertising and real estate business and as of 2012 was residing in Sag Harbor, N.Y., and Key West, Florida. David's partner (husband), David Neal Hartman, died in October 2010, following a nearly 41-year relationship.[176]

10. **JOHN FRANCIS**[3] **KEANE, JR.** (*John Francis*[2], *Daniel*[1]) was born in Bridgeport, Fairfield County, Connecticut, 27 June 1898.[177] He died in Westhampton, New York, in September 1970.[178] He married in Braidwood, Will County, Illinois, 16 March 1927, as her second husband, **VICTOIRE SHAW (LE CARON) KELLEY**, who was born in Rockville Center, New York, 25 May 1903, and died in New York City in April 1970, daughter of Charles and Victoire Flechelle (Sprague) Le Caron.[179] She married first in Brooklyn, New York, 10 November 1922, Samuel Charles Kelley, son of Edward and Catherine (_____) Kelley.[180]

John attended Bridgeport High School and began his secondary education at the College of the Holy Cross. Halfway through his freshman year there, in 1917, John transferred to Harvard University. In 1917, while at Harvard, John joined the Students' Army Training

Camp, and attended Officers' Training Camp in Plattsburgh, New York. He registered for the World War I draft, noting that he was a student at Harvard and a corporal in the SATC.[181] On 16 September 1918 he was commissioned as a second lieutenant in field artillery, and was sent to the Field Artillery Central Officers' Training School and Camp Zachary Taylor in Kentucky on 26 September 1918. He was honorably discharged on 11 December 1918.[182]

On September 9, 1919, while a student at Harvard, John witnessed the Boston Police Strike. Literally overnight, the streets of Boston were in full disarray. The experience had an impact on John throughout his life; he repeatedly reminded his children, "Don't take guff from cops," as they were growing up.

He received an AB *cum laude* in 1921 and an MBA, also from Harvard, in 1922. Soon afterward, on 9 June 1922, he applied for a U.S. passport, noting that he had visited Quebec in December 1921 and January 1922. His scheduled travel included study abroad with stops in France, Belgium, Greece, Spain, Portugal, Austria, and Italy.[183]

Shortly after graduating from Harvard, John met Victoire Shaw Le Caron, a descendant of the Sprague family of New England. The couple married and settled in Brooklyn, where John worked to bring European technologies to the United States, securing patents for Waterman's Pen and the technology that would become Ford Motor Company's automobile alternator. John traveled extensively to Europe during these years, and on 24 December 1926 he sailed on the SS *Adriatic* from Liverpool, England, arriving at New York on 2 January 1927.[184] At the time, he was living at 17 Battery Place in New York City. John traveled overseas again in 1928, when he sailed on the SS *Aquitania* from Southampton, England, arriving at New York on 4 May 1928.[185] While overseas he was required to cross the English Channel by airplane, a harrowing journey in the 1920s due to the high headwinds.

He was very successful in his work in the 1920s, amassing large sums of stocks and options. As part of his work John was heavily involved in mini loans to support and sustain his customers. He had also been extended a considerable amount of credit, as the majority of his wealth was tied to his extensive stock holdings. His newfound wealth and success would soon disappear, almost overnight. The October 1929 stock market crash left many of the companies John was involved with in receivership or bankrupt. His stock values depleted, John was unable to repay any of his debts. However, he refused to declare bankruptcy and promised to repay his full debt, no matter how long it took. He kept his promise, continually making payments until the debts were paid off in 1960.

Following the stock market crash, John was determined to succeed on Wall Street, and joined Delafield and Delafield as an investment manager. John's specialty was the bond market, and he worked for the rest of his life in estate planning and even continued to manage portfolios until shortly before his death.

Even in the midst of the Great Depression, John and Victoire, who was known as "Buddy," continued to raise their family at 332 Maple Street in Brooklyn, spending time each summer on Long Island with their Grandmother Sprague. The children attended St. Francis of Assisi School, located directly across the street from their home.

The family was deeply affected by the destruction of Pearl Harbor on 7 December 1941. Their son (Shirley) Thomas had joined the U.S. Navy only a few months before, on 26 August. After the family spent the summer with Buddy's mother on Long Island, John told his children that they would not be returning to New York City. He had acquired a farm in Manorville. (In fact, John had asked his mother-in-law to borrow the car to travel to Manorville to secure a house, but was denied the request. Not to be stopped, he rode a bicycle 6 miles from the city to Manorville to secure the property.) He purchased a house and 100 acres of land for $3,000 that would provide them with a vegetable garden. Though the area is remembered as being quite rural, with no running water, John quickly settled his family there, himself commuting back and forth to New York City each weekend. While living costs continued to rise in New York City, John was determined to ensure his family was self-sustaining.

With the move to Manorville, Buddy learned to manage a spartan home (no running water, no central heat) and take care of farm animals and gardens. Once the children were grown, she moved to New York City to be with her husband. She took a job working with Lieutenant Governor Malcolm Wilson, Chairman of the New York World's Fair.

John continued to work in investments for the rest of his career; he worked with several clients up until his death in 1970. He and Buddy died within months of each other.

For their children's memories of John and Buddy, see Appendix II (page 121), the transcript of a November 2011 conversation.

Child of Samuel Charles and Victoire Shaw (Le Caron) Kelley:

19   i.   SHIRLEY THOMAS KEANE, b. New York City 26 Aug. 1924 as Shirley Thomas Kelley;[186] m. 20 Aug. 1948 PATRICIA CATHERINE McHUGH.[187]

Children of John Francis and Victoire Shaw (Le Caron) Keane:

20   ii.   VICTOIRE LE CARON[4] KEANE, b. New York City 20 Dec. 1927; m. (1) New York ca. 1944 GEORGE GUYDISH; m. (2) New York ca. 1952 FRANK JABLONKA; m. (3) New York ca. 1959 JOHN FENWICK AIRD; m. (4) Conn. ca. 1968 GEORGE BOSSERT; m. (5) Calif., 29 March 1981, RICHARD BARTH; m. (6) Calif., ca. 2006, KURT MANN.[188]

21   iii.   JOHN FRANCIS KEANE III, b. New York City 11 Oct. 1931; m. Belmont, Middlesex Co., Mass., 15 Nov. 1958 MARILYN TEAGAN.[189]

22   iv.   KEVIN THOMAS KEANE, b. New York City 28 Feb. 1933;[190] m. Johnson City, Broome Co., N.Y., 27 June 1959 ELIZABETH ANN RICE.[191]

23   v.   SUSAN KEANE, b. New York City 25 March 1937; m. (1) DONALD PARSONS; m. (2) Newport Beach, Orange Co., Calif., 19 April 1975 ROBERT J. TRIVISON.[192]

24   vi.   ANDRÉE FLORENCE KEANE, b. New York City 15 Oct. 1940; m. New York City 27 Oct. 1962 PETER JOSEPH SHIELDS, JR.[193]

11. DANIEL AUGUSTINE[3] "GUS" KEANE (*John Francis[2], Daniel[1]*) was born in Bridgeport, Fairfield County, Connecticut, 30 October 1899.[194] He died in Boston, Suffolk County, Massachusetts, 15 October 1961.[195]

Gus went to high school in his hometown of Bridgeport and furthered his education with another year at the College of the Holy Cross in Worcester, Massachusetts.[196] Rev. D. Augustine Keane, SJ, entered the Jesuit Order at St. Andrew's Episcopal Church in Poughkeepsie, Dutchess County, New York, in 1918.[197] Gus returned to Weston College in 1928 to study theology so he could become a priest; he was ordained in 1931.[198] He studied scholastic philosophy at Weston College and received an MA in education from Boston College.[199] He earned a doctorate in philosophy from the Pontifical Gregorian University in Rome, Italy.[200]

Gus's teaching career began at Boston College High School, where he taught third-year students from 1925 to 1928.[201] As Father Keane, he served as a Jesuit faculty member at Weston College, from about 1933 to 1936.[202] He then succeeded Rev. James T. McGovern, SJ, as principal of BC High on 14 February 1936, at the age of 37.[203] He was principal and board member for fifteen years, during which time he doubled enrollment and led the raising of $5 million to build a new school on Morrissey Boulevard in the Dorchester section of Boston.[204] On 30 May 1950, the Archbishop of Boston, Richard James Cushing, laid the cornerstone of the new main building, with Father Keane acting as master of ceremonies.[205] During his tenure as principal, Father Keane delivered many eulogies and high-profile sermons.[206] He was often mentioned in the local newspapers for his role in the school's religious retreats, events, and graduation ceremonies.[207]

On 21 June 1951, Father Keane took over as rector and headmaster of the Cranwell Preparatory School in Lenox, Massachusetts, succeeding Rev. Joseph R. N. Maxwell, SJ, who became president of Boston College.[208] According to the *Springfield Union,* "The appointment of Father Keane was made by Very Rev. John Jansens, father general of the Society of Jesus in Rome, Italy."[209] Under Father Keane's leadership, the school gained new buildings for classrooms and a senior dorm.[210] In November 1956, Father Keane began expanding the athletic facilities of Cranwell Prep.[211] A month later, the school celebrated the most successful fall sports campaign in its history by presenting the Father Keane Trophy. The "senior football fathers" donated this "huge golden football trophy" in honor of the undefeated season and Father Keane's role in the school and athletic field expansions.[212]

In August 1958, Father Keane returned to BC High as a guidance counselor, ending his long career as a teacher of Latin, English, and Greek.[213] His legacy remains in his epistemology work, since "adopted by the Jesuits as a standard text" and in the fond memories of BC High and Cranwell Prep students and faculty touched by his lifelong commitment to Jesuit education.[214]

Within the family, Gus was a popular uncle. His niece, Susan (Bray) Walker, recalls, "As children, we greatly anticipated his visits because he always had lots of stories and brain twisters for us. When we would fall into a brain twister trap, he would laugh heartily. He was a natural-born teacher."[215]

Father Keane died at BC High on 15 October 1961. His detailed obituary ran in both the *Boston Globe* and the *Bridgeport Post* the following day.[216] The requiem Mass took place at the Immaculate Conception Church on Harrison Avenue in Boston on 18 October 1961, and burial was at Weston College Cemetery in Weston, Middlesex County, Massachusetts.[217]

12. PAUL ANTHONY³ KEANE (*John Francis², Daniel¹*) was born 21 December 1900 in Bridgeport, Fairfield County, Connecticut.[218] He died in Fairfield, Fairfield County, Connecticut, 15 November 1975.

He was buried at St. Michael's Cemetery in Stratford, Fairfield County, where he is interred in the John F. Keane family plot.[219] He married at Bridgeport, 29 June 1928. **DOROTHY ENOLA KEANE**, who was born there 21 March 1905, daughter of James and Bridget (Burns) Keane. She died 12 August 1995 in West Palm Beach, Palm Beach County, Florida, and is buried in the Keane family plot in St. Michael's Cemetery, next to her husband.[220]

During their teenage years, Paul and his twin brother, Joe, worked and trained at their father's haberdashery. Consistent with the family tradition of seeking higher education, the twins matriculated at the College of the Holy Cross. During their junior year, they arranged to finish their senior year at Harvard College. Their father, grieved by the recent death of his wife while dealing with his own terminal illness, died in 1922. As a result, the twins had to withdraw from college to manage the family business. According to the family, "It was a given that Paul and Joe would make sure that their two younger brothers, Bob and Frank, graduate college." The twins responsibly fulfilled this commitment."[221] In 1926, the brothers opted to close the family business in light of Bridgeport's shifting business environment. The twins were free to pursue their respective career paths.

Paul saw opportunity at John F. Woodruff Co., a men's clothing store in nearby Danbury, Connecticut, where he served as vice president. Several years after Paul's marriage to his longtime sweetheart, Dorothy Enola Keane, Mr. Woodruff unexpectedly closed the business.

Throughout the Great Depression, Paul was employed as a marketing representative for Investors Syndicate. In 1940 Paul found his true career path when he joined Fletcher Thompson Architects Inc., a prominent Bridgeport architectural and engineering firm. A short time later, he was named treasurer of the firm. Paul retired in 1970, after twenty-nine years of service. He also invested in and became president of Homesites Inc., a successful townhouse-style apartment complex. Overseeing his investment kept him busy throughout his retirement.

Paul was a Fourth Degree Knight and, for a number of years, served as financial secretary for the Park City Council No. 16 Knights of Columbus. He was active in the Holy Name Society of Our Lady of the Assumption Catholic Church, and a member of Civitan International and the Algonquin Club.

Paul's daughters, Betty and Dottie, remember their father as a wonderful parent. Dottie believes that she and Betty were inspired by the exemplary way their father lived his life. Every morning and every evening Paul would kneel in the confines of the master bedroom to pray quietly.

Betty notes that Paul was "an outstanding husband, father, and friend. He always had time for family and friends. He nurtured us in every way. He was compassionate to all. His sense of humor was renowned and his friends and family were the beneficiaries of his joy of life. Current events were a continual interest, and his keen mind and his many interests made him an enjoyable companion in any group."[222]

Paul's wife, Dorothy, lost her mother at the age of 2. Her widowed father, James, resolved to raise her, together with her three brothers, alone. He tried to spend time each evening to listen to and counsel Dorothy, his favorite child.

Dorothy graduated from the College of New Rochelle, Westchester County, in 1927 with a BS in biology. She received a teaching certificate in Connecticut and discovered that she had a natural aptitude for teaching. She taught basic and advanced biology and chemistry at the high school level, mostly at Central High School in Bridgeport. Always maintaining an orderly classroom, she was able to reach out and motivate all her students at all learning levels. Dorothy retired in 1971.[223]

According to Dorothy's daughters, she would often repeat three maxims to them: "(1) Look for the good in a person. No matter how a person behaves there is good in everyone. (2) Use the soft word. (3) Be willing to step back to let one's spouse go forward." Betty and Dottie remember their mother as an outstanding wife and a true complement to her husband. "She was a loving mother, intelligent and beautiful—a woman ahead of her time."[224]

Children of Paul Anthony and Dorothy (Keane) Keane:

25   i.   ELIZABETH ANNE[4] "BETTY" KEANE, b. Bridgeport 8 Aug. 1929; m. Fairfield 28 Dec. 1954 ROBERT PHILIP ROSSBAUM.[225]

26   ii.   DOROTHY MARIE "DOTTIE" KEANE, b. Bridgeport 16 May 1932; m. Fairfield August 1958 HERBERT CARL ACHTMEYER, JR.[226]

13. JOSEPH ALOYSIUS[3] "JOE" KEANE (*John Francis[2], Daniel[1]*) was born in Bridgeport, Connecticut, 21 December 1900,[227] and died in Dallas, Texas 26 July 1992 of throat cancer.[228] He married, about 1940, **KATHERINE "KAY" LYONS,** daughter of Thomas and Mary (Curley) Lyons of West Roxbury, Massachusetts. She was born 11 October 1906 and died in Dallas 1 August 1997 of congestive heart failure.[229]

Like his twin brother Paul, Joe worked at his father's store before attending the College of the Holy Cross. The brothers shared a room at school, indulging in at least one "oatmeal contest" to see who could eat the most oatmeal. Joe lost to his brother Paul, who ate seventeen bowls in a victory still remembered by the family.[230]

When his father died in 1922, Joe and his brother Paul were asked to return to Bridgeport to take part in the family business. As secretary of the company, Joe had the difficult task of delivering news of the store's closing to members of the Bridgeport community in 1926. Still the twins made sure their younger brothers could graduate from college.

After the store's closing, Joe moved to New Jersey, though his nieces and nephews still looked forward to his visits to the Keane home in Bridgeport. Whenever he visited, "we could eat as many banana splits as we wanted. And that was a big deal," remembered his niece, Susan (Keane) Trivison.[231]

Before marrying, Joe lived at 332 Maple Street in Brooklyn with his brother, John Francis Keane, Jr., and his family. His nephews John and Kevin Keane remember seeing the sights of New York City with Uncle Joe, traveling to the *Queen Mary,* the Statue of Liberty, and Ebbets Field to watch the Dodgers play on the weekends.

Joe was an accountant. Kay, a graduate of Lesley College, was a gym teacher.

Children of Joseph Aloysius and Katherine (Lyons) Keane:[232]

27 i. ANNE BARBARA[4] "NANCY" KEANE, b. East Orange, N.J., 5 March 1942; m. Cohasset, Mass., 7 September 1985, ROBERT MEDLIN.

ii. THOMAS PATRICK "TOMMY" KEANE, b. 1943; d. New Orleans, La., 16 Aug. 1981 of leukemia. He was a bartender; in later years he went by the name Shane Keane.

14. ROBERT JOSEPH[3] "BOB" KEANE (*John Francis[2], Daniel[1]*) was born in Bridgeport, Connecticut, 6 February 1905[233] and died about 1967.[234] He married, 9 June 1929, **MARIE ROWAN,** who was born 9 June 1908, daughter of _____ and Mary (Müller) Rowan.[235]

Bob attended the College of the Holy Cross, but then transferred to and graduated from Fordham University. While there, he met Marie Rowan, who lived nearby in the Bronx. After they married, they lived on Park Avenue in Bridgeport, Connecticut. Their daughter, Patricia, was born prematurely — at Royal Hospital in the Bronx — while they were visiting Marie's mother. In 1935 the family moved to Kings

Highway in New Rochelle, New York, and in 1936 to Byron Lane in Larchmont, New York. Bob and Marie lived there until they died.

Bob was a salesman; he sold Rexair and Electrolux vacuum cleaners and eventually insurance. He was known to many in the family as "the jokester of them all." He carried a little book full of jokes for every occasion; a niece recalls, "We all couldn't wait to hear all the jokes."[236]

Children of Robert Joseph and Marie (Rowan) Keane:[237]

28   i.   PATRICIA[4] KEANE, b. Bronx, N.Y., 24 April 1932; m. 20 Nov. 1954 JOHN CORNELIUS "JACK" SPARKMAN.

29   ii.   ROBERT JOSEPH KEANE, JR., b. New Rochelle 6 Oct. 1936; m. (1) DEANNE PFEIFFER, m. (2) CHRISTINA ANNE "JUSTY" (CARLO) GALLUP.

15. DANIEL JOSEPH[3] KEANE (*Michael Joseph[2], Daniel[1]*) was born in New Haven, New Haven County, Connecticut, 3 February 1895.[238] He died in Middletown, Middlesex County, Connecticut, 21 October 1969.[239] He married, between 1920 and 1928, **CORINA YOUNG,**[240] who was born in Texas about 1901 and died in Brownsville, Cameron County, Texas, 24 February 1974; she was buried at the Buena Vista Burial Park.[241] Daniel and Corina divorced before 1930.[242] She married second in Brownsville, Cameron County, Texas, 23 April 1934, John N. McCoy.[243]

Daniel attended Hillhouse High School in New Haven and received multiple scholarships to attend Yale University. He graduated in 1916. While at Yale he was a member of the Waylaid Debating Club, and served in it as secretary in 1915 and 1916. He also participated on the university debate team in 1916. After his graduation, he lived at 189 Columbus Avenue in New Haven and told Yale he was "undecided as to his future work," but noted an interest in studying law.[244]

While his future career path was undecided in 1916, Daniel soon joined the United States Army, serving as a second lieutenant of cavalry from Plattsburgh. He soon became attached to the 13th Cavalry and commanded a remount depot, which took him to Texas, where he was promoted to major. For his service during World War I, seeing action on 8 and 9 January 1918, he was awarded the Mexican Service Medal.[245]

In 1919, Daniel lived with his parents at 49 Putnam Avenue in New Haven, but by 1920 he had rejoined the army as a soldier, stationed at Camp Furlong, Luna County, New Mexico.[246] After this, he worked in the music business. It is possible that met his future wife, Corina Young, while stationed at San Antonio. Soon after their marriage, the couple moved from San Antonio to New Haven, returning to San Antonio by 1925. They divorced before 1930.[247]

Daniel returned a World War II draft registration card that noted his address as 280 East Main Street in Bridgeport and his nearest relative as Mrs. Margaret Keane, of 24 Coram Street in Hamden, Connecticut. At that time, Daniel had returned to the music business and was employed by Bridgeport Brass Company.[248]

Child of Daniel Joseph and Corina (Young) Keane:

    i.   JOHN JOSEPH YOUNG[4] KEANE, b. Brownsville 21 Sept. 1928;[249] m. 14 June 1974 Cameron Co. MARIE S. SOLIZ.[250]

        John lived with his mother in Brownsville and attended St. Joseph's Academy, where he graduated in 1946 with the second highest scholastic honors.[251]

        In 1951, he graduated from the 5th Armored Division's leaders school at Camp Chafee in Arkansas, while assigned to the 529th Field Artillery Observation Battalion in Fort Sill, Oklahoma.[252]

        At the time of his grandmother's death in 1953, John was stationed in Italy. Following his service in the military, he attended the University of Texas, where he received a bachelor's degree in civil engineering in 1965.[253] As of this writing, he was living in Brownsville.[254]

16. **JAMES LOUIS[3] KEANE** (*Michael Joseph[2], Daniel[1]*) was born in Bridgeport, Fairfield County, Connecticut, 9 January 1896.[255] He died in Newington, Hartford County, Connecticut, 12 March 1970.[256] He married in Connecticut, about 1930 or 1931, **NANCY VERONICA O'CONNELL**,[257] who was born in England 13 January 1908,[258] and died in Avon, Hartford County, Connecticut, 4 August 1990.[259]

James pursued a degree at Yale University alongside his brother, Daniel Joseph, while also working as an electrical engineer; he graduated in 1916. In 1914 he had enlisted in the Coast Artillery Corps; in 1916 he was on border service with the Connecticut National Guard. During World War I, James served in the army; he was promoted to captain and was stationed with the 1st Coast Artillery in Fort McKinley, Maine, and later at Fort Monroe, Virginia. He was later transferred to Company A of the 2nd Aviation Instructions Company, followed by the 50th Aero Squadron, which served in Clamecy, France.[260]

After the war, James continued to serve in the U.S. military; Captain James L. Keane is recorded as leaving Antwerp, Belgium, 31

July 1920 aboard the U.S.A.T. *Pocahontas,* destined for Hoboken, New Jersey.[261] He is also recorded aboard the USS *Siberia Maru,* which sailed from Yokohama, Japan, in October 1926 and arrived at the port of San Francisco 15 Oct. 1926.[262]

In 1930, James was working as an engineer for an insurance company in Hartford, lodging in the household of Roger Lane on Denison Street in Hartford.[263]

On 28 October 1931, James and his wife sailed from Hamilton, Bermuda, aboard the SS *Carinthia.*[264] By 1942, the couple had moved to Newington, where they were living at 2727 Berlin Turnpike. James was employed at Aetna Casualty and Surety Company of Hartford.[265]

Child of James Louis and Nancy Veronica (O'Connell) Keane:

   i. JAMES[4] KEANE, JR., b. Conn. ca. 1933.[266]

17. SYLVESTER JOHN[3] KEANE (*Michael Joseph[2], Daniel[1]*) was born in New Haven, New Haven County, Connecticut, 31 December 1900.[267] He died in San Antonio, Bexar County, Texas, 10 February 1981.[268] He married in San Antonio, 17 December 1938, GRACE WILMA BECK,[269] who was born in Runge, Karnes County, Texas, 26 September 1906.[270] She died in Texas 29 January 1988 and is buried with her husband at the Fort Sam Houston National Cemetery in San Antonio.[271]

Sylvester served as a captain in the United States Army during World War I, beginning his service 3 January 1919. In 1921, he applied for a U.S. passport, indicating he was planning to travel and study in France, Belgium, Italy, and Switzerland. His application noted that he stood 5 feet, 4 inches, with a high forehead, medium mouth, square chin, straight-medium nose, a smooth face, and had brown eyes, brown hair, and a light complexion.[272]

He retired from the army on 31 January 1939 and then attended Yale University, where on 19 June 1940 he received a master's degree in engineering.[273]

Children of Sylvester John and Grace Wilma (Beck) Keane:

   i. MICHAEL SYLVESTER[4] KEANE, b. San Antonio 2 Jan. 1940;[274] m. Dordrecht, Holland, HERMINA HENDRIKA VAN'T SPIJKER.[275]

      Michael received a BA from the Univ. of Texas at Austin, an MS from the Univ. of Göttingen, and a PhD from the Univ. of Erlangen-Nürnberg. An internationally known and recognized professor of mathematics, Michael lectures around the world, frequently visiting

Holland and other European countries. On the faculty of Wesleyan Univ. in Middletown, Conn, he focuses on mathematical physics, operator algebras, probability theory, and topological dynamics.[276]

ii.   KAROLEN STELLA KEANE, b. San Antonio 25 Dec. 1943;[277] m. 6 June 1964 THOMAS WESTBROOK GLASS.[278]

Karolen attended Jefferson High School and the Univ. of Texas, where she was the treasurer of the Alpha Chi Omega Sorority and a member of the Texas Stars, Alpha Lambda Delta, and Tau Beta Sigma Sororities.[279]

She and Thomas divorced 12 August 1981. Karolen was residing in San Antonio as of this writing.[280]

iii. SARAH MARGARET KEANE, b. San Antonio 28 Dec. 1947;[281] m. San Antonio 16 April 1966 WILLIAM KENNETH CLARK,[282] b. Bexar Co. 20 March 1939.[283]

Fourth Generation

18. **Susan Keane**[4] **Bray** (*Margaret M.*[3] *Keane, John Francis*[2], *Daniel*[1]) was born in Bridgeport, Fairfield County, Connecticut, 21 January 1930. She married at the Church of Assumption in Fairfield, Fairfield County, 4 January 1958, **John David Walker,** who was born in Boston, Massachusetts, 17 June 1927, son of Clarence Cook and Grace Euphemia (Tompkins) Walker. The ceremony was officiated by Susan's uncle, the Reverend Daniel Augustine Keane.[284]

Susan attended Unquowa School in Fairfield and Fairfield High School. While attending Fairfield High, she was a member of the National Honor Society and elected to the student council. In 1948 she graduated from the Northampton School for Girls. She received a BA from Smith College, Northampton, Massachusetts, in 1952.

Until 1960, Susan worked as an advertising copywriter for McCann Erickson Advertising Agency. She has been an active community volunteer, serving as president of the Scarsdale Chapter of American Field Services and as library chair, vice president, and president of the Parent Teacher Association of her children's school. In addition, she was the treasurer and newsletter editor for the Scarsdale Village Club and was elected to the school board nominating committee as well as the nominating committee for village trustees. In 1985 and 1986 she served as president of the Westchester Smith [College] Club.

Susan has devoted a great deal of service to Arc of Westchester, an organization dedicated to "empower children and adults with developmental disabilities to achieve their potential based on personal choices, abilities and interests." She has served on the organization's board of directors and was vice president. She has also served as chair or a member of various committees within the organization, including the Governance and Executive committees as well as the Capital Campaign and Hawthorne Project committees. In 2007 Susan received the Katzenberg Award for outstanding service and in 2009 received the Kingsley Family Partnership Award.

John graduated in 1945 from Wellesley High School in Wellesley, Massachusetts, from which he received first prize in English. Following his graduation, he served in the U.S. Navy, in the Asia Pacific Service, from 1945 to 1946. He received a BA, *cum laude,* from Amherst College in Amherst, Massachusetts, in 1950. In 1951 he received an MA in English literature from Columbia University.

Engaged in the advertising business, John has worked as a copywriter for Fletcher Richards, Inc., and was associate creative director for Communications Counselors Network. Before his retirement he was vice president and management supervisor at Ogilvy & Mather.

John has also served as treasurer and a trustee for Scarsdale Adult School and was an active baseball, soccer, and basketball coach for Scarsdale Recreation Children's Athletics.

Children of John David and Susan Keane (Bray) Walker:

     i. ELIZABETH GRACE[5] WALKER, b. New York City 6 Feb. 1960. She attended Adams School in New York City and BOCES in Rye Lake, N.Y., and in 1981 she graduated from Westlake High School in Thornwood, N.Y. Currently an associate at eDocNY, a document storage company, she has also worked at MetLabs and Caldor.

        A recipient of multiple prizes in swimming from the Special Olympics, in 2005 Elizabeth was named artist of the month by Arc of Westchester, where she serves as a member of the Agency Customer Service Committee, a self-advocacy group. Her mother notes, "Elizabeth is developmentally disabled. She is happy, cooperative, likes to help with cooking and take part in community activities. She enjoys being with her nieces and nephews."

30   ii. DAVID BRAY WALKER, b. New York City 10 Jan. 1963; m. Lexington, Davidson Co., N.C., 16 July 1994 ELIZABETH MOFFITT CAMPBELL.

31   iii. WILLIAM ALEXANDER WALKER, b. New York City 20 June 1964; m. New York City 19 Aug. 1995 AMY LYNN WALSH.

19. SHIRLEY THOMAS KEANE was born in New York City 26 Aug. 1924, son of Samuel Charles and Victoire (Le Caron) Kelley. He later assumed the surname of Victoire's second husband, John Francis Keane. He died probably at Bayonne, Hudson County, New Jersey, 21 March 1982.[285] He married **PATRICIA CATHERINE MCHUGH,**[286] who was born at Jersey City, Hudson County, New Jersey, 1 March 1921, and died probably at Matawan, Monmouth County, New Jersey, March 7, 2001.[287]

Shirley, who later was known as Thomas S. Keane, enlisted in the U.S. Navy in 1941 and was honorably discharged 14 November 1945. He was later a longshoreman and a ship navigator with Exxon Corporation. At the time of his application to the Sons of the American Revolution in 1952, he was working for the Erie Railroad and living in Jersey City.[288]

His daughter Linda recalls that he had many stories about World War II, and that the war had a lasting effect on him. She also recalls, "He loved all his sisters, but had a special fondness for sister Vicky."[289]

Children of Shirley Thomas and Patricia Catherine (McHugh) Keane:

i. LINDA SUSAN KEANE, b. Greenport, Suffolk Co. (Long Island), N.Y. 21 Feb. 1950; m. (1) 21 Feb. 1970 RICHARD CHRISTENSEN, div. 1979; m. (2) 21 June 1980 RICHARD SMITH.

   Linda lived in a farmhouse on Long Island until she was 6 years old. "The smells of asparagus, strawberries, and fresh-cut grass still bring me back," she writes. "Bouncing on the back of the farm truck, dirt everywhere, laughing with Uncle John and Kevin (my godfather)."[290]

   Linda graduated from Brookdale Community College. Since 1995 she has been personal assistant and cook for the Rev. John Scully at the Church of St. Clement, Matawan, N.J.

   Children of Richard and Linda (Keane) Christensen:

   1. *Richard Joseph Christensen,* b. 31 Oct. 1972. Cook and manager, Laurel Bay Rehab and Nursing Home.
   2. *David Michael Christensen,* b. 15 Sept. 1973; m. 9 Sept. 2000 *Christine Crane.* Veteran of the U.S. Navy; finance manager, Bob King Volkswagen, Wilmington, N.C.

      Child of David Michael Christensen and Michelle Coleman:

      A. *David Michael Christensen,* b. 12 Dec. 1997.

      Children of David Michael and Christine (Crane) Christensen:

      B. *Molly Christensen,* b. 11 Jan. 2003.
      C. *Flynn Christensen,* b. 18 Jan. 2006.

Children of Richard and Linda (Keane) (Christensen) Smith:

1. *Kerrin Glynn Smith,* b. 6 Jan. 1981. Graduated from Georgian Court College, N.J. Officer in charge, PMR Gabbs Post Office, Gabbs, Nev.

2. *Shannon Rose Smith,* b. 11 Dec. 1982. Graduated from Stetson Univ., Fla. Employed in institutional sales, First Eagle Investment Management, New York City.

ii. TIMOTHY KEANE, b. 6 Feb. 1957; m. 1991 PATRICIA POSO, who d. in 2011. He worked as a property manager in N.J. and is retired in Fort Lauderdale, Fla.

iii. DANNY KEANE, b. 25 Jan. 1960; m. 19 May 1984 KATHY BAUER. A graduate of Rutgers University, Danny served in the U.S. Army, 101st Airborne Div. He retired from General Motors and is CEO of Middle River Sober Living, LLC, Fort Lauderdale, Fla.

Children of Danny and Kathy (Bauer) Keane:

1. *Danny Keane,* b. 4 Jan. 1985; m. 3 Sept. 2010 *Kathleen* _____.

Child of Danny and Kathleen (_____) Keane:

A. Eloise Violet Keane, b. 17 Aug. 2012.

2. *Christopher Keane,* b. 9 May 1986.

iv. GLYNN MARIE "DOLLY" KEANE, b. 7 Oct. 1963; m. 10 Nov. 1985 DANIEL DUGAN. She is enrolled in a master's program at the Univ. of North Carolina at Wilmington.[291]

Children of Daniel and Glynn Marie (Keane) Dugan:

1. *Daniel Dugan, Jr.,* b. 12 May 1987; m. 16 Oct. 2010 *Amanda Chase.* He graduated from Rensselaer Polytechnic Institute and is employed by KAO as a process engineer.

Child of Daniel and Amanda (Chase) Dugan:

A. *Oliver Dugan,* b. 10 June 2010.

2. *Conor Thomas Dugan,* b. 21 April 1990. Student, and student government president, at Univ. of North Carolina at Charlotte.

20. **VICTOIRE LE CARON**[4] **KEANE** (*John Francis*[3–2], *Daniel*[1]) was born in New York City, New York County, New York, 20 December 1927. She married first, in New York, about 1944, **GEORGE GUYDISH;** second, in New York, ca. 1952, **FRANK JABLONKA;** third, in New York ca. 1959, **JOHN FENWICK AIRD**, born 28 December 1930 and died 24 September 1997, son of John Bryson and Florence (Young) Aird;[292] fourth, in Connecticut, ca. 1968, **GEORGE BOSSERT;** fifth, in California, 29 March 1981, **RICHARD BARTH;** and sixth, in California, ca. 2006, **KURT MANN.** [293]

Victoire attended St. Francis of Assisi Grade School in New York City and graduated from Bishop McDonald Memorial High School in Brooklyn, New York. She worked in the real estate industry.

Children of Victoire Le Caron (Keane) (Guydish) (Jablonka) (Aird):

32   i.   GEORGE[5] GUYDISH, JR., b. New York 1 Nov. 1945; m. CATHY WINNUBST.

     ii.   VICTOIRE KATHERINE AIRD, b. Southampton, Suffolk Co., N.Y. 30 Dec. 1952. She received a full scholarship to the Univ. of Southern California, where she earned a bachelor's degree. She works in advertising and has received numerous national and international awards.

     iii.   WENDY JANE AIRD, b. Southampton 2 Oct. 1954; m. Chicago, 16 March 1995, DAVID ROY PERCHES, who was b. Los Angeles, Calif. 6 June 1948 and d. 20 Dec. 2003 of a heart attack. Wendy attended the Univ. of California, Los Angeles, where she received a full scholarship, and works for Expedia.com.

33   iv.   ANDRÉE AIRD, b. Southampton 31 Oct. 1956; m. (1) 11 July 1986 ZANE OWEN JOHNSON; m. (2) Orange Co., Calif., 2000, RUSSELL GORDON PRIMROSE.

34   v.   JOHN FENWICK AIRD II, b. New York City 3 March 1960; m. (1) 18 June 1983 ALISA MICHELLE WILLMS; m. (2) 21 Dec. 1996 PATRICIA RENEE (HAINES) ARNOLD.

21. **JOHN FRANCIS**[4] **KEANE III** (*John Francis*[3–2], *Daniel*[1]) was born in New York City, New York County, New York, 10 October 1931.[294] He married in Belmont, Middlesex County, Massachusetts, 15 November 1958, **MARILYN TEAGAN**, who was born in Boston, Suffolk County, Massachusetts, 20 December 1933, daughter of John and Gladys M. (McGuinness) Teagan.

John attended Center Moriches High School and then Harvard College, where he graduated in three years, *magna cum laude,* with a degree in economics. He attended Harvard Business School and received an MBA in 1954. He received a commission from the U.S. Navy and was discharged as a lieutenant in 1957.

John then joined Arthur D. Little, Inc., as a consultant, where he spent three years before joining IBM's Data Processing Division. It was here where he learned about computers and developed a keen sense of salesmanship. In late 1965, John sensed that there was a budding need for guiding and assisting customers in the productive use of this new technology. He left IBM and formed Keane Associates, Inc.

The company was successful and spread its influence to India, Canada, England, and most of the fifty states. The company grew to more than 11,000 employees and became a member of the New York Stock Exchange. Revenues exceeded $1 billion. In 2007 Keane Associates was sold to the private equity group of Citibank, and then to NTT, a Japanese company.

John's wife, Marilyn, earned her AB degree in government and history from Tufts University. She then joined IBM, where she helped clients prepare to add computers to their businesses and taught the use of data processing to IBM'ers from 1955 to 1960.

Children of John Francis and Marilyn (Teagan) Keane, all born in Boston:

35　　i.　JOHN FRANCIS[5] KEANE IV, b. 19 Feb. 1960; m. Cambridge, Mass., ANNE-MARIE WELDON.

36　　ii.　BRIAN TEAGAN KEANE, b. 6 Feb. 1961; m. Hartford, Conn., ELIZABETH FURNIVALL.

37　　iii.　VICTOIRE LE CARON KEANE, b. 24 May 1965; m. Cambridge, Mass., KENNETH LANG.

22. **KEVIN THOMAS[4] KEANE** (*John Francis*[3–2], *Daniel*[1]) was born in New York City, New York County, New York, 28 February 1933. He married in Johnson City, Broome County, New York, 27 June 1959, **ELIZABETH ANN RICE**, who was born 14 November 1935 in Johnson City, daughter of Richard and Elizabeth (Dowling) Rice.[295]

From 1955 until 1958, Kevin served in the U.S. Air Force Strategic Command as an observer, working with navigation, bombing, and as an electronics engineer before retiring as a captain. He received an AB in economics from Harvard University and an MBA from Harvard Business School in 1960.

He began his business career with a manufacturer of heating, ventilating and air conditioning equipment and three years later was given the opportunity to acquire a manufacturer and distributor of truck equipment.

In 1970 he was invited and agreed to lead the start-up and development of an aerospace company that has become a global leader in manufacturer of advanced, high-performance lighting, electrical power, avionics databus products, and automated test systems.

Once retired from active management, he continued as Chairman of Astronics Corporation; Modpac Corporation, formerly a subsidiary of Astronics; and Triform Camphill, a non-profit organization serving people with special needs.

Elizabeth received a BS from Cornell and an MEd from Boston University.

Children of Kevin Thomas and Elizabeth Ann (Rice) Keane, all born in Buffalo, Erie Co., N.Y.:

38   i.   KEVIN[5] KEANE, b. 11 Sept. 1961; m. ALISON ROSENFIELD.
39   ii. ROBERT S. KEANE. b. 29 March 1963; m. HEATHER MCAVOY.
40   iii. DANIEL G. KEANE, b. 12 May 1965; m. LESLIE FERNANDES.
        iv. DAVID W. KEANE, b. 14 March 1967.
41   v.   PATRICIA KEANE, b. 21 Nov. 1968; m. NATHAN DOWDEN.

23. SUSAN[4] KEANE (*John Francis*[3–2], *Daniel*[1]) was born in New York City, New York County, New York, 25 March 1937. She married first DONALD PARSONS, who was born 31 December 1937. She married second at Newport Beach, Orange County, California, 19 April 1975, ROBERT J. TRIVISON, who was born in Cleveland, Cuyahoga County, Ohio, 12 December 1919, son of Charles and Theresa (Masiello) Trivison.[296]

Susan, a former wig designer, has owned and operated a real estate company in California for more than twenty-five years. Her husband, Robert, served in the U.S. Army Air Corps from 1943 until 1945. A graduate of John Carroll University, Robert received degrees in business and accounting before attending Cleveland Marshall Law School. While at John Carroll University, he was president of the Commerce Club and a member of Alpha Sigma Nu.

Robert has worked as a business executive at several companies, and was a senior vice president at ITT–Cannon and Electronic Components.

Children of Donald and Susan (Keane) Parsons:

    i.   DONALD KEANE[5] PARSONS, b. Norfolk, Va., 1 Oct. 1956. He works in sales and marketing for Spanish-language media. His partner, Ismael Lomba, died 13 April 2010, after a 25-year relationship.

42   ii.   KAREN PARSONS, b. 9 Dec. 1960; m. 16 March 1985 RONALD EVERETT KEITH.

24. ANDRÉE FLORENCE[4] KEANE (*John Francis[3-2]*, *Daniel[1]*) was born in New York City, New York County, New York, 15 October 1940. She married in New York City, 27 October 1962, **PETER JOSEPH SHIELDS, JR.,** son of Peter Joseph and Dorothy (Streuber) Shields. He was born in Erie, Erie County, Pennsylvania, 28 July 1938. They later divorced.[297]

Andrée graduated from Sacred Heart Academy in Sag Harbor, New York, and Mount Ida College in Newton, Massachusetts. She currently owns a real estate company and as of 2011 resided in Chicago, Illinois.

Her former husband, Peter, served in the U.S. Army Reserve. He graduated from St. James Preparatory School in Hagerstown, Maryland, and received a BS from New York University. He is a business consultant.

Children of Peter Joseph and Andrée Florence (Keane) Shields:

    i.   VICTOIRE KEANE[5] SHIELDS, b. New York City 5 April 1963. She graduated from Miami Univ. in Oxford, Ohio, and works as a private banker.

    ii.   PETER JOSEPH "PJ" SHIELDS, b. New York City 16 Oct. 1964; d. Bloomingdale, DuPage Co., Ill., 12 March 1975. He is buried in Erie, Pa.

43   iii.   JULIE GODDARD SHIELDS (twin), b. Naperville, DuPage Co., 26 Oct. 1972; m. Hinsdale, DuPage Co., 14 October 1995, ANDREW DARIEN THOMPSON.

44   iv.   HOLLY STREUBER SHIELDS (twin), b. Naperville 26 Oct. 1972; m. Hinsdale, 7 Oct. 2000, JUSTIN TRAVIS HAYNA.

25. ELIZABETH ANNE[4] "BETTY" KEANE (*Paul Anthony[3]*, *John Francis[2]*, *Daniel[1]*) was born in Bridgeport, Fairfield County, Connecticut, 8 August 1929. She married at Fairfield, Fairfield County, 28 December 1954, **ROBERT PHILIP ROSSBAUM,** who was born in Bridgeport 2 November 1929, son of Gustave and Amalia (Westphal) Rossbaum. He died 16 February 2003 in Glastonbury, Hartford County, Connecticut, where he was buried 22 February 2003.[298]

Betty received a BS from the College of New Rochelle in 1951 and taught public school until 1962. Her teaching experience included teaching in a one-room school in Hutchinson, Texas. She is an active volunteer for the Hartford Hospital Auxiliary and is a tutor for the public school system in Glastonbury. She is also a Camp Fire Girl leader and a member of the Glastonbury Town Committee (Republican).

Robert was an aviator in the U.S. Navy and received a BA from the University of Bridgeport in 1951. He received his MD in 1962 from Seton Hall University School of Medicine, now the University of Medicine and Dentistry of New Jersey. He was a partner in Hartford Anesthesiology Associates and retired after thirty years. Active in the American Medical Association, he was also a member of the Hartford County Medical Association and served on the board of directors of the Hartford Anesthesiology Associates. For many years Robert was a popular coach for the Little League of Glastonbury.

Children of Robert Philip and Elizabeth Anne (Keane) Rossbaum:

45   i.   ROBERT PHILIP[5] ROSS, b. Worcester, Worcester Co., Mass., 16 Dec. 1962; m. New Britain, Hartford Co.,17 June 2006, MAGGIE JULIE SZCZEPANSKI.

46   ii.   KATHLEEN KEANE ROSS, b. West Hartford, Hartford Co., 3 Dec. 1964; m. Glastonbury 21 Nov. 1992 PAUL MICHAEL VELLA.

26. DOROTHY MARIE[4] "DOTTIE" KEANE (*Paul Anthony[3]*, *John Francis[2]*, *Daniel[1]*) was born in Bridgeport, Fairfield County, Connecticut, 16 May 1932. She married in Fairfield, in August 1958, **HERBERT CARL ACHTMEYER, JR.,** who was born in New Haven, New Haven County, Connecticut, 9 January 1932, son of Herbert Carl and Doris Tomlinson (Cotter) Achtmeyer.[299]

Dottie received a BS from the College of St. Elizabeth in Morristown, New Jersey. She was the chief therapeutic dietician at St. Vincent's Hospital and also a homemaker. She is a member of the Legion of Mary and the Sylvester Cancer Foundation at the University of Miami. In addition, Dottie was a volunteer for the Westport, Connecticut, school system.

Herbert received an AB from Brown University and served in the U.S. Army in military intelligence from 1954 until his discharge, as a first lieutenant, in 1958. Before retiring, he was a vice president of the Employee Benefits Department at Johnson & Higgins.

An active volunteer, Herbert has been a scoutmaster for the Boy Scouts of America and served as a cadet leader for the Girl Scouts. He was also an employee benefit instructor at New School, a New York university, and was clerk of session at the First Presbyterian Church in Miami, Florida. He has also been a catechism teacher at St. Rita Catholic Church in West Palm Beach, Florida.

As of 2013, Dorothy and Herbert were residing in Wellington, Florida.

Children of Herbert Carl and Dorothy Marie (Keane) Achtmeyer:

    i.   PAUL HERBERT[5] ACHTMEYER, b. Hartford, Hartford Co., Conn., 27 April 1960; d. Hartford 6 May 1980; bur. St. Michael's Catholic Cem., Stratford, Conn. An honor student, Paul was active in athletics, excelling in track, wrestling, and cycling. At the time of his death he was a sophomore at the Univ. of Connecticut.

47   ii.   CAROL ELIZABETH ACHTMEYER, b. Hartford 3 Feb. 1962.

48   iii.   SUSAN ELLEN ACHTMEYER, b. Bridgeport 12 Jan. 1965; m. Austin, Travis Co., Texas, 29 June 1991 DAVID FIELD MONTGOMERY.

27. ANNE BARBARA[4] "NANCY" KEANE was born in East Orange, New Jersey, 5 March 1942 and died in Dallas, Texas 10 June 2001. She married in Cohasset, Massachusetts, 7 September 1985, **ROBERT MEDLIN.** He was born in Columbus, Georgia, 18 January 1953, son of John Robert Medlin, Sr., and Moleyne (James) Medlin. He married, second, 29 April 2006, Janet Liese.[300]

Nancy graduated from Boston College, received a master's degree from Cornell University, and graduated from nursing school at Columbia University. She was Director of Nursing at the diabetes hospital at the University of Alabama at Birmingham. From 1982 to 1985 she worked as a stockbroker at Merrill Lynch and at Sterne Agee & Leach in Birmingham. From 1985 to 1989 she was director of clinical programs for a psychiatric hospital in Birmingham.

Bob received a BBA from the University of Georgia in 1974. From 1974 to 2002 he worked at PriceWaterhouse/PriceWaterhouseCoopers in Atlanta, Paris, Birmingham, and Dallas. He is a licensed CPA in Georgia, Alabama, and Texas. Since 2002 he has worked for FTI Consulting, where he is Senior Managing Director.

Children of Robert and Anne Barbara "Nancy" (Keane) Medlin:

    i.   KATHERINE ELIZABETH[5] MEDLIN, b. Dothlan, Ala., 6 Aug. 1986.

    ii.   MICHAEL KEANE MEDLIN, b. Orange County, Fla., 2 April 1990.

28. **PATRICIA**[4] **KEANE** (*Robert Joseph*[3], *John Francis*[2], *Daniel*[1]) was born in Bronx, New York, 24 April 1932. She married, 20 November 1954, **JOHN CORNELIUS "JACK" SPARKMAN,** who was born 16 April 1930, son of Drake Hoyt and Kathryn (Tierney) Sparkman. He died 13 May 2007 of lung cancer.[301]

Pat lived in New Rochelle and Larchmont, New York. She graduated from the Ursuline School in New Rochelle and received a BS in nursing from the College of Mount Saint Vincent in Riverdale, New York. She and Jack both grew up on Byron Lane in Larchmont. When first married, they lived in Pelham, and New Rochelle, New York, before finally moving to Uxbridge Road in Edgemont (Scarsdale), New York, in 1965.

After their children were grown, Pat worked as a psychiatric nurse on a children's unit. She is the founder of Family Ties of Westchester, a family-oriented support group that provides support services to families of children in Westchester with social, emotional, and behavioral difficulties.

Jack graduated from Manhattan College in New York City in 1952 and served in the U.S. Army's chemical corps at Fort McClellan in Anniston, Alabama, from 1952 to 1954. He received a law degree from Columbia University in 1954. His son, John Jr., was born while he was taking the bar exam. Jack worked as a trust and estates lawyer at Carter Ledyard & Milburn, 2 Wall Street, New York City, his entire career.

Jack was an avid sailor and raced for many years. (His father, Drake Sparkman, founded the naval architecture firm Sparkman & Stephens.) He and Pat boated throughout the Northeast, the St. Lawrence, and the Chesapeake Bay. After 2003, they continued to travel, by automobile.

In 2000 Pat and Jack retired to Groton, Connecticut. Together, they made seven long trips around the United States and Canada. Pat loves to be on the road and continues to travel throughout the world.

Children of John Cornelius and Patricia (Keane) Sparkman:

 i. SUSAN MARIE[5] SPARKMAN, b. New Rochelle 25 Aug. 1955; m. Katonah, N.Y., 10 Oct. 2001 ANTHONY L. SPERANDIO, b. Bronx, N.Y., 9 March 1951, son of Lawrence and Josephine (Fraulo) Sperandio. Susan Sparkman-Sperandio received a BA from Barnard College in 1977; while there, she spent a year in Italy. She worked for many years in the food industry in New York City; she owned Susan Marie caterers and specialized in fashion shoots. Since 1998 she began a career in real estate in Scarsdale. Her husband, Anthony, owns A–Z Roofing, which does roofing, waterproofing, and brick restoration on commercial buildings. They live in Katonah, N.Y.

Anthony has two sons: Steven and Michael Sperandio.

49   ii.   JOHN CORNELIUS SPARKMAN, JR., b. New Rochelle 3 July 1957; m. 24 Feb. 1958 AMY DUNBAR; div.

29. ROBERT JOSEPH⁴ KEANE, JR. (*Robert Joseph³, John Francis², Daniel¹*) was born at New Rochelle, New York 6 October 1936. He died at Stamford, Connecticut 4 June 2012 and is buried there in Queen of Peace Cemetery. He married first, in 1960, **DEANNE PFEIFFER.** He married second, at South Salem, New York, 28 March 1981 **CHRISTINA ANNE "JUSTY" (CARLO) GALLUP,** who was born at Stamford 30 Sept. 1935, daughter of John Joseph and Isabelle (Genovese) Carlo. Justy was married previously to Arthur J. Gallup, Jr.; they divorced in 1979.[302]

Bob developed diabetes at the age of 3 and was one of the first children to receive insulin. Bob graduated from the College of the Holy Cross in 1954 with a BS in accounting. A certified public accountant in New York and Connecticut, he was controller, treasurer, and vice president of Sotheby's International Realty, Inc., in Greenwich, Connecticut; and treasurer, corporate secretary, and director at Fletcher-Thompson, Inc., in Bridgeport, Connecticut. Bob also was an instructor and author, presenting accounting seminars and writing articles for architects and engineers.

Justy Keane received a BS from the University of Connecticut in 1957.

Children of Robert Joseph Keane, Jr., and Deanne (Pfeiffer) Keane:

50   i.   KEVIN ROBERT⁵ KEANE, b. 29 Nov. 1962; m. 1988 SALLY CARLSON; div.

51   ii.   CAROLYNN MARIE KEANE; b. 2 July 1964; m. JAMES A. HAYMAN.

      iii. MARIANNE PATRICIA KEANE, b. 12 Nov 1965.

Children of Arthur J. and Christina Anne "Justy" (Carlo) Gallup:

      i.   JON T. GALLUP, b. Stamford, Conn., 27 Sept. 1959. Constable, Stamford, Conn.; state marshal, State of Connecticut; chairman, Stamford Transit District; District 14 representative, Stamford Democratic Committee.

      ii.   ROBERT CHRISTOPHER GALLUP, b. Stamford 6 March 1963; m. (1) Hopewell Junction, N.Y., 1 June 1991, SHARON ANAGNOS, b. 9 April 1963, dau. of Peter and Katherine (Miller) Anagnos; m. (2) Lewisboro, N.Y., STACY (WARE) MCKINLEY, b. Pittsburgh,

Penn., 2 March 1963, dau. of Jay and Sandy (_____) Ware. She was previously married to Michael McKinley. An accountant, Robert is a graduate of Univ. of Hartford; Stacy has a BA from Alfred University and is a corporate recruiter.

Children of Robert Christopher and Sharon (Anagnos) Gallup:

1. *Kristy Lynn Gallup,* b. Norwalk, Conn., 9 Sept. 1995; New Canaan High School class of 2013.
2. *Casey Samantha Gallup,* b. Norwalk 5 June 1999.

Children of Michael and Stacy (Ware) McKinley, stepchildren of Robert Christopher Gallup:

1. *Britney Ware McKinley,* b. Wellsville, N.Y., 24 Jan. 1992; student at University of Connecticut—Stamford.
2. *Tessa Suzanne McKinley,* b. Wellsville 29 Nov. 1994; student at Suffolk University, Boston, Mass.
3. *Michaeleen Star McKinley,* b. Wellsville 24 Oct. 1995.

FIFTH GENERATION

30. **DAVID BRAY**[5] **WALKER** (*Susan Keane*[4] *Bray, Margaret M.*[3] *Keane, John Francis*[2], *Daniel*[1]) was born in New York City, New York County, New York, 10 January 1963. He married at Grace Church in Lexington, Davidson County, North Carolina, 16 July 1994, **ELIZABETH MOFFITT "BOBBIE" CAMPBELL**, who was born in Lexington 9 February 1963, daughter of Roy C. and Mary Hill (Moffitt) Campbell.[303]

David graduated from Scarsdale High School in 1981. He received a BA, *cum laude,* from Amherst College in 1985. While at Amherst he was the captain of the crew team, vice president of the Glee Club, and a member of Chi Psi fraternity. He received an MBA in 1990 from the Wharton School at the University of Pennsylvania, where he was also captain of the crew team.

David is a managing director at J. P. Morgan Investment Bank, where he is global head of automotive banking.

Children of David Bray and Elizabeth Moffitt (Campbell) Walker:

    i.   ANNIE[6] WALKER, b. 15 Aug. 1996.
    ii. CATHERINE WALKER, b. 22 May 1998.
   iii. SARAH WALKER, b. 8 April 2000.

31. **WILLIAM ALEXANDER**[5] **WALKER** (*Susan Keane*[4] *Bray, Margaret M.*[3] *Keane, John Francis*[2], *Daniel*[1]) was born in New York City, New York County, New York, 20 June 1964. He married at the Church of St. Luke in the Fields in New York City, 19 August 1995, **AMY LYNN WALSH**, who was born 30 June 1965, daughter of George Vincent and Catherine Mary (Frank) Walsh.[304]

William graduated from Scarsdale High School in 1982 and received a BA, *magna cum laude,* from Amherst College in 1986. While there he was co-captain of the college's swim and water polo teams and was a member of the Psi Upsilon fraternity. He received a law degree, also *cum laude,* from the University of Michigan, where he served as article editor of the *Michigan Law Review* from 1990 to 1991.

William worked as a law clerk for the Honorable Louis L. Stanton, U.S. District Court for the Southern District of New York, from 1991 until 1993, when he became an associate at Paul, Weiss, Rifkind, Wharton, and Garrison. As of 2012, William is an attorney and senior manager for Fiduciary Trust Company International.

Children of William Alexander and Amy Lynn (Walsh) Walker:

   i.   HENRY[6] WALKER, b. 30 March 1998.

   ii.   JOHN WALKER, b. 2 June 2001.

32. GEORGE[5] GUYDISH, JR. (*Victoire[4], John Francis[3-2], Daniel[1]*) was born in New York City, New York County, New York 1 November 1945. He married **CATHY WINNUBST**; they later divorced.[305]

Children of George and Cathy (Winnubst) Guydish:

   i.   MICHAEL THOMAS[6] GUYDISH, b. 17 July 1970; m. 8 June 2002 LISA HOLMES.

       Children of Michael Thomas and Lisa (Holmes) Guydish:

       1.   *Kara[7] Guydish* (twin), b. 19 March 2003.

       2.   *Colette Guydish* (twin), b. 19 March 2003.

   ii.   CHRISTOPHER THOMAS GUYDISH, b. 7 Jan. 1974; d. 6 July 2007 of brain cancer; m. 9 June 2001 CLARE LOGAN. He was a deputy sheriff in Suffolk County, New York. His children have participated in the annual Northport–East Northport [New York] Relay for Life, a fundraiser for the American Cancer Society, as a team called "Daddy's 400 Club." (Christopher's badge number was 400.)

       Children of Christopher Thomas and Clare (Logan) Guydish:

       1.   *Corey Thomas[7] Guydish,* b. 16 Dec. 2003.

       2.   *Meghan Rose Guydish,* b. 13 July 2005.

   iii.   THOMAS GUYDISH, b. 8 May 1980; unmarried.

33. ANDRÉE[5] AIRD (*Victoire[4], John Francis[3-2], Daniel[1]*) was born in Southhampton, Suffolk County, New York, 31 October 1956. She married first, 11 July 1986, **ZANE OWEN JOHNSON,** who was born 1 September 1950; they divorced in 1996. She married second,

20 May 2000, **RUSSELL GORDON PRIMROSE,** who was born in Santa Ana, California 26 June 1955.[306]

Andrée has a degree in interior design. She has spent most of her career in the lumber industry, selling to architects and builders. Russell also works in the lumber industry, in wholesale domestic sales. They live in San Clemente, California.

Child of Russell Gordon Primrose, stepchild of Andrée (Aird) (Johnson) Primrose:

i.   TIANA LEA PRIMROSE, b. 2 Sept. 1981.

   Child of Tiana Lea Primrose and Billy Robert Macdonald:

   1.   *Remmi Primrose Macdonald,* b. 13 Sept. 2010.

Children of Zane Owen and Andrée (Aird) Johnson:

ii. TREVOR RAY[6] JOHNSON, b. 27 June 1989. He is a student at Saddleback College, Mission Viejo, Calif.

iii. MEGAN LE CARON JOHNSON, b. 19 Oct. 1991. She is a student in the pre-veterinary program at Colorado State University.

34. **JOHN FENWICK AIRD II** (*Victoire*[4], *John Francis*[3-2], *Daniel*[1]) was born in New York City, New York County, New York 3 March 1960. He married, 18 June 1983, **ALISA MICHELLE WILLMS,** who was born 4 November 1963 in La Mirada, California. They divorced 1 June 1995. He married second, 21 December 1996, **PATRICIA RENEE (HAINES) ARNOLD,** who was born 14 September 1966 in Galion, Ohio. They divorced 4 February 2010. As of 2012, John is working as a car salesman.[307]

Children of John Fenwick and Alisa Michelle (Willms) Aird:

i.   JOHN FENWICK[6] AIRD, b. Mission Viejo, Calif. 17 Dec. 1983.

ii. AISLINN KIRSTI AIRD, b. Poway, Calif. 11 Oct. 1988.

Child of John Fenwick and Patricia Renee (Haines) (Arnold) Aird:

iii. MORGAN VICTOIRE AIRD, b. Laguna Beach, Calif. 12 June 1997.

Child of Patricia Renee (Haines) Arnold, stepchild of John Fenwick Aird:

i.   CHRISTIAN JOSHUA ARNOLD, b. San Clemente, Calif., 25 Sept. 1991.

35. **JOHN FRANCIS[5] KEANE IV** (*John Francis*[4-2], *Daniel*[1]) was born in Boston, Massachusetts, 19 February 1960. He married in Cambridge, Massachusetts, **ANNE–MARIE WELDON.**[308]

Children of John Francis and Ann Marie (Weldon) Keane, all born in Newton, Massachusetts:

  i. JOHN FRANCIS[6] KEANE V, b. 5 Feb. 1998.
 ii. BRENDAN WILLIAM KEANE, b. 13 June 1999.
iii. PATRICK TEAGAN KEANE, b. 4 May 2003.
 iv. KAITLIN VICTOIRE KEANE, b. 26 Nov. 2004.

36. **BRIAN TEAGAN[5] KEANE** (*John Francis*[4-2], *Daniel*[1]) was born in Boston, Massachusetts, 6 February 1961. He married in Hartford, Connecticut, **ELIZABETH FURNIVALL.**[309]

Children of Brian Teagan and Elizabeth (Furnivall) Keane, all born in Boston:

  i. SARAH LIBERTY[6] KEANE, b. 8 Aug. 1993.
 ii. ALEXANDER FURNIVALL KEANE, b. 7 July 1995.
iii. VICTOIRE MARIE KEANE, b. 12 Dec. 1996.

37. **VICTOIRE LE CARON[5] KEANE** (*John Francis*[4-2], *Daniel*[1]) was born in Boston, Massachusetts, 24 May 1965. She married in Cambridge, Massachusetts, **KENNETH LANG.**[310]

Children of Kenneth and Victoire Le Caron (Keane) Lang, all born in Boston:

  i. MARIN ELIZABETH[6] LANG, b. 25 Feb. 1998.
 ii. CHRISTOPHER KEANE LANG, b. 5 Oct. 1999.
iii. JULIA TEAGAN LANG, b. 27 Sept. 2001.
 iv. GRACE VICTOIRE LANG, b. 26 Dec. 2003.
  v. CLAIRE LE CARON LANG, b. 13 March 2006.

38. **KEVIN[5] KEANE** (*Kevin*[4], *John Francis*[3-2], *Daniel*[1]) was born in Buffalo, Erie County, New York, 11 September 1961. He married **ALISON ROSENFIELD,** who was born in New York, New York County, New York, 7 November 1962.[311]

Children of Kevin and Alison (Rosenfield) Keane:

  i. NATHAN[6] KEANE (twin), b. 9 Sept. 1988.
 ii. TREVOR KEANE (twin), b. 9 Sept. 1988.
iii. LILY KEANE, b. 29 June 1991.
 iv. HENRY KEANE, b. 8 June 1997.

39. **ROBERT⁵ KEANE** (*Kevin⁴, John Francis³⁻², Daniel¹*) was born in Buffalo, Erie County, New York, 29 March 1963. He married **HEATHER McAVOY,** who was born in Thailand 5 March 1962.[312]

Child of Robert and Heather (McAvoy) Keane:

    i.   SABRINE⁶ KEANE, b. Paris, France, 30 June 1996.

40. **DANIEL⁵ KEANE** (*Kevin⁴, John Francis³⁻², Daniel¹*) was born in Buffalo, Erie County, New York, 12 May 1965. He married **LESLIE FERNANDES,** who was born in Framingham, Middlesex County, Massachusetts, 8 September 1962.[313]

Children of Daniel and Leslie (Fernandes) Keane, all born in Buffalo:

    i.   STEPHANIE⁶ KEANE, b. 17 Feb. 2000.
    ii. VICTORIA KEANE, b. 30 Sept. 2002.

41. **PATRICIA⁵ KEANE** (*Kevin⁴, John Francis³⁻², Daniel¹*) was born in Buffalo, Erie County, New York, 21 November 1968. She married **NATHAN DOWDEN,** who was born 11 November 1969.[314]

Children of Nathan and Patricia (Keane) Dowden, all born in Boston, Massachusetts:

    i.   MAX⁶ DOWDEN, b. 23 Sept. 1997.
    ii. OWEN DOWDEN, b. 13 April 2005.
    iii. CHARLOTTE DOWDEN, b. 8 Feb. 2007.

42. **KAREN⁵ PARSONS** (*Susan⁴ Keane, John Francis³⁻², Daniel¹*) was born 9 December 1960. She married, 16 March 1985, **RONALD EVERETT KEITH,** who was born 31 July 1958. She is a business owner.[315]

Children of Ronald Everett and Karen (Parsons) Keith, all born at Newport Beach, Calif.:

    i.   COLIN EVERETT⁶ KEITH, b. 27 July 1990.
    ii. ANDRÉE LE CARON KEITH, b. 31 Aug. 1993.
    iii. SPENCER JAMES KEITH, b. 6 April 1995.

43. **JULIE GODDARD⁵ SHIELDS** (*Andrée⁴, John Francis³⁻², Daniel¹*) was born in Naperville, DuPage County, Illinois, 26 October 1972. She married in Hinsdale, DuPage County, 14 October 1995, **ANDREW**

Darien Thompson, who was born in Galesburg, Knox County, Illinois, 31 December 1972, son of Harold J. and Deborah Ann (Beck) Thompson.[316]

Julie received her BA and MBA from the University of Illinois and works as a real estate broker.

Children of Andrew Darien and Julie Goddard (Shields) Thompson:

    i. Hannah[6] Thompson, b. Ill. 18 April 1998.

    ii. Michael Thompson, b. Calif. 7 Aug. 1999.

    iii. Benjamin Thompson, b. Ariz. 23 Jan. 2002.

44. **Holly Streuber[5] Shields** (*Andrée[4], John Francis[3-2], Daniel[1]*) was born in Naperville, DuPage County, Illinois, 26 October 1972. She married in Hinsdale, DuPage County, 7 October 2000, **Justin Travis Hayna,** who was born in DeKalb, DeKalb County, Illinois, son of John Allen and Trudy Lee (Troxell) Hayna.[317]

Holly received a BS from the Univ. of Illinois and a DVM from that university's College of Veterinary Medicine. She is a veterinarian.

Children of Justin Travis and Holly Streuber (Shields) Hayna:

    i. Connor[6] Hayna, b. Minn. 29 June 2003.

    ii. Luke Hayna, b. Fla. 11 March 2005.

45. **Robert Philip[5] Ross** (*Elizabeth Anne[4] Keane, Paul Anthony[3], John Francis[2], Daniel[1]*) was born in Worcester, Worcester County, Massachusetts, 16 December 1962. He married in New Britain, Hartford County, 17 June 2006, **Maggie Julie Szczepanski.**[318]

Robert received a BS from Northeastern University in Boston, Massachusetts, in 1987 and a JD from Suffolk Law School in Boston in 1991. A practicing attorney, as of 2012 he is a partner in the law firm of Hurd, Horvath & Ross in Palm Beach Garden, Florida.

Children of Robert Philip and Maggie Julie (Szczepanski) Ross:

    i. Derek Tyler[6] Ross, b. 1994.

    ii. Shannon Taylor Ross, b. 1997.

    iii. Kyle Hunter Ross, b. 2007.

    iv. Megan Elizabeth Ross, b. 2008.

    v. Jackson Tanner Ross, b. 2010.

46. Kathleen Keane[5] Ross (*Elizabeth Anne[4] Keane, Paul Anthony[3], John Francis[2], Daniel[1]*) was born in West Hartford, Hartford County, Connecticut, 3 December 1964. She married in Glastonbury, Hartford County, 21 November 1992, **Paul Michael Vella, MD**, son of Paul and Rose (_____) Vella.[319]

Kathleen received a BA from Providence College, *magna cum laude*, in 1987 and received her JD from Boston College Law School in 1990.

She is a practicing attorney, and serves on the staff of the Freedom of Information Commission for the State of Connecticut.

Children of Paul Michael and Kathleen Keane (Ross) Vella:

    i.   Paul Michael[6] Vella, Jr., b. June 1996.
   ii. Kathryn Elizabeth Vella, b. April 2000.

47. Carol Elizabeth[5] Achtmeyer (*Dorothy Elizabeth[4] Keane, Paul Anthony[3], John Francis[2], Daniel[1]*) was born in Hartford, Hartford County, Connecticut 3 February 1962.[320]

She received a BS in nursing from Villanova University in Philadelphia, Pennsylvania, and an MS in nursing from the University of Washington in Seattle. She is a nurse practitioner in Seattle and a medical informatics researcher. She has published a number of medical research papers.

Child of Carol Elizabeth Achtmeyer:

    i.   Jamie Price[6] Achtmeyer.

48. Susan Ellen[5] Achtmeyer (*Dorothy Elizabeth[4] Keane, Paul Anthony[3], John Francis[2], Daniel[1]*) was born in Bridgeport, Fairfield County, Connecticut, 12 January 1965. She married in Austin, Travis County, Texas, 29 June 1991, **David Field Montgomery**, who was born in Austin 31 May 1948, son of Berthem and Sybil Field (Nichols) Montgomery.[321]

Susan received a BS from Florida International University in Miami. She is a practicing occupational therapist and a volunteer for the Brentwood Christian School in Austin.

Children of David Field and Susan (Achtmeyer) Montgomery:

    i.   Stephane Paul[6] Montgomery, b. 29 March 1992.
   ii. Christian Patrick Montgomery, b. 11 March 1997.
  iii. Joel Michail Montgomery, b. 30 July 2001.

49. **JOHN CORNELIUS[5] SPARKMAN, JR.** (*Patricia[4] Keane, Robert Joseph[3], John Francis[2], Daniel[1]*) was born 3 July 1957. He married **AMY DUNBAR,** who was born 24 February 1958. They later divorced.[322]

An excellent sailor, John set the spinnaker on the America's Cup boat *Enterprise.* He graduated from Boston College in 1986, worked for Bainbridge and Patagonia, and now is the Managing Publisher of the *Christian Science Journal, Sentinel,* and *Herald* at the Christian Science Publishing Society in Boston, Massachusetts. He lives in Brookline, Massachusetts.

Children of John Cornelius and Amy (Dunbar) Sparkman:

    i.   JOHN BARRETT[6] SPARKMAN, b. 15 June 1991. He is a student at Tufts University and has a pilot's license.

    ii.   JAMES NOAH SPARKMAN, b. 15 July 1993. Noah is a student at Boston University, where he competes on the rowing team.

    iii.   JOSHUA TRUETT SPARKMAN, b. 30 Aug. 1996. He lives in Old Lyme, Conn., with his mother. He is home schooled.

50. **KEVIN ROBERT[5] KEANE** (*Robert Joseph[3-4], John Francis[2], Daniel[1]*) was born 29 November 1962. He married in 1988 **SALLY CARLSON** of Worcester, Massachusetts, who was born 22 June 1961. They divorced in 1998.[323]

Kevin received a BA in philosophy and economics from Colgate University. At the time of publication, he was working for IBM Corporation's Software Group. He is worldwide Synergy Sales Leader for Enterprise Marketing Management.

Children of Kevin Robert and Sally (Carlson) Keane:

    i.   TIMOTHY ALBERT[6] KEANE, b. 5 June 1991. He received a BA from Boston University in 2012, in computer science and economics.

    ii.   LAUREN MARIE KEANE, b. 19 Nov. 1993. She attends Boston University.

51. **CAROLYNN MARIE[5] KEANE** (*Robert Joseph[3-4], John Francis[2], Daniel[1]*) was born 2 July 1964. She married **JAMES A. HAYMAN** of Georgetown, Massachusetts.

Both Carolynn and James graduated from McGill University in 1986. James received an MD and an MBA from the University of Chicago.[324]

Child of James and Carolynn Marie (Keane) Hayman:

    i.   ANNA MARIE[6] HAYMAN, b. 3 Sept. 1996.

Keane cousins, 2003. *Left to right:* Kevin Keane, David Bray, Susan (Keane) Trivison, Susan (Bray) Walker, John F. Keane III, Bob Keane.

William, Elizabeth, and David Walker, after Elizabeth's high school graduation, 1981.

Susan (Bray) Walker's immediate family, 2002. *Rear:* David and Bobbie Walker, Susan and John Walker, Elizabeth Walker, Will and Amy Walker. *Front:* Catherine, Sarah, Annie, John, Henry.

Walker cousins, Thanksgiving 2011. *Left to right:* Henry and John, sons of Will Walker; Annie, Sarah, and Catherine, daughters of David Walker.

Bob and Justy Keane on their wedding day, 1981.

Bob and Justy with his children (*left to right*) Marianne, Carolynn, and Kevin.

Kevin Robert Keane with his children, Timothy and Lauren.

Right: James and Carolynn (Keane) Hayman with their daughter, Anna Marie.

Marianne Keane.

Left: Joe and Kay (Lyons) Keane with their daughter Nancy (Keane) Medlin and her children, Katherine (*bottom*) and Michael. *Right:* Robert and Nancy Medlin.

Left: Elizabeth "Betty" (Keane) Rossbaum with her husband, Robert, and their children, Kathleen and Robert Ross. *Right:* Children of Bob and Maggie (Szczepanski) Ross: Derek, holding Kyle; Jack; Shannon, holding Megan.

Children of Paul and Kathleen (Ross) Vella. *Left:* Kathryn. *Right:* Paul, Jr.

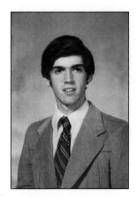

Clockwise from above: Dorothy (Keane) Achtmeyer and her husband, Herbert; their children, Paul Achtmeyer, Carol Achtmeyer, and Susan (Achtmeyer) Montgomery with her children *(top to bottom)* Joel, Christian, and Stephane.

Jamie Achtmeyer, daughter of Carol Achtmeyer (also shown).

Above: Marie Keane with her granddaughter, Susan Sparkman. *Right:* Anthony Sperandio and Susan Sparkman-Sperandio.

Above: Patricia (Keane) Sparkman (*center*), with her daughter, Susan Sparkman-Sperandio and son, John Sparkman, Jr. *Right:* Jack and Patricia Keane Sparkman, ca. 2000.

Children of John Sparkman, Jr.: Noah, Truett, and Barrett Sparkman.

Siblings: John, Susan, Victoire, Andrée, and Kevin.

Left: Victoire (Keane) Barth and four of her children: Wendy, Kathy, and John Aird, and Andrée (Aird) Primrose. *Above:* Wedding of Russell Primrose and Andrée (Aird) Johnson, 2000: Trevor Johnson, Megan Johnson, Russ, Andrée, Tiana Primrose.

Left: Christopher Guydish, grandson of Victoire (Keane) Barth and her first husband, George Guydish. *Above:* Christopher with his wife, Clare, and children, Meghan and Corey.

Victoire (Keane) Barth with grandchildren Megan and Trevor Johnson.

Right: John and Marilyn (Teagan) Keane with John, Brian, and Victoire, 1971.

Right: John and Marilyn Keane with Victoire, Brian, and John.

Left: John Keane with his sons John and Brian in front of the Keane Associates office, Charlestown, Massachusetts.

John and Marilyn (Teagan) Keane with their children and grandchildren, 2011. *Back row:* John, Anne-Marie, Elizabeth, Brian, Victoire, John, Marilyn, and Alexander Keane; Kenneth and Victoire Lang. *Middle row:* Sarah Keane, Marin and Christopher Lang, Brendan Keane, Julia Lang, John Keane. *Front row:* Claire Lang, Kaitlin and Patrick Keane, Grace Lang. Photo by Caroline Bolick.

Grandchildren of John and Marilyn (Teagan) Keane, 2008. *Left to right:* Sarah, Alexander, Victoire, Marin, Christopher, John, Brendan, Julia, Grace, Patrick, Kaitlin, Claire.

Kevin and Elizabeth (Rice) Keane with their children and grandchildren. *First row, left to right:* Robert Keane, Owen Dowden, Patricia (Keane) Dowden, Charlotte Dowden, Max Dowden, Kevin Thomas Keane, Elizabeth (Rice) Keane, Henry Keane, Kevin Keane, Victoria Keane, Daniel Keane, Stephanie Keane. *Second row, left to right:* Heather (McAvoy) Keane, Sabrine Keane, Nathan Dowden, David Keane, Trevor Keane, Alison (Rosenfield) Keane, Lily Keane, Nathan Keane, Leslie (Fernandes) Keane.

Left: Robert and Susan (Keane) Trivison (*right*) with Susan's son Don Parsons (*second from left*) and his partner Ismael Lomba (*left*). *Right:* Susan (Keane) Trivison's daughter Karen (Parsons) Keith with her family: Colin, Andrée, Karen, Spencer, and Ron Keith.

Andrée (Keane) Shields (*rear*) and her family, ca. 2003. *Front, left to right:* Michael Thompson, Julie (Shields) Thompson, holding Ben Thompson, Hannah Thompson, Holly (Shields) Hayna, holding Connor Hayna. *Middle, left to right:* Andrew Thompson, Eddie Carr and Vickie Shields, Justin Hayna.

Connor (*left*) and Luke Hayna, ca. 2009.

Shirley Thomas Keane and his wife, Patsy (McHugh) Keane.

Above: Linda (Keane) Smith, at home on Long Island, 1950s. *Above right:* Shirley Thomas Keane with sons Timothy and Danny. *Right:* Shirley Thomas and Patsy Keane's four children: Tim, Danny, Glynn, and Linda.

Glynn (Keane) Dugan and Dan Dugan, with Daniel and Conor Thomas.

Linda (Keane) Smith (*front*) and her children, David Christensen, Kerrin Smith, Shannon Smith, and Richie Christensen.

Danny and Kathy (Bauer) Keane with their sons, Chris (*left*) and Danny (*right*).

Keane-Le Caron reunion, Chatham, Massachusetts, 2003.

APPENDIX I

THE
Geary/Sheahan Families

FIRST GENERATION

1. **JOHN FRANKLIN**[1] **GEARY** was born in Ireland sometime around 1800. He married, before 1832, **HANNAH HOOKE**, who was born in Maryland.[1]

While a record of John's arrival in the United States has not been found, it is probable he arrived before 1830, eventually settling near Maryland and the District of Columbia. No record of the marriage or death of John or his wife Hannah has been located in the records of the District of Columbia, though it is possible they were living in nearby Virginia or Maryland at the time of those events.

Though John and Hannah have not yet been located in any federal census records, it is known that they were living in the District of Columbia around 1832, when their presumed first child, a daughter, Margaret C. Geary was born, and were in Maryland by January 1843, when their daughter Susan F. Geary was born.

It is possible that the family moved up to New York City during the 1850s, as their daughter Margaret had made her way to Bridgeport, Connecticut, by 1856 and their daughter Susan had met Spencer C. Platt, the son of a prominent New York businessman, by 1861.[2]

Children of John Franklin and Hannah (Hooke) Geary:

2   i.   MARGARET C.[2] GEARY, b. District of Columbia abt. 1832;[3] m. (1) prob. Conn. abt. 1855 DANIEL SHEAHAN;[4] m. (2) prob. Conn. abt. 1867 HUBERT LYNCH.[5]

3.   ii. DR. SUSAN F. GEARY, b. Md. Jan. 1843;[6] m. (1) prob. New York City bef. 1861 SPENCER C. PLATT;[7] m. (2) N.J. 7 April 1896 REV. DR. THOMAS SNOWDEN THOMAS.

SECOND GENERATION

2. **MARGARET**[2] **C. GEARY** (*John Franklin*[1]) was born in Washington, D.C., about 1832.[8] She died likely in Port Byron, Cayuga County, New York, after 1894.[9] She married, about 1855, **DANIEL SHEAHAN**,[10] who was born in Ireland and died, possibly in Huntington, Fairfield County, Connecticut, before 1867.[11] Margaret married second, likely in Connecticut, about 1867, **HUBERT LYNCH**,[12] who was born in Ireland about 1837. He died, likely in Connecticut, after 1880.[13]

Daniel was a shoemaker. He had come to Bridgeport, Connecticut, from Ireland sometime before 1856.[14] Following Daniel's death, Margaret married Hubert Lynch, who had arrived from Ireland before 1860. In September 1867, legal guardians were appointed to Margaret's children from her first marriage: E. L. Walker as guardian of Daniel Sheahan, then 9, and Lewis Curtis as guardian of Jeremiah Sheahan, age 11, and Susan Sheahan, age 8. The arrangement was difficult for Margaret, and that same month she petitioned the court to remove Lewis Curtis as the guardian of Jeremiah and Susan:[15]

> The application of Margaret Lynch of Birmingham in Derby in New Haven County respectfully requests that on the 3rd day of September 1867 Lewis Curtis of Huntington was by your Hon. Court appointed guardian of her two children Jeremiah and Susan Sheehan, now age 11 yrs and Susan now aged 8 years the said applicant then being insane and incapable of taking care of sd children. She says that she has now recovered her mental and physical health and is fully competent and able to take charge and care of sd children and to bring them up and support them — and further that said Lewis Curtis has not and does not take such care of sd children, nor give them such attention, as such guardian, as their tender

years require. She therefore prays that the said appointment
of Lewis Curtis may be rescinded and that he be removed
from sd guardianship and that she or some other suitable
person may be appointed guardian of sd children.

At some point Margaret withdrew her petition, though Lewis
Curtis remained the legal guardian of Jeremiah and Susan until 2
February 1872, when he submitted a petition to the court to resign,
noting that the two children often stayed with their mother, Margaret,
in another district.[16]

Based upon the accounting delivered to the courts by both E. L.
Walker and Lewis Curtis, the children still resided with their mother,
now known as Margaret Lynch, for much of the time. In fact, Susan
was living with Margaret and her second husband, Hubert Lynch, in
Orange, New Haven County, Connecticut, in 1870. Jeremiah, now 14,
was working a few houses away on the railroad and living with the
Harry D. Benson family.[17]

E. L. Walker petitioned the court to be removed as the guardian
of Daniel Sheehan 1 May 1872, noting that Daniel was now living in
Norwalk, Connecticut, and no longer residing with him.[18]

Margaret moved back to Bridgeport sometime after 1872. She was
working in the house of Thomas Hawley in 1878, when she petitioned
the Governor of Connecticut to support her daughter's enrollment at
the Perkins Institute for the Blind.[19] It is possible that by 1880 she
was boarding at 101 William Street in Bridgeport, as a "Mrs. Margaret
Lynch" is recorded there in the 1880 and 1881 City Directories.[20]

In 1880 her husband Hubert Lynch was living in the household of
John G. Pete in Huntington, though Margaret and her children are not
enumerated there.[21] It is possible that he is the same Hubert Lynch who
sold land located in Trumbull, Fairfield County, to LeGrand G. Beers in
1893 and to Nellie Lynch of Monroe, Fairfield County, in 1894, though
no definitive connections have been established.[22]

It is possible that Margaret and Hubert had separated by 1882, as
she returned to using her first husband's surname and moved her family
to Waterbury, Connecticut, where she worked as a nurse while residing
at 92 North Main.[23] In 1883 Margaret had moved to 67 Dublin Street;
she returned to Bridgeport in 1884.[24] She returned to Waterbury in
1886, again working as a nurse, this time at 8 Wall Street.[25] By 1887, she
and her children had moved to 40 Scoville Street.[26] In 1888, Margaret,

her son Daniel Joseph, and her daughter Susan Elizabeth moved to Fair Haven, New York.[27]

In 1893, Margaret moved to 72 West Liberty Street, where she lived with her son-in-law John Francis Keane and her daughter Susan until 1894. She then moved to Port Byron, New York.[28] As her son Daniel and sister Susan F. (Geary) Platt owned land in the area, it is possible Margaret went to spend her remaining years there. She likely died before 1900.[29]

Children of Daniel and Margaret C. (Geary) Sheahan:

4   i.   JEREMIAH F.[3] SHEAHAN, b. Bridgeport 7 March 1856;[30] m. Waterbury 9 Feb. 1880 MARY J. RYAN.[31]

5   ii. DANIEL JOSEPH SHEAHAN, b. Waltham, Middlesex Co., Mass., 6 Sept. 1858;[32] m. Waterbury 26 June 1889 ANNIE KENNEY.[33]

6   iii. SUSAN ELIZABETH SHEAHAN, b. Mass. Sept. 1861;[34] m. Red Creek, Wayne County, N.Y., 19 Aug. 1891 JOHN FRANCIS KEANE.[35]

Child of Hubert and Margaret C. (Geary) (Sheahan) Lynch:

     iv. MARY C. LYNCH, b. Conn. abt. 1867/1868; d. Conn. 7 July 1869/1870.[36] Mary is noted as the daughter of Hubert and Margaret Lynch buried in St. Mary's Cemetery, Milford, Conn.[37]

3. **DR. SUSAN F. GEARY** (*John Franklin*[1]) was born in Maryland in January 1843.[38] She died at the Methodist Episcopal Church Home in Manhattan, New York County, New York, 27 May 1911.[39] She married first, likely in New York City, before 1861, **SPENCER C. PLATT,**[40] who was born in New York City about 1833, son of Nathan C. and Jane (Plumber) Platt. He died in Neptune Township, Monmouth County, New Jersey, 3 September 1892.[41] She married second, in New Jersey, 7 April 1896, **REV. DR. THOMAS SNOWDEN THOMAS,** who was born in Maryland 28 July 1828, son of Thomas S. and Ann (Sewall) Thomas.[42] He died in Philadelphia, Philadelphia County, Pennsylvania, 2 October 1907.[43]

Susan likely traveled with her older sister Margaret from Maryland to New York — though no record of the family has been found there before 1860. Around that time she met Spencer C. Platt, son of Nathan C. Platt, a wealthy jeweler and New York City chamberlain. The Platt family was well connected within New York City, and their considerable wealth was in part due to the discovery of gold in California. A profile in the 3 March 1886 issue of the *New York Herald* profiles the family:[44]

When the Platts—Nathan and George—made their thousands in New York, there was no assay office there. The mint was in Philadelphia, nearly a hundred miles away, and those who had made their return trip from California, around Cape Horn, after a four months' voyage in the famous clipper ships of the time, did not care to make another railroad trip to sell their 'ore.' They carried it around their waists, had it sewed in the lining of their clothes or in satchels or in their pockets, and even before they divested themselves of their mining clothes or indulged in the luxuries incident to a return home, they tramped down to Liberty Street three or four hundred strong and sold their 'diggings.' Old Mr. Platt (George) weighed the ore, figured the value, and gave the Californian his check for the amount. At that time it was well known that the Platts kept a large cash balance on hand in the growing business of the city. Nathan and George, when quite young, came to the city about 1810 from Huntington, L.I., and engaged in the manufacture of gold and silver thimbles in what is now known as Chatham square. They met with success there, manufactured other articles, and had so expanded their business, that, about 1830, they purchased 4 and 6 Liberty street, a part of the well-known Grant-Thurburn estate, whose seed-store and garden form part of the history of New York. It was here in Liberty Street that they became prominent jewelers in New York. They opened an assay office just previous to the California excitement, and their stamp on a bar of gold was considered, here and abroad, as good as that of the U.S. mint. The 'forty-niners' from California rapidly increased their business, and in a few years they owned additional property on Maiden Lane and Nassau street.

When the Civil War erupted, New York City conducted a registration of all those eligible for military duty within the city. Spencer and Susan were married by then, living in the city's 6th Congressional District, where Spencer completed his registration, noting that he was married and a jeweler.[45] The couple continued to live in New York City throughout the Civil War; a report of the 1865 federal tax records notes that Spencer C. Platt was taxed $44.50 for a mansion house, a gold watch, and a silver plate.[46]

Susan enrolled at the New York Medical College for Women when it opened its doors in November 1863. Started by Dr. Clemence S. Lozier, the school was chartered under the University of the State of New York and was the first college in New York City where women could study medicine. At its beginning the school had just eight faculty members and seven students. Dr. Lozier oversaw the school for the next twenty-five years, seeing graduates begin to practice across the United States. Susan had become a pioneer student by attending the school. As one historian stated, "no longer did men students hiss and jeer as visiting women students came to amphitheaters for clinical instruction."[47] While at the college Susan studied the emerging science of homeopathy, graduating in 1867 with a degree in homeopathic medicine.[48] The college was the first school in the world to teach homeopathic medicine to women, making Susan one of the world's first female homeopathic doctors specifically trained as such.

In the 1870 U.S. Census, Susan appears with her husband, Spencer, living in a hotel in Brooklyn, Kings County, New York.[49] The record indicates that Spencer was a jeweler. Spencer and Susan split their time between New York City and the Platt family's farm, located near Auburn in Cayuga County, New York. While in upstate New York, Susan joined the Auburn First United Methodist Church, where she is listed as a member on 2 November 1876 while living on Williams Street.[50]

In 1880, Susan was working in Norwalk, Fairfield County, Connecticut, in the household of Bradley O. Banks with her nephew, Daniel Joseph Sheahan.[51]

Susan and her husband were deeply involved in the litigation regarding the estate of Spencer's father, Nathan C. Platt. Nathan and his brother George W. Platt jointly owned Platt and Brothers, a successful silversmith and jewelry business in New York City. In addition, Nathan owned several individual pieces of property in Wayne and Cayuga Counties in upstate New York, as well as land on Nassau Street in New York City. Nathan's interests in the partnership were valued at $221,097 (the equivalent of just over $5.3 million in 2010) in February 1860, and his Nassau Street property was valued at $125,000. His land in Cayuga and Wayne Counties was valued between $75 and $150 per acre.

Nathan was already serving as the city chamberlain when he became president of the Artisans' Bank in New York City. Soon after, the City of New York deposited money into the Artisans' Bank, which some thought was under the direction of Nathan himself. In an attempt to avoid a scandal, Nathan was forced to ensure that the city's money was withdrawn, and the bank failed in 1860. According to court documents, Nathan's "courage was broken, his spirit was mortified, his power of will was enfeebled, and his energy and mental capacity were weakened."[52] In the resulting chaos, Nathan inadvertently transferred large portions of his business directly to his brother. By 1861, with his health quickly failing, he had also given up large portions of his land and other assets. As much of the property was acquired on credit, the family was fearful that the "creditors would strip him of everything."

When Nathan died, on 7 July 1863, his sons, Spencer C. and William H. Platt, began the process of reclaiming their father's lost property from their uncle. The lawsuit alleged that George W. Platt intended to "'wipe out' the feeble partner" and that the property had been "procured by the overmastering influence of the defendant, and by hopes and expectations which he led his brother to cherish of protection and restitution." William and Spencer Platt both testified to the events of 1 July 1861, when George had threatened Nathan that he would "cut him off as a brother and give him further trouble" if the documents were not signed.

The brothers won their case and the subsequent appeal in October 1873, with the court noting, "[T]he relation of blood and that of trust growing out of the partnership indicated, when taken in connection with the brother's feeble state, the existence of dominion and influence, and called for proof of the purity of the transactions." The court ruled that Spencer and William "established affirmatively the existence of undue influence, which not being controverted by defendant, the transfers should be set aside."[53]

Though Spencer and his brother were victorious, the estate continued to be embroiled in legal controversy for the next several years. Spencer, along with his brothers William and Nathan C., Jr., were named as executors of their father's estate, with William taking the majority of the responsibility through an agent, William R. Martin. Their sister, Catherine (Platt) Cooke, brought a lawsuit against her brothers and their wives (including Susan F. (Geary) Platt) noting that she had "received no part of the money" from her father's estate and attempted to block any further sale of property. The court, on appeal, found that the executors could sell the property, as the will of Nathan C. Platt did not create any kind of trust, which would have included all of his children.[54]

In 1880, Spencer and Susan began selling portions of the Platt family farm; on March 22 of that year, they sold a large section of the property to Chrysler of Fair Haven for $270.[55] Pending the court's decisions and likely in an effort to consolidate their property, Spencer and Susan sold another portion of the land to Emelia Kayser for $1 in February 1883,[56] and she resold that property for $1 the same day.[57]

As the lawsuit and its appeals continued to work their way through New York's courts, Spencer and Susan were able to purchase, for just over $400, part of the Platt farm that had been presented for public sale in 1887.[58]

In addition, the brothers were sued by Edward N. Martin, a relative of William R. Martin, who had been the attorney for William, Spencer, and Nathan C. Platt, Jr., during their earlier litigation with their uncle George. Martin sued Spencer and his brothers for breach of contract, as he wasn't given 50 percent of the estate as he had been promised originally. However, Martin was found to have conducted himself improperly and the suit was dismissed in 1886.[59] Martin appealed the decision, and Susan F. Platt became a respondent herself in an appeal heard in April 1887, in which the court's earlier findings were upheld. Susan and her sister-in-law Annie (wife of William Platt) were also joint plaintiffs in an effort to recover a portion of their father-in-law's estate that was used as a settlement in another lawsuit, which had previously been brought by Aaron Degrauw. This suit was eventually, after appeal, settled in their favor.[60]

After achieving full legal control over a portion of the Platt family's property in Cayuga County, Susan sold portions of it to her nephews. First, on 18 June 1888, Susan sold just over 100 acres to Daniel J. Sheahan, who was living in Fair Haven at the time, for $303.50.[61] A few months later, on 19 December 1888, she sold part of the Platt family farm to Jeremiah F. Sheahan, who was also living in Fair Haven. That property, which sold for $111, included land in the town of Sterling, consisting of about 10 acres, which bordered the land she previously sold to Daniel.[62] Susan sold additional land to Jeremiah on 12 December 1892 for $10 with the condition that he "quietly enjoy the said premises."[63]

Sometime during the summer of 1892, Susan and Spencer moved from upstate New York to Neptune Township, where Spencer died on 3 September 1892 from a softening of the brain.[64]

After the death of her husband, Susan sought to sell her remaining property in Cayuga County, advertising in the *Fair Haven Register* on numerous occasions:

> A part of the 'Platt Farm' on the west shore of Little Sodus Bay, Fair Haven, N.Y., consisting of 58 acres, (18 cleared and 40 woodland) a beautiful new dwelling house containing nine rooms and attic and good cellar, two good wells on the premises. Splendid view of the bay and lake. Suitable for a farm or family summer resort. Price $4,500, part cash and balance on mortgage. Enquire of
>
> W4   DR. SUSAN F. PLATT
> Box 2342   Ocean Grove, N.J.[65]

She succeeded in part, selling a portion of the property to Phillip Michael in April 1893 for $200.[66]

Susan spent much of her widowhood in New Jersey, where she met Rev. Dr. Thomas Snowden Thomas. She married him there on 7 April 1896. Rev. Thomas was a minister of the Methodist Episcopal Church and had served as chief clerk of the Maryland House of Delegates from 1860 to 1861. He was also the U.S. hospital chairman during the Civil War. At the time he and Susan were married, he was the editor of the *Peninsular Methodist,* a weekly newspaper circulated in Delaware and Maryland.[67]

Susan and her second husband were living in Neptune in 1900, where they were enumerated in the U.S. Census.[68] Shortly thereafter, the couple moved to Philadelphia, where Rev. Dr. Thomas died 2 October 1907 at his daughter's home.[69] The notice of his funeral was published in the *Philadelphia Enquirer,* 5 October 1907:[70]

FUNERAL OF REV. DR. T. S. THOMAS

> The funeral of Rev. Dr. T. Snowden Thomas will be held this afternoon at his late residence 1902 Wallace Street. The services will be attended by members of the Philadelphia conference. Up to a few weeks ago Dr. Thomas lived at 1708 Vine Street but during the last

week of his illness he was moved at his daughter's request
to her residence. His second wife, who was at his bedside
during his last moments, was Dr. Susan F. Platt, a graduate
of the New York Medical College and Hospital.

After her second husband's death, Susan returned to New York City.
In 1910 she was living at the Methodist Church Home on Connecticut
Avenue.[71] She died there 27 May 1911 and was buried 29 May 1911
next to her first husband, Spencer, in the Platt family plot in Greenwood
Cemetery.[72]

THIRD GENERATION

4. **JEREMIAH F.**[3] **SHEAHAN** (*Margaret C.*[2] *Geary, John Franklin*[1]) was born in Bridgeport, Fairfield County, Connecticut, 7 March 1856.[73] He died likely in New Haven, New Haven County, Connecticut, after 1930.[74] He married in Waterbury, New Haven County, 9 February 1880, **MARY J. RYAN**,[75] who was born in Wolcottville, Litchfield County, Connecticut, in July 1861.[76] She died in Bridgeport about 1919.[77]

After the death of Jeremiah's father, Lewis Curtis was made the boy's legal guardian, though court documents illustrate that he and his sister spent a great deal of time with their mother Margaret and her second husband, Hubert Lynch, between 1867 and 1880.[78]

Around 1883, Jeremiah moved to Waterbury, where he was working as a clerk at 90 Bank Street;[79] in 1884, he was living at 64 Prospect Street.[80] Between 1885 and 1888, Jeremiah held a number of positions. He worked as a traveling agent, a letter carrier, and a delivery clerk for Simon Bohl, respectively. In 1888, he was living at 13 Pond Street, but on 19 December of that year Jeremiah purchased about 10 acres of land located in Sterling, Cayuga County, New York, from his aunt Susan F. (Geary) Platt for $111. These acres bordered the land she had previously sold to his brother, Daniel.[81] He also received additional land from his aunt on 12 December 1892 for $10 with the condition that he "quietly enjoy the said premises."[82]

Jeremiah and his wife Mary returned to Bridgeport in 1893, having sold their property in Sterling to William H. Hollenbeck for $500 on 22 March 1893.[83]

By 1894, Jeremiah was working for the New York and New Haven Railroad Company and living at 187 South Avenue in Bridgeport.[84] In 1896 he was employed at the railroad freight depot;[85] he worked there until 1898, when he joined the America Manufacturing Company.[86]

In 1900, Jeremiah and Mary were still living in Bridgeport, where Jeremiah worked as a laborer in the "loco-mobile."[87] He and Mary separated around 1907, and in 1910 Jeremiah was living with his brother-in-law John F. Keane in Bridgeport.[88]

Sometime around 1922, Jeremiah moved to New Haven, where he worked as a steward at the Hotel Essex and resided at 179 Meadow Street.[89] In 1925, he moved to Boston, Massachusetts, but had returned to New Haven by 1927.[90]

By 1930, Jeremiah was living in St. Andrew's Home for the Aged on Winthrop Avenue in New Haven.[91]

Children of Jeremiah F. and Mary J. (Ryan) Sheahan:

    i.   SUSAN E.[4] SHEAHAN, b. Waterbury 17 April 1881.[92] *No further record.*

7   ii. EDWARD JEROME SHEAHAN, b. Waterbury 9 June 1882;[93] m. abt. 1907 AMELIA MCCARTHY.[94]

    iii. MARGARET ELIZABETH SHEAHAN, b. Waterbury 24 Jan. 1885;[95] d. Bridgeport 15 Jan. 1900.[96]

5. **DANIEL JOSEPH**[3] **SHEAHAN/SHEEHAN** (*Margaret C.*[2] *Geary, John Franklin*[1]) was born in Waltham, Middlesex County, Massachusetts, 6 September 1858.[97] He died in New Haven, New Haven County, Connecticut, 31 January 1941.[98] He married in Waterbury, New Haven County, 26 June 1889, **ANNIE KENNEY**,[99] who was born in New Orleans, Orleans Parish, Louisiana, about 1864,[100] daughter of _____ and Bridget (_____) Kenney. She died, likely in New Haven, between 1920 and 1930.[101]

After the death of Daniel's father, E. L. Walker became the boy's legal guardian until 1 May 1872, by which time Daniel had moved to Norwalk, Fairfield County, Connecticut.[102]

In 1880, while working as a farm laborer, Daniel was living with his aunt Susan F. (Geary) Platt. At the time she was working as a physician in the home of Bradley O. Banks in Norwalk.[103]

By 1882, Daniel had moved with his mother to Waterbury, where he was working as a hostler at 68 North Main Street. In 1884 he was working as a foreman for F. E. Benham while living at 19 Kingsbury Street.[104]

In 1885 he started Sheehan and Madden, a livery, feed, boarding, and exchange stable located at Cole Corner on South Elm Street. The company specialized in "Ladies' and Gentle's Driving Horses."[105] The business closed only two years later, and in 1887 Daniel was working for American Pin Company.[106] He moved to Fair Haven, Cayuga

County, New York, with his mother and sister Susan in 1888. In 1889, he returned to Waterbury, where he married Annie Kenney, a native of New Orleans.[107]

On 18 June 1888, Daniel bought just over 100 acres of land in Sterling, Cayuga County, from his aunt Susan for $303.50.[108] Shortly before 1892, Daniel, now a farmer, his wife Annie, and their young son Spencer moved from their home in Connecticut to the land he had acquired in Sterling.[109]

Daniel sold 60 acres of his land to Mary Elizabeth Smith on 29 June 1893 for $3,000,[110] and in turn purchased around 30 acres for $2,500 from Mary Elizabeth Smith and her husband, John, on 1 July 1893.[111] There, Daniel lived next to his aunt and his brother Jeremiah.

By 1900, the family had moved to the nearby town of Throop, where their youngest son, Spencer, was at school.[112] In 1905, the New York state census recorded Daniel, his wife, Anna, who was working around the house, and their children Spencer, Walter, Bertha, and William as still living in Throop. Three of their children, Spencer, Walter, and Bertha, were attending school there.[113]

Sometime after 1905, Daniel and his family returned to Connecticut, purchasing a home in Waterbury, where Daniel was working as a building carpenter in 1910.[114] In 1920, Daniel's mother-in-law Bridget Kenney, who had come to the United States in 1840, was living with the family in their home on Terrace Avenue.[115]

Following the death of his wife between 1920 and 1930, Daniel moved to the house of Margaret Shaw, where he started a decorating company. Sometime around 1938, he became a resident of the Little Sisters of the Poor on 238 Winthrop Avenue in New Haven; he remained there until his death on 31 January 1941.[116] He was buried at St. Lawrence Cemetery in West Haven, New Haven County.

Children of Daniel Joseph and Annie (Kenney) Sheahan/Sheehan:

8   i.   SPENCER ALFRED[4] SHEEHAN, b. Fair Haven, Cayuga Co., 14 Aug. 1890;[117] m. bef. 1920 HELEN _____.[118]

9   ii.   WALTER J. SHEEHAN, b. Auburn, Cayuga Co., 29 July 1894;[119] m. prob. N.Y. bef. 1928 BELLE ENSINE.[120]

      iii. BERTHA SHEEHAN, b. N.Y. 16 July 1896;[121] d. Jan. 1964;[122] unmarried.

10   iv. WILLIAM DANIEL SHEEHAN, b. prob. Auburn 20 Sept. 1900.[123]

      v.   _____ SHEEHAN, b. N.Y. bet. 1890-1900; d. N.Y. bef. 1900.[124]

6. **Susan Elizabeth[3] Sheahan** (*Margaret C.[2] Geary, John Franklin[1]*) was born in Massachusetts in September 1861[125] and died in Bridgeport, Fairfield County, Connecticut, 15 June 1921.[126] She married in Red Creek, Wayne County, New York, 19 August 1891, **John Francis Keane**.[127] *See Part III of text, John Francis Keane, Sr. (no. 4, page 60).*

FOURTH GENERATION

7. EDWARD JEROME[4] SHEEHAN (*Jeremiah F.[3], Margaret C.[2] Geary, John Franklin[1]*) was born in Waterbury, New Haven County, Connecticut, 9 June 1882.[128] He died at St. Elizabeth Hospital in Chicago, Cook County, Illinois, 24 July 1937, and was buried at Mr. Carmel Cemetery in Proviso, Cook County.[129] He married, about 1907, AMELIA MCCARTHY,[130] who was born in Madison, Dane County, Wisconsin, 23 January 1883.[131] She died in Chicago 15 May 1930.[132]

Edward applied for a U.S. passport 6 August 1913, reporting his residence as 408 77th Street in Brooklyn, Kings County, New York, where he was working as a mechanical instructor. His application description notes that he was 31 years old, stood 5 feet, 11 inches, and had blue eyes. It also notes that he had a high forehead, small mouth, small chin, light hair, light complexion, Roman nose, and a long thin face.[133]

By 1918, Edward was working for the Noiseless Typewriter Company at 252 Broadway in New York City. Edward completed his World War I draft registration card on 12 September 1918, reporting his address as 408 77th Street in Brooklyn.[134]

According to the 1920 United States Federal Census, Edward was a manager of a typewriter company, residing with his wife and daughter in Brooklyn.[135] However, by 1929, the family had moved to Chicago, renting a house at 400 North Austin Boulevard.[136]

Edward and Amelia sailed from Havana, Cuba, aboard the SS *Virginia* on 18 March 1929, arriving in San Francisco, California.[137] In 1930, Edward and Amelia were living on Greenwood Avenue in Chicago, where he was a partner in a typewriting shop.[138] Soon after, Edward opened his own real estate business, which he operated until his death in 1937.[139]

Child of Edward Jerome and Amelia (McCarthy) Sheehan:

11   i.   BEATRICE MARIE[5] SHEEHAN, b. New York City 18 Dec. 1907;[140] m. Chicago 3 July 1930 DR. THOMAS FRANCIS GALLAGHER.[141]

8. **Spencer Alfred**[4] **Sheehan** (*Daniel Joseph*[3], *Margaret C.*[2] *Geary, John Franklin*[1]) was born in Fair Haven, Cayuga County, New York, 14 August 1890.[142] He died in Hobart, Delaware County, New York, in April 1972.[143] He married, before 1918, **Helen** _____, who was born in New York about 1896.[144] She died after 1930.[145]

Spencer completed his World War I draft registration card in 1917 while living at 34 Terrace Avenue in Waterbury, New Haven County, Connecticut. At the time he was working as a shipper at the American Pin Leg Company and was noted as being tall and slender with gray eyes and light brown hair.[146]

By 1920, Spencer and his wife Helen were living near his parents, Daniel and Annie (Kenney) Sheahan/Sheehan, in Waterbury with Gertrude Tangloff, a boarder.[147] A decade later, Helen and their children, Wilbur J. and Spencer, were still living in Waterbury, though Spencer was not residing in the household.[148]

Children of Spencer Alfred and Helen (_____) Sheehan:

    i.   Wilbur J.[5] "Bill" Sheehan, b. Conn. 7 Aug. 1918;[149] d. prob. Hot Springs, Garland Co., Ark., 6 March 2004;[150] m. Bexar Co., Texas, 22 Feb. 1983 Helen P. Bliss.[151]

        Bill served in the U.S. Army during World War II, from 1942 until he was honorably discharged in 1946. Afterwards, he attended the College of Engineering at the Univ. of California, Berkeley, graduating in 1950. He then joined the Army Corp of Engineers working in Saudi Arabia, Afghanistan, Libya, Italy, and Spain. He retired in 1975 and moved to San Antonio, Texas, where he met his wife, Helen. They moved to the Hot Springs Village community in 1992.[152]

    ii.   Spencer Francis Sheehan, b. prob. Waterbury 24 Sept. 1922;[153] m. Lois _____.[154]

        He served in the U.S. Navy during World War II, aboard the USS *Benham* in 1945 and 1946, and as of 2004 was living in Waterbury.[155]

9. **Walter J.**[4] **Sheehan** (*Daniel Joseph*[3], *Margaret C.*[2] *Geary, John Franklin*[1]) was born in Auburn, Cayuga County, New York, 29 July 1894.[156] He died in St. Petersburg, Pinellas County, Florida, 29 January 1964 and was buried at Memorial Park Cemetery in St. Petersburg.[157] He married, likely in New York, before 1928, **Belle Ensine**,[158] who

was born in New York 29 October 1892. She died in Pinellas County 2 January 1976.[159]

Walter attended the Massachusetts Institute of Technology (MIT) in Cambridge, Massachusetts. After graduating from MIT, he worked for many years in Syracuse, New York, before moving to St. Petersburg, Florida. At the time of his death, he also had a stepson, Wendell B. Deane, who was living in St. Petersburg.[160]

Child of Walter J. and Belle (Ensine) Sheehan:

    i.   WALTER J.[5] SHEEHAN, b. N.Y. 8 Dec. 1929;[161] d. Seminole, Pinellas Co., 6 Nov. 1995;[162] m. Fla. Sept. 1956 ELIZABETH _____.[163] They divorced 20 July 1979.[164]

        During the Korean War, Walter served as a sergeant in the U.S. Air Force.[165]

10. **WILLIAM DANIEL[4] SHEEHAN** (*Daniel Joseph[3], Margaret C.[2] Geary, John Franklin[1]*) was born, likely in Auburn, Cayuga County, New York, 20 September 1900.[166] He died, likely in St. Petersburg, Pinellas County, Florida, 14 June 1998.[167]

In addition to his children noted below, William was also the stepfather of Janet W. Hecker of Tallahassee, Florida, and Gerald Carroll of Newbury Park, California.[168]

Children of William Daniel Sheehan:

    i.   WALTER B.[5] SHEEHAN, res. Port Byron, N.Y., 1998.[169]

12   ii. WILLIAM DANIEL SHEEHAN, JR.; m. MARTHA _____.[170]

FIFTH GENERATION

11. **BEATRICE MARIE**[5] **SHEEHAN** (*Edward Jerome*[4], *Daniel Joseph*[3], *Margaret C.*[2] *Geary, John Franklin*[1]) was born in New York City, New York County, New York, 18 December 1907.[171] She died in Augusta, Richmond County, Georgia, 1 March 1988.[172] She married in Chicago, Cook County, Illinois, 3 July 1930, **DR. THOMAS FRANCIS GALLAGHER,**[173] who was born 29 December 1905 in Chicago.[174] He died in Augusta 20 June 1984.[175]

After their marriage they sailed aboard the SS *Statendam,* which returned to New York City from France on 30 August 1930.[176]

Beatrice worked as a chemist for much of her life, and in 1931 published "A study of the biuret reaction of an amino alcohol, epichloramine," at the University of Chicago.[177] Thomas was a biochemist. They moved to Augusta around 1980.[178]

Children of Dr. Thomas Francis and Beatrice Marie (Sheehan) Gallagher:

    i.   DR. BRIAN B.[6] GALLAGHER, res. Augusta, Ga.[179]

    ii. DR. THOMAS F. GALLAGHER, JR., res. Omaha, Neb.[180]

12. **WILLIAM DANIEL**[5] **SHEEHAN, JR.** (*William Daniel*[4], *Daniel Joseph*[3], *Margaret C.*[2] *Geary, John Franklin*[1]) married, before 1977, **MARTHA _____.**[181] They divorced in November 1997, after which William continued to live in St. Petersburg, Pinellas County, Florida; he was residing there as of 2004.[182]

Child of William Daniel and Martha (_____) Sheehan:

    i.   CHRISTOPHER A.[6] SHEEHAN, b. prob. St. Petersburg 14 March 1977.[183]

CONVERSATION WITH CHILDREN OF

John and Victoire
(Le Caron) Keane

ON NOVEMBER 4, 2011, the children of John and Victoire (Le Caron) Keane met for an annual siblings reunion in California and reminisced about family stories to family historian Maureen Taylor.

What do you remember about your mother?

Kevin: There are DAR [Daughters of the American Revolution] papers on our mother's side. And those are very obviously accurate and historically available.

Andrée: I do have all the original DAR papers.

Kevin: John, you and I are on record because we're members of the SAR [Sons of the American Revolution], the William Floyd Chapter, in Patchogue, Long Island. Do you remember?

John: I remember that, but I don't remember anything about any of the papers or anything.

Kevin: Well, I remember when you and I were marched in to sign up as charter members of the William Floyd Chapter of the SAR, Sons of the American Revolution. In Patchogue.

I believe there are two streams of genealogies that go back to the regional DAR, because one is the Goddard family. And I believe the other is the Sprague family.

John: Yes, that's right.

Kevin: And so, those are New England families that are historically important.

So, in general, all of you were born in the New York City area, correct?

John: Yes.

Kevin: All of us, if I'm not mistaken, were born in Flower Hospital in New York City, which I think is now part of [another] major hospital in New York. [It] was a significant hospital system in the Upper East Side. And our mother's uncle, or like our grandmother's brother, was Dr. Shirley Sprague. And he was a well-known physician in New York. And, in my memory, he is credited has having delivered more babies than anybody in the history of the records in New York at Flower Hospital, at the time. Because he was a prominent, I guess, what in today's world would be obstetrician and pediatrician. I mean, he was well-known.

Did all of you grow up in New York City as well?

John: We grew up in Brooklyn, now, until I was ten years old. And then we moved out to Long Island . . . [in] 1942.

Do you have any childhood memories of growing up and being in Brooklyn?

Kevin: I have two memories. One is our father's brother, who is Joseph, one of the six children — six boys, I guess — and he was a bachelor at the time and lived at the house in Brooklyn, on 332 Maple Street . . . , which is across the street from St. Francis of Assisi School and Church and grade school. So I mention that because there's a small story there which may be of interest, may not be.

But Uncle Joe lived with us for a period of time. And, on every opportunity he had, typically on a weekend, he would take John here and myself somewhere around New York, because he loved to do that with his nephews, John and I. And we would, one week, go to the Statue of Liberty, another week on the *Queen Mary*. Another week we'd go to Ebbets Field and watch the Dodgers play and so forth. And that was an early part of our life prior to our move out to Long Island.

The other small story, very small, is I remember being in grade school — and I can't tell you what grade, but it had to be the fourth grade or fifth grade, when we were quite young. But, as a class, we were not very good. And the teacher, who was a very disciplined nun, decided she was going to march us over to some other location in punishment. It was like, in our minds, going to the dungeon, someplace where we were going to be punished for our lack of, you know, being a proper child.

We lived directly across the street from that grammar school. And, as I can recall, walking in line with our classmates towards this imprisonment, if you will. And, at the last moment in my desperation, which was total fear, I broke off the line, and I just ran, as fast as I could, to the street, and across the street, and home into the house, and much, I guess, to the surprise of my mother. But I just didn't want to be locked up and punished.

And I can remember that as being an experience in life that . . . has always stayed with me. . . . It just meant that we weren't very good kids, probably, in terms of the classroom environment. But that's a piece of our childhood which I remember.

John: I could tell you a story. At the St. Francis of Assisi Church, they had a yard out in front of it with a big steel fence. And behind the fence were chestnut trees. And all the kids had games that you'd get your chestnut, and you'd try to make it as hard as possible, put it on a string. And then you would challenge another person, and he'd hold up his chestnut. And you would hit his chestnut with your chestnut.

So I was going over, at the time of year that there were chestnuts there, to leap a few others' chestnuts. And I was under the fence, and along comes the monsignor. He said, "Come over here, young man." And he said, "What are you doing there?" I said, "Getting my chestnuts." He said, "What grade are you in?" I said, "I'm in the fourth grade." "I want you to go back in school on Monday. And I want you to tell your teacher that you were out here. And I've been talking to you about those chestnuts. And you tell her what you were doing so wrong." I figured, "Oh my goodness."

And so, I went home. And the whole weekend, I was thinking, how am I going to handle this? And I figured, well, I just won't do anything. But gee, then I'm going to have to face up to God. And this is the monsignor telling me to do something. I'm disobeying it. And so it was my first moral dilemma. [*laughter*] But I didn't tell anybody. [*laughter*]

Why do you think your family moved from Brooklyn to Long Island?

John: Well, that was a very good reason. My father worked on Wall Street. And each summer, we would take the whole family out to Long Island and visit, live, with my grandmother. And my mother would be out there also. And my oldest brother [Shirley Thomas Keane], who was seven years older than I, had gotten into a little problem. And he joined the Navy on August 26th. . . . And then Pearl Harbor broke out. And we were out in my grandmother's [the next] summer.

And the next thing I knew is, my father was saying that we're not going back to New York. "We've got a house over in Manorville. And that's where you're going to go to school. And you're going to reside down here." I try to imagine, as an adult, how it must have felt when your country has gone into war. And he felt that, out in the country, you could survive with your gardens and vegetables and so forth, where in the city, that'd be much more difficult.

And he then stayed in New York, worked in New York. He would come out Friday evening, and then he'd go back into New York on Monday mornings. I think that was it. And then, it was a great way, I know for Kevin and I. It was a little bit more difficult for the girls growing up out in the country. But we didn't have any running water. They paid, I think, three thousand dollars, purchased the house plus a hundred acres of land. So you could imagine. . . . We had an outhouse, that's right. [*laughter*]

Kevin: So it was very rural.

John: It was very rural.

Andrée: I'd like to capitalize on what John just said. And this is my recollection, that my father was quite successful at an early age and lost a lot of money in the stock market, when the stock market crashed. And so I think he felt that, in order for us to be healthy, he felt that we should be brought up on Long Island. Because basically, we couldn't afford to live in New York anymore. And I was only two at the time, so this is all memory.

But he borrowed that money from my grandmother.

John: That's correct.

[*simultaneous conversation*]

Susan: And then he paid her back.

[*simultaneous conversation*]

Kevin: No memory.

Which grandmother? Grandmother Keane?

John: Grandma Le Caron, which is my mother's mother.

Susan: When he did go out, and decided to buy some property, he asked my grandmother if he could borrow her car. And she said no. [*laughter*] He took a bicycle and drove over to Manorville.

John: About six miles.

Susan: That's right. On the bike. But also, when we were growing up, we had to have animals that produced. We had to grow things that produced. So, like we had chickens and goats and —

Kevin: a cow —

Susan: cow, pigs, cats, dogs, yeah.

It sounds like both the crash of the stock market and losing just about everything he had, and with the war, he wanted to make sure his family was self-sufficient.

John: Yes.

Andrée: Exactly. And now I understand .... But when he went bankrupt, so to speak, he told somebody at the company that he was going to pay the whole thing back. And it took him until, I think, 1960 — and apparently, from what I understand, he paid the whole thing back.

John: Yep.

Andrée: Is that correct?

Kevin: That is correct.

In 1929 — let me go back to the early twenties. His early experience in life involved, after finishing graduate school, at some point [getting] into the business of . . . seeking companies in Europe, who were developing patents, and . . . he would be the agent to bring that patented technology into the country, for which he received basically very little cash but lots of stock or stock options.

I'll give you two examples. He apparently, in my vague memory, was responsible for bringing into the United States the patent for the Waterman pen.

The second thing that I vaguely remember, he was responsible for securing the patent rights to the first of the — in the thirties — of the Ford Motor Company['s] current technology for the automobile alternator. And that was very important. And it was of considerable value, in terms of options and whatever.

When the 1929 crash occurred, all of that disappeared, because the companies went into receivership and bankruptcy and [were] involved with mini loans. And, as a consequence, he had a lot of obligations because he was, like [in] the current financial crisis, he was cash-shy. And I recall — perhaps with John here — a conversation with our father, when we asked—we had to be of college age at this point—"What happened? And why did you go to Wall Street?" And I think, in summary, his comment was — these are my words — "If you can't beat them, you join them." And he went to Wall Street and secured a job with a company known as Delafield and Delafield. And his specialty was in the bond market. And he was actually an investment manager for portfolios at Delafield and Delafield — maybe estate planning, but . . . for the bond portfolios.

And he had a number of clients which survived his time with Delafield and Delafield, even past the point where Delafield and Delafield merged into another firm, whose name I don't remember. But he, almost to the latter part of his life, before he passed away — he was seventy-two when he passed away. But maybe when he was in his sixties, he still managed two or three of the portfolios.

[*simultaneous conversation*]

Susan: He became ill. But before he was ill, he took care of . . . one of his clients, almost [right] before he passed away.

Kevin: Yes. Because now Susan, in making her comments, may add a lot to it. Because when our father passed away, Susan was the one who worked with the attorney, in all the probate preparations and filings — and so was using a lot of that stuff in detail. But basically, that was his history.

Now, getting to the point that Andrée talked about, he also said — and the question was, in your career, why did you stay at Wall Street? — "I've joined them. I'm learning about it." But he also made a comment, many years ago, that it was his mission, commitment in life, to pay back every cent that he owed during the crash. In other words, every bit. . . . He never went into bankruptcy. And that was a matter of principle. And I think that has guided us in our own attitudes, in many respects. At least I feel that way.

So, because he was cash poor, he had accumulated debts. Because, of course, you bought things on credit from various companies. And so, his goal was to repay all of that debt.

Kevin: Absolutely.

John: That's right.

Your father traveled quite a bit. . . . He had a U.S. passport. He went to Quebec. He went to France and Belgium and Greece and Spain and Portugal, all those places. Did he ever talk about that?

Kevin: One little very short story. I recall, when I was finishing college, I was in the Air Force ROTC. And I was going to go on active duty after graduation into the Air Force, which I did. And, during that time period — this was 1955 to 1958 — I ended up in the Strategic Air Command. And I flew excessively in Europe. And I remember John, when I was home at one point, telling me that what I did, he did back in the twenties. And from England, he would fly in the Sopwith Camel, I think is the name of the plane, across the English Channel, to get into France and Germany. And, at that point, to see companies, to negotiate his opportunities, and then bring them eventually back to the United States.

So you're very correct. He did a lot of traveling in Europe. But I thought that was the uniquely interesting thing, that he flew on those post–World War I airplanes, which are open-cockpit planes, which are double-wing. You've probably seen them, remember them. . . . And he used to fly, periodically, across the English Channel. And I thought that was very impressive. Still is impressive to me.

He wasn't a pilot, but he would be a passenger?

Kevin: A passenger.

John: Right.

Andrée: And I remember, he always talked about flying over the English Channel.

Kevin: Well, there you go.

Andrée: And he talked about how long it took because of the headwinds. But . . . somehow I always envisioned him in his plane, these horrible winds, and [taking] twice as long trying to get across. And he talked about how dangerous it was, basically.

Kevin: And it's only twenty miles across. . . .

Andrée: I didn't know why he was there, but I remember him being in a plane trying to cross the darn channel. But it took too long.

What are your significant memories of your mother or your father?

Susan: Getting back to during the war [World War II], when we were young, we had these drills in case the atom bomb came . . . or the war came. Remember?

And where to go, and what to do. I mean we just —

Kevin: Blackouts.

Susan: And the blackouts, everything.

Kevin: John, you remember well? Talk about the cars and taping the headlights halfway.

John: Oh, yeah.

Kevin: Describe some of that. Remember going to the Navy? Let us do this that night. We had walked down to the Dosiak(?) and to the field there, where they had the radar, the search lights. Remember that?

John: Yes.

Kevin: Civil Defense, yeah.

John: Yeah. John was not involved.

Kevin: No.

John: Incidentally, Maureen, you probably have noticed we call our parents John and Buddy. Buddy is our mother, and John is our father.

Kevin: And that was on their insistence. I recall questioning that. None of our friends called their parents by their first name. Specifically to our mother: "Why are you being called Buddy?" She said, "I was always called Buddy. And that's the way I want it." And it was Buddy and John.

Susan: Her dad named her that. And it was a cartoon character.

What was the name of the cartoon character?

Susan: Buddy.

Andrée: Buddy.

John: I would say Bunk was Buddy's brother, our uncle. And Bunk was also a cartoon character. So it was Buddy and Bunk, and I don't know who else.

Kevin: Interesting. I didn't know that.

Andrée: I did not know that.

Susan: And the other thing about John — even though he had a very large family, and a lot of responsibilities, he'd come out on weekends. And every Sunday, there was a farmer across the street. And his son, he had a thing about education, my father did. And he took three hours out of a Sunday, every Sunday, to teach [the farmer's son]. And, to this day, [the son] talks about it. Now he's an engineer and everything — that he would have never been educated or where he is [without my father]. My father insisted. And he would only come out on weekends, and he spent three hours a week tutoring this young man.

John: He came out on weekends. And, from the first thing on Saturday morning, it was "Up John, up Kevin."

Susan: "Up Susan, up Andrée." [*laughter*]

John: And we were like indentured servants. We cleared the land.

Kevin: That's right. We planted the crops.

Susan: I pulled the thing while he did the plowing.

Andrée: I crawled under the house to help locate some plumbing. [*laughter*] I was the littlest one, and I could crawl under the house, into the crawl space.

Susan: But then you had to build a cesspool.

John: We built cesspools.

Susan: And the pigpens.

Andrée: That was sophisticated.

Kevin: We burned all the stumps when we dug up the trees. And I remember, when I was in high school, I liked to play baseball a great deal. And we had formed a team. And our team would play other teams in a ten-mile radius of where we lived. But we wouldn't dare tell John that we've got a commitment to play at two o'clock in the afternoon. But half the time we'd come up, going to a baseball game about twenty minutes late. And everybody was standing by, waiting for us to arrive. [*laughter*]

Because you had chores to do.

Kevin: That's right.

That's interesting that your dad wanted you to live on Long Island, on this farm, and do all the work. But do you know, did he ever talk about why he wanted to do that? I mean, does this come from his father and his grandfather . . . ?

Kevin: He wanted a work ethic. . . . Father John would say, "I want this and this and this done." And I could remember brother John saying, "We've got to get out there now, and we've got to get it done." And we would work like hell to get it done so we could get out of there to go to the ballgame. And that's why we were late. You know, we just couldn't get it all done on time. And you will recall, there were many instances.

But . . . he felt that we had to earn everything that we had to benefit by. And, as a result . . . he would push the boys, [brother] John and I, to find work and do things. In brother John's case, he worked for two or three years — I don't remember how long — on a vinery, which John will describe to you. I ended up saying, "I want to grow hybrid flowers."

And he loaned me the money to buy the seeds for hybrid delphinium flowers. And he helped me build a hothouse, a very small structure, to germinate the seeds, and then planted them. And we planted three acres of these flowers.

And the short story is, we ended up selling them during college years to the wholesale flower markets in New York City through an intermediary, who was about six miles away in Eastport, a town nearby. My point is, this is how we earned money to get to college, among other things. And we also did the same thing in growing asparagus plants from seed, and then planted about an acre and a half — am I correct? —

John: Yes, yes —

Kevin: — of asparagus, which all of us [planted]. Vicky, you were already out of the house.

Victoire: Yes, yes.

Kevin: You and Andrée and John and I were all involved in the asparagus business. Now, this will get to another series of stories which John can tell better than I can. Because one of the consequences of that is, we had to deliver the asparagus. We would be up at the crack of dawn, cut the asparagus, bunch them like you buy them in the store in bunches. There were little mechanical devices by which you did it. And you'd take these bunches and deliver them to a store.

Female voice: We had our own stand.

Kevin: But when the store opened, then we'd go to school. And, at that age, we were old enough to drive a car. And we had a license. So we delivered them. I can recall delivering these. But . . . the store opened like at eight o'clock. And, by the time they got the stuff and I got to school, I was five or ten minutes late getting into school.

And John remembers other stories even better than this, that I can remember — [having] to go to the principal's office. And the principal was a fellow by the name of Halleck Wood. And, among other things . . . Halleck Wood said we were awful as sons, in that we were never on time for school. And we would never make it anywhere. We wouldn't get into college. You know, we were doomed if we didn't straighten out. And John is laughing here, but he'll tell stories about it, because he got the same story. And the thing is, the principal couldn't accept the fact we were just trying to do our responsibilities as a family, to deliver the product to the store.

Now our parents were of the mind that this is good and healthy. And we agreed. And it was a very concerted commitment to make things happen.

John: I'm going to turn to something else. I started working on the farm when I was eleven years old.

Kevin: I was nine. I know.

John: And, I mean, that was from seven in the morning until six at night. And I remember when I first went over to Harold Carter, our next door neighbor, and said, "I'd like to pick some potatoes." And he looked at me, and I was about up to his kneecaps, and said, "Well, I don't know whether you can or not. But why don't you come with me?" And we went across the street. And he dug up a row of potatoes and said, "Now, would you pick those and put them in those bags?" And he wanted to see whether I could lift up a half-a-bushel basket and put it in the bags. I said, "Okay. You're on." And I could earn four cents a bushel.

Now, in a day I'd probably pick forty bushels, which was not too much. But I was generally the only white person on the field. And a couple of the black guys would come up and I'd say hi to them. And they'd stop and say, "Goddamn, what a worker." [*laughter*] And I felt like a million dollars.

Female voice: Yeah.

John: And then, my first check that I remember getting was about for about eighteen dollars. I came down on a Saturday morning. And John said, "I understand you got a check." I said, "Yeah." I was pretty proud of it. And he said, "Well, I've been thinking about it. I want you to take one-third of that check and give it to your mother."

Kevin: Yep.

John: "For the family." And then I thought, "Holy smokes. That leaves me with only twelve dollars." "Then I want you to take another third of the check, and I want you to put it in the bank for your college. And then you can keep a third." [*laughter*] I was absolutely crushed. I was in tears and so forth. But that's the way I went right through high school.

Kevin: That's the way it was. [*simultaneous conversation*]

John: It was part of the money I used going to college. But it was a very subtle way of inculcating work, frugality. We had to save for the future. And I think it was a wonderful thing. I don't think any one of us really regrets it very much.

Susan: I have to say one thing. And John — my brother John. Everybody in town was amazed because you went in with the migrant workers. And you were one of the very few people that they accepted. Remember that?

John: Yeah.

Susan: I mean, it was unbelievable.

Kevin: Because as a young teenager, you worked as hard or harder than anybody on that vinery or anything else. That's absolutely right.

I have a couple of other questions for you. I was looking at your father's family. There was the loss of so many siblings. So many of his siblings, his sisters and brothers, died.

Kevin: Three of them died over three months.

Did he ever talk about that?

John: Yes. I think it was diphtheria. And they were all very young children.

Kevin: Early 1900s.

John: Yeah. He talked about it.

Andrée: Well, the stories that I remember being told to me are that, at that time, the Keanes had three children. This is talking about my grandparents. And one of the children, or perhaps two, became ill with diphtheria. So they decided that they would split — the parents split. And one parent took one child . . . was it to Waterbury? There were two children. And then, you know, the correspondence then was only by mail. So one wrote to the other and said, basically, "How are the children doing?" Or "How is the child doing?" And I don't know how this worked out, but [my grandmother] wrote back to my grandfather [and] said, "Oh, John passed away last night." And then she received a letter saying, "Oh" — I don't know the other two boys' names at the time — but they passed away too. Which was so sad, because the three of them, as my brother John said, had died. But they were separated, hoping that they would not be contagious.

John: This was 1890 to 1895, because John was then born as the first child after they died in 1898. Yeah. So that's about the time period.

Did your father ever talk to you about where this work ethic and this desire for education came from? I mean, did he ever talk about his parents?

John: That was the thing that really got me. He talked about the importance of education as far as we were concerned, but never reflected on his own family, or even reflected on how extensive the education of his brothers and sister were. And that's one thing that really got me on this whole family —

Kevin: In that respect, however, as you may already know, all of the brothers went to Holy Cross. And one went to Fordham. One daughter went to Smith, the only daughter, the oldest child at that point, Margaret. She went to Smith. This was back in the early teens, 1900 and whatever it was. And John ended up going to Harvard. We talked about this last night. He apparently violated the parietal rules or something at Holy Cross and was suspended from the school. Then he got mad and quit and applied to Harvard and finished up at Harvard after half of his freshman year at Holy Cross.

But they were all educated. It seemed to be part of the natural process in the family, at that point in time. And I agree with John, I don't recall really any conversations or incentives or, you know, statements about it, in any way.

So he never really talked about his father or anything?

John: No, he never really did.

There were no funny things attributed to him, like you're working out in the field, and he's telling you, "Oh, my father did this," or "My father did that," or a few of the funny things?

John: He never did.

Andrée: In my recollection, if he ever talked about either parent, it was usually his mother.

Susan: That's right.

Andrée: But never the father, that I remember. I mean, I always thought all his wonderful wisdom started and ended with him, you know.

He died before all of you were born, your grandfather?

Female voice: Yes, oh yes.

John: Only one thing I can remember hearing about my grandfather was that he used to collect Irish immigrants that had recently come over to this country, and put them in his wagon, and try to get them assimilated into the American way of life. And that's about all I know about that. And I don't know who it was, whether it was John that mentioned it to me, or whether it was Paul, or Joe, or who.

Your grandfather — he's the one with the haberdashery in Bridgeport — was a fairly successful businessman.

John: He was.

He had his own company, John F. Keane and Company.

John: We had no idea whether he went to college or where got his zest for education that he imparted to his siblings.

Kevin: It's an interesting question, because in hindsight, it's pretty clear that the grandparents were very supportive, apparently, of all their children persevering and getting through college. And how that happened, and why, there's just no recollection, nothing.

And was there anything that you remember being in your house that might have come from the Keane Company?

Kevin: In the latter years of his life — John and I were probably college age at that time — I remember our father talking about and fantasizing about the Keane Family coat of arms, which he then reduced down to designs of fish on a plate. Do you recall? Can you help me on that, Susan or Andrée?

Susan: Yes, because the fish meant Christianity. That's right.

Kevin: I think it was pure fantasy.

Andrée: I know exactly what Kevin is talking about. I think he even had my mother reproduce it on a plate, too, because she had been taking some painting lessons at the time.

Susan: Oh, that's right.

Andrée: But he claimed that was the Keane Coat of Arms. And he explained it to me at the time, and I couldn't tell you what it was. But I don't know if anybody has [it] — do you have a copy of that Coat of Arms?

Kevin: I do not. But I might just comment that we had the occasion, my wife and I, to go to Carrigaholt in Ireland, at the mouth of the Shannon River. And apparently, as you may know . . . it was a fishing location. And a lot of people's livelihood was based on the sea.

And somehow or other, that connection was all part of. Oh, and there was one amusing comment I remember, over the years — and I think everyone here will remember it — is that I can recall Buddy and John, our mother and father, talking about, and maybe in jest, if you want to find a family fortune, you'll find it under a black rock in Ireland.

Victoire: I heard about this.

Kevin: So we went to Ireland, and we went to the beach. And the whole beach is black rocks. [*laughter*]

Victoire: That's true. And he said when you go there, it'll be —

Kevin: You remember that, Vicky?

Victoire: The third rock. The third rock, it'll bring you great happiness.

Kevin: Well, there [were] millions of rocks. [*laughter*]

Victoire: There were always three when he talked. That was when Buddy was in the hospital, probably another baby. [*laughter*]

Kevin: So these were probably just amusing comments they made to us, you know, and obviously have no relationship to anything except fun.

Well, it's all part of your family history. John, you can correct me if I'm wrong, but I think John started this investigation to learn more about the family's roots in Ireland, and find out about how the family came over, and why, and all of that. And, you know, your cousin David Bray had a lot of information. What's missing is any reminiscences, so it's great to have these stories.

John: County Clare and Carrigaholt. When we had an office over in Dublin, I remember a representative of the Irish government saying, "What did you say your last name was?" I said, "Keane." "Oh, you must be from County Clare." And that I guess there was a lot of Keanes out of County Clare. And [Dottie, the wife of] Paul, our father John's brother . . . was a Keane.

Kevin: It was his cousin.

Victoire: Yes, his cousin.

John: And there was a second one [who] was a Keane.

Kevin: Yes, you're right. That's true.

John: So there was some intermarriage, although it was not close. It was appropriate.

Kevin: Small comment. We traveled a couple times in Ireland. And I remember, after we were in Carrigaholt, I noticed that the local bar . . . was a saloon with the name Keane. And, as we traveled, became aware [that in] almost every town we seemed to be in, a half a dozen of them had saloons which had the name Keane.

And we made a point of stopping at a number of them, taking a picture of them, sometimes with the people, the proprietors, and identifying ourselves. We had a few extra beers in the process. [*laughter*] But we did this with friends of ours, who are not important in this conversation. But we traveled together. And they got a big kick out of this, and they made a big deal out of taking the photos and all that stuff. But, there were a lot of Keanes in the saloon business in Ireland. [*laughter*] They're all over the place. . . .

I have one final question for today, which is, did your father use any what you might consider unusual expressions?

Female voice: Yes. Don't take guff from cops. [*laughter*]

Don't what?

Kevin: Don't take guff from cops.

Female voice: Don't take guff from cops. [*simultaneous conversation*]

Andrée: I think that that came from when he was in college at Harvard; there was a policeman's strike.

Kevin: Oh yes, it was a policeman's strike.

Andrée: And a lot of the college kids became interested —

Kevin: — like they do today —

Andrée: Some of these kids would give them a rough time. But, from our perspective, I thought [the expression] meant, don't put up with any baloney from anybody. [*simultaneous conversation*] We were all raised with that mantra.

Kevin: Exactly.

Susan: This is Susan. One of the things which was incredible to me: you know, most parents [would give] a child a spanking or whatever. Our father would [give] three little taps, just little taps on the head. And that was worse than beating us. [*laughter*] And if we got the three taps, we'd cry. And that was terrible.

Andrée: And one time we had next door neighbors. And they had twin girls. And we were all playing. And one of them had done something that wasn't appropriate or whatever. And my father went over, and he tapped one of them on the head to say that was a no-no. And he had the wrong twin. But the girl went home absolutely hysterically crying, because Mr. Keane had tapped her on the head. [*laughter; simultaneous conversation*]

Susan: That was the worst thing that could happen.

Kevin: That was rejection. Yes.

The stories that you've told about your dad are really lovely and do flesh out the person. . . . You've already told me that he went to Holy Cross and then to Harvard.

John: I found out, this morning, he started college at Holy Cross. But I did not know this myself. And he was heading up a panty raid. And that's why he was bounced out of Holy Cross and applied to Harvard.

Kevin: Just a related thing. This history of all the boys going to Jesuit schools — Holy Cross or Fordham, the oldest or second oldest —

Female voice: second oldest —

Kevin: — the second oldest son after the first one passed away was Father Augustus Keane, who became a Jesuit priest. And, just as a point of interest, he had a lifelong commitment in education at Boston College. . . .

John: Boston College High.

Kevin: Oh, Boston College High, okay. And then, he eventually retired in his last assignment to being rector of Cranwell Preparatory School, which today is a resort. But it was a Jesuit prep school in New England, outside of Lenox, Massachusetts, for many years.

Anyway, what I'm saying is that the Irish Catholic influence was very strong in the family, and was probably a significant piece of the value system that existed in those years, right down through to our parents. So just a comment.

John: We've chatted about John our father, and how he affected our lives. I would like to direct some attention to Buddy, our mother. I think she was the most understated, but most effective element in all of our lives. Just think for a moment, of her versatility — going from a city girl to Manorville, in a house with no running water, no central heat, and an outhouse, and having to manage a home with a goat, a cow, two pigs, two dogs, three cats, and a hundred and fifty chickens, plus several major gardens. We don't talk about it, but can you imagine any of your wives or wives of your friends doing this, plus going to work on local farms during the summer and fall, picking vegetables, tying cauliflower, or weeding cranberry bogs? Then she was working with the Title Company in Riverhead. And to top it all, when we all left home, and Buddy joined John in New York City, the next thing we heard was that she was working for Lieutenant Governor Malcolm Wilson in his job as Chairman of the New York World's Fair. To me, Buddy is my role model for versatility, and one that our children can look up to.

It's been lovely speaking with all of you this afternoon.

John: It was really great to have you on the other end of the line. You know, without you, we would not have come up with any of these things.

Kevin: It was a great pleasure.

Keep talking.

CHARTS

DESCENDANTS OF
DANIEL AND MARGARET
(KEANE) KEANE

DESCENDANTS OF

Edward and Margaret (Keane) Bray

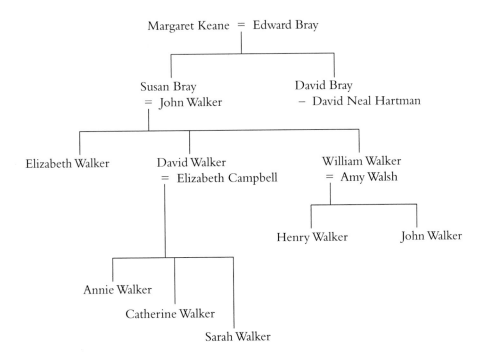

DESCENDANTS OF

John and Victoire (Le Caron) Keane

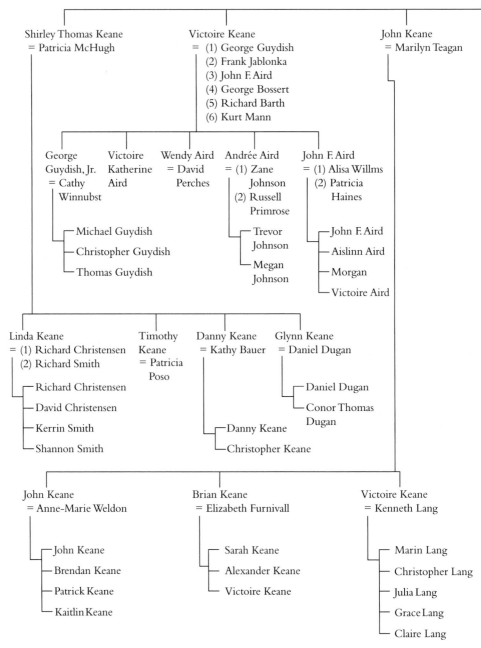

Shirley Thomas Keane
= Patricia McHugh

Victoire Keane
= (1) George Guydish
  (2) Frank Jablonka
  (3) John F. Aird
  (4) George Bossert
  (5) Richard Barth
  (6) Kurt Mann

John Keane
= Marilyn Teagan

George
Guydish, Jr.
= Cathy
  Winnubst

Victoire
Katherine
Aird

Wendy Aird
= David
  Perches

Andrée Aird
= (1) Zane
  Johnson
  (2) Russell
  Primrose

John F. Aird
= (1) Alisa Willms
  (2) Patricia
  Haines

- Michael Guydish
- Christopher Guydish
- Thomas Guydish

- Trevor
  Johnson
- Megan
  Johnson

- John F. Aird
- Aislinn Aird
- Morgan
- Victoire Aird

Linda Keane
= (1) Richard Christensen
  (2) Richard Smith

Timothy
Keane
= Patricia
  Poso

Danny Keane
= Kathy Bauer

Glynn Keane
= Daniel Dugan

- Richard Christensen
- David Christensen
- Kerrin Smith
- Shannon Smith

- Danny Keane
- Christopher Keane

- Daniel Dugan
- Conor Thomas
  Dugan

John Keane
= Anne-Marie Weldon

Brian Keane
= Elizabeth Furnivall

Victoire Keane
= Kenneth Lang

- John Keane
- Brendan Keane
- Patrick Keane
- Kaitlin Keane

- Sarah Keane
- Alexander Keane
- Victoire Keane

- Marin Lang
- Christopher Lang
- Julia Lang
- Grace Lang
- Claire Lang

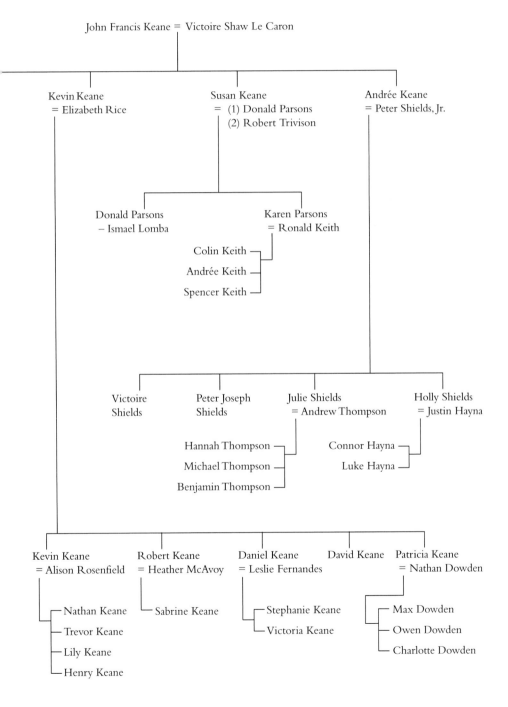

John Francis Keane = Victoire Shaw Le Caron

Kevin Keane
= Elizabeth Rice

Susan Keane
= (1) Donald Parsons
  (2) Robert Trivison

Andrée Keane
= Peter Shields, Jr.

Donald Parsons
– Ismael Lomba

Karen Parsons
= Ronald Keith

Colin Keith
Andrée Keith
Spencer Keith

Victoire
Shields

Peter Joseph
Shields

Julie Shields
= Andrew Thompson

Holly Shields
= Justin Hayna

Hannah Thompson
Michael Thompson
Benjamin Thompson

Connor Hayna
Luke Hayna

Kevin Keane
= Alison Rosenfield

Robert Keane
= Heather McAvoy

Daniel Keane
= Leslie Fernandes

David Keane

Patricia Keane
= Nathan Dowden

Nathan Keane
Trevor Keane
Lily Keane
Henry Keane

Sabrine Keane

Stephanie Keane
Victoria Keane

Max Dowden
Owen Dowden
Charlotte Dowden

145

DESCENDANTS OF
Paul and Dorothy Enola (Keane) Keane

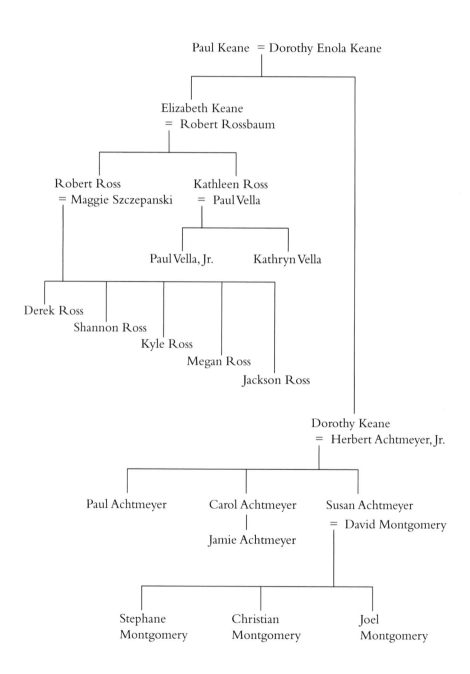

Paul Keane = Dorothy Enola Keane

Elizabeth Keane
= Robert Rossbaum

Robert Ross
= Maggie Szczepanski

Kathleen Ross
= Paul Vella

Paul Vella, Jr.   Kathryn Vella

Derek Ross

Shannon Ross

Kyle Ross

Megan Ross

Jackson Ross

Dorothy Keane
= Herbert Achtmeyer, Jr.

Paul Achtmeyer   Carol Achtmeyer   Susan Achtmeyer
= David Montgomery

Jamie Achtmeyer

Stephane
Montgomery

Christian
Montgomery

Joel
Montgomery

DESCENDANTS OF

Joseph and Katherine "Kay" (Lyons) Keane

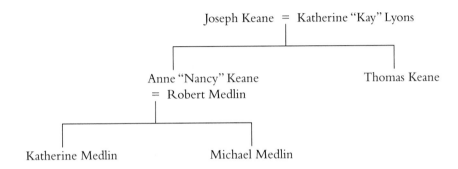

Joseph Keane = Katherine "Kay" Lyons

Anne "Nancy" Keane
= Robert Medlin

Thomas Keane

Katherine Medlin

Michael Medlin

DESCENDANTS OF

Robert and Marie (Rowan) Keane

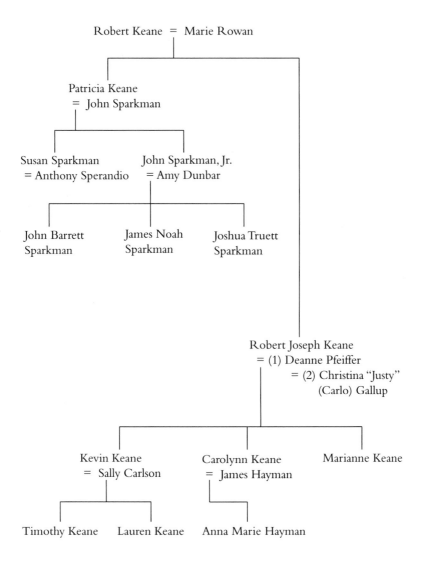

Robert Keane = Marie Rowan

Patricia Keane
= John Sparkman

Susan Sparkman
= Anthony Sperandio

John Sparkman, Jr.
= Amy Dunbar

John Barrett
Sparkman

James Noah
Sparkman

Joshua Truett
Sparkman

Robert Joseph Keane
= (1) Deanne Pfeiffer
= (2) Christina "Justy"
(Carlo) Gallup

Kevin Keane
= Sally Carlson

Carolynn Keane
= James Hayman

Marianne Keane

Timothy Keane   Lauren Keane

Anna Marie Hayman

NOTES

PART I

1   John Lloyd, *A Short Tour; or, an Impartial and Accurate Description of the County of Clare with Some Particular and Historical Observations* (Ennis, Ireland: John Busteed and George Trinder, printers, 1780), accessed through the Clare County Library website, *www.clarelibrary.ie/eolas/coclare/history/lloyds/lloyds_tour_index.htm*, November 2011.

2   Information in this section is from Rev. P. White, *History of Clare and the Dalcassian Clans of Tipperary, Limerick, and Galway* (Dublin: M. H. Gill and Son, Printers, 1893).

3   *The Parliamentary Gazetteer of Ireland: Adapted to the New Poor-law, Franchise, Municipal and Ecclesiastical Arrangements, and Compiled with a Special Reference to the Lines of Railroad and Canal Communication, as Existing in 1814–45*, vol. 2 (Dublin: A. Fullarton and Co., 1846), p. 360.

4   Kilcloher Townland, Kilballyowen Parish, Rahona Electoral Division, *General Valuation Revision Lists, Kilrush Rural District (Clare), 1856–1945*, Family History Library (FHL) Microfilm 819463.

5   Clare County Library, "County Clare — An Introduction," *Clare History*, online at *www.clarelibrary.ie/eolas/coclare/history/countclr.htm*, accessed November 2011.

6   Pat O'Brien, "The Penal Laws in Clare," *Clare History*, online at *www.clarelibrary.ie/eolas/coclare/history/penal_laws_clare.htm*, accessed November 2011.

7   Tony Downes, "The 1798 Rebellion in County Clare," *Clare History*, online at *www.clarelibrary.ie/eolas/coclare/history/clare_1798_rebellion.htm*, accessed November 2011.

8   Clare County Library, "County Clare — An Introduction," *Clare History*, online at *www.clarelibrary.ie/eolas/coclare/history/countclr.htm*, accessed November 2011.

9   Kilcloher Townland, Kilballyowen Parish, Rahona Electoral Division,
      *General Valuation Revision Lists, Kilrush Rural District (Clare), 1856–
      1945,* FHL Microfilm 819463.

10   Senan Scanlan, "Inhabitants of Scattery Island, Shannon Estuary,
      Co. Clare," *Clare Genealogy,* online at Clare County Library website,
      *www.clarelibrary.ie/eolas/coclare/genealogy/don_tran/fam_his/scattery/
      inhabitants_1850.htm,* accessed November 2011.

11   Ibid.

12   "The Little Ark of Kilbaha," *Clare History,* online at Clare County
      Library website, *www.clarelibrary.ie/eolas/coclare/history/kilbaha.htm,*
      accessed November 2011.

13   "Children's History Page," online at St. Cuan's National School
      website, *kilbahaschool.com/Kilballyowen.htm,* accessed November 2011.

14   Carrigaholt (County Clare) Catholic Parish Registers, microfilmed by
      the National Library of Ireland, 1973, FHL Microfilm 926099.

15   Helen Litton, *The Irish Famine: An Illustrated History* (Dublin:
      Wolfhound Press, 2006).

16   Senan Scanlan, "Vandelerus of Kilrush County Clare," *Clare History,*
      online at Clare County Library website, *www.clarelibrary.ie/eolas/coclare/
      genealogy/don_tran/fam_his/vandeleurs/famine.htm,* accessed November
      2012.

17   A. M. Hodge and R. Rees, *Union to Partition: Ireland, 1800–1921*
      (Newtownards, Ireland: Colourpoint Books, 1995).

18   "Emigration & Education Statistics, 1931, Co. Clare," *From Ireland,*
      online at *www.from-ireland.net,* accessed November 2011.

19   Clare County Library, "County Clare — An Introduction," *Clare
      History,* online at *www.clarelibrary.ie/eolas/coclare/history/countclr.htm,*
      accessed November 2011.

20   Clare County Council, "CSO publishes census 2011 preliminary
      results," online at *www.clarecoco.ie/community/news/cso-publishes-census-
      2011-preliminary-results.html,* accessed November 2011.

21   1901 Irish Census, National Archives of Ireland, *www.nationalarchives.ie,*
      accessed September 2011.

22   1911 Irish Census, National Archives of Ireland, *www.nationalarchives.ie,*
      accessed September 2011.

23   O'Cathain Festival 2010, online at *www.ocathainfestival.com,* accessed
      September 2011.

24 Irish Surname Search: *Keane, O'Kane, O'Cahan, (MacCloskey, MacEvinney)*, online at *www.goireland.com*, accessed September 2011.

25 Thomas Jefferson Westropp, "Kilkee and Its Neighborhood," *Journal of the North Munster Archaeological Society* 3, no. 4 (1915).

26 Antoinette O'Brien, "Clare Heritage Center [Report on the Daniel and Margaret Keane Family for the New England Historic Genealogical Society]," dated 9 January 2012, ref. 26937.

27 A rood is one quarter of an acre; a perch is one fortieth of a rood, or 1/160th of an acre.

28 Antoinette O'Brien, "Clare Heritage Center [Report on the Daniel and Margaret Keane Family for the New England Historic Genealogical Society]," dated 9 January 2012, ref. 26937.

29 Sincere thanks to Judy Lucey, Archivist at the New England Historic Genealogical Society and an expert on Irish genealogy, for providing background information on Griffith's Valuation and for helping with interpretation of the records.

30 James R. Reilly, "Is There More in Griffith's Valuation Than Just Names?" *The Irish at Home and Abroad* 5, no. 2 (1998), p. 58.

31 Kilcloher Townland, Kilballyowen Parish, Rahona Electoral Division, *General Valuation Revision Lists, Kilrush Rural District (Clare), 1856–1945*, FHL Microfilm 819463.

32 Antoinette O'Brien, "Clare Heritage Center [Report on the Daniel and Margaret Keane Family for the New England Historic Genealogical Society]," dated 9 January 2012, ref. 26937.

Additional References

Clare Local Studies Project, *Poverty Before the Famine: County Clare, 1835* (Ennis, Ireland: CLASP Press, 1997).

John Grenham, *Tracing Your Irish Ancestors*, 3rd ed. (Baltimore: Genealogical Publishing Company, 2006).

National University of Ireland, Galway, *Landed Estates Database*, *landedestates.nuigalway.ie*, accessed May 2012.

John O'Donovan and Eugene Curry, *The Antiquities of County Clare: Ordnance Survey Letters, 1839* (Minneapolis: Irish Books and Media, 2000).

John O'Hart, *Irish Pedigrees; or The Origin and Stem of the Irish Nation* (Dublin: McGlashan and Gill, 1876).

Kieran Sheedy, *The United Irishmen of County Clare* (Ennis, Ireland: Clare Education Centre, 1998).

PART II

1   For more information regarding the immigration experience, see
     Kerby M. Miller, *Emigrants and Exiles: Ireland and the Irish Exodus to
     North America* (New York: Oxford University Press, 1985).

2   Passenger and Crew Lists of Vessels Arriving at New York, New York,
     1820–1897, NARA Microfilm Publication M237, roll 231, line 37.

3   Jane Eliza Johnson, *Newtown's History and Historian, Ezra Levan Johnson*
     (Newtown, Conn.: privately printed, 1917).

4   Harlan Jessup, Email correspondence, October 2012. Mr. Jessup is a
     professional genealogist based in Newtown, Connecticut

5   Cited in "History of Newtown, Connecticut," Wikipedia, online at
     http://en.wikipedia.org/wiki/History_of_Newtown,_Connecticut, accessed
     November 2012.

6   Ibid.

7   Rev. William Byrne, D.D., *History of the Catholic Church in the New
     England States*, vol 2 (Boston: The Hurd and Everts Co., 1899), p. 274.

8   New York Belting and Packing Co., National Register of Historic
     Places Inventory — Nomination Form. Received 28 April 1982,
     entered 2 June 1982.

9   Joseph M. Keane household, 1900 U.S. Census, New Haven County,
     Conn., city of New Haven, NARA Microfilm Publication T623, roll
     145, enumeration district 360, p. 15B, dwelling 185, family 308.

10   Newtown, Fairfield County, Connecticut: Births, 1867, p. 106.

11   Daniel Kane [Keane] household, 1870 U.S. Census, Fairfield County,
     Conn., town of Newtown, NARA Microfilm Publication M593, roll
     98, p. 728B, dwelling 582, family 604.

12   Newtown, Fairfield County, Connecticut: Births, 1870, pp. 4–5 and
     Newtown, Fairfield County, Connecticut: Deaths, 1870, pp. 448–449.

13   Newtown, Fairfield County, Connecticut: Births, 1872, pp. 16–17 and
     Newtown, Fairfield County, Connecticut: Deaths, 1876, pp. 476–477.

14   Daniel Keane household, 1880 U.S. Census, Fairfield County, Conn.,
     town of Newtown, NARA Microfilm Publication T9, roll 94,
     enumeration district 115, p. 35C, dwelling 315, family 250.

15   Dennis C. Gately Keane household, 1880 U.S. Census, Fairfield County,
     Conn., town of Newtown, NARA Microfilm Publication T9, roll 94,
     enumeration district 115, p. 44D, dwelling 383, family 432.

16   Elisha Carlton Sanford, *Thomas Sanford, the Emigrant to New England;
     Ancestry, Life, and Descendants,* vol. 2 (Rutland, Vt: The Tuttle Company,

1911), p. 386; Henry Sanford household, 1880 U.S. Census, Fairfield County, Conn., town of Newtown, NARA Microfilm Publication T9, roll 94, enumeration district 116, p. 2C, dwelling 346, family 361.

17   The tombstone of Daniel and Margaret Keane can be found at St. Rose's Cemetery in Newtown, Conn.

18   Elisha Carlton Sanford, *Thomas Sanford, the Emigrant to New England; Ancestry, Life, and Descendants,* vol. 2 (Rutland, Vt: The Tuttle Company, 1911), p. 386.

19   1887 Bridgeport, Connecticut, City Directory, p. 226; newspaper clippings in possessions of the Keane family (likely from the *Bridgeport Post* and the *Bridgeport Telegram*).

20   George C. Waldo, Jr., ed., *History of Bridgeport and Vicinity* (Chicago: S. J. Clarke and Co., 1917).

21   1890 Bridgeport, Connecticut City Directory, p. 255.

22   1891 Bridgeport, Connecticut, City Directory, p. 280.

23   1892 Bridgeport, Connecticut, City Directory, p. 319.

24   *Official Letter Book of Gov. Richard D. Hubbard, October 1877–January 1879* (Hartford, Conn.: Connecticut State Library, 1934), *passim.*

25   Correspondence between D. Joshua Taylor and Jane Seymour-Ford, Research Librarian, Perkins School for the Blind, 12 March 2009. Susan was enumerated at the Perkins School in the 1880 census: "Perkins School," 1880 United States Federal Census, Suffolk County, Massachusetts, city of Boston, NARA Microfilm Publication T9, roll 557, enumeration district 687, sheet 48B, dwelling 270, family 475.

26   1886 Waterbury, Connecticut, City Directory, p. 217.

27   1887 Waterbury, Connecticut, City Directory, p. 242.

28   Letter in the possession of David Bray. "Aunt and Uncle Platt" are likely Spencer and Susan (Geary) Platt (see p. 106). Cousins Fannie and Kittie have not been identified; records of Spencer and Susan Platt do not list any children.

29   Bridgeport, Connecticut, Land Records, vol. 103, p. 463.

30   Bridgeport, Connecticut, Land Records, vol. 158, p. 654.

31   Interview with Dorothy Keane Achtmeyer.

32   Undated newspaper clipping, in possession of the Keane family.

33   Newtown, Fairfield County, Connecticut: Deaths, 1898, pp. 234–235; Bridgeport, Fairfield County, Connecticut: Deaths, 1898, pp. 278–279.

34   Interview with Elizabeth Keane Rossbaum.

35   Interview with Dorothy Keane Achtmeyer.

36   Interview with Dorothy Keane Achtmeyer.

37   Interview with Susan Bray Walker.

38   Interview with Dorothy Keane Achtmeyer.

39   "John F. Keane Dies Following Brief Illness," *Bridgeport Telegram,*
      30 September 1922, p. 21.

40   Interview with Dorothy Keane Achtmeyer.

41   "John F. Keane Dies Following Brief Illness," *Bridgeport Telegram,*
      30 September 1922, p. 21.

42   Undated newspaper clipping, in possession of the Keane family.

43   Unidentified and undated newspaper clipping, in possession of the
      Keane family.

44   "About SVC," St. Vincent's College, online at *www.stvincentscollege.edu,*
      accessed August 2011.

45   Interview with Patricia Keane Sparkman.

46   "Physical Checks Slated for 10,000 Pupils Here," *Bridgeport Post,*
      6 October 1957, p. 8.

47   Brooks Mather Kelley, *Yale: A History* (New Haven, Conn.: Yale Uni-
      versity Press, 1999).

48   Robert S. Oliver, ed., *History of the Class of Nineteen Hundred and
      Sixteen of Yale College: Yale University, Class of 1916* (New Haven, Conn.:
      Yale University Press, 1916) and *Alumni Directory of Yale University:
      Graduates and Non-Graduates 1920* (New Haven, Conn.: Yale Uni-
      versity Press, 1920), p. 320.

49   George Henry Nettleton, ed., *The Book of Yale Pageant, 21 October
      1916, in Commemoration of the Two-Hundredth Anniversary of the Removal
      of Yale College to New Haven* (New Haven, Conn.: Yale University Press,
      1916), p. 211.

50   Anthony J. Kuzniewski, *Thy Honored Name: A History of the College of
      the Holy Cross, 1843–1994* (Washington, D.C.: Catholic University of
      America Press, 1999), 227.

51   John Francis Keane, Sr., to Paul A. and Joseph A. Keane, 25 September
      1919. Original in the possession of Betty Keane Rossbaum.

52   John Francis Keane, Sr., to Paul A. and Joseph A. Keane, 9 October
      1919. Original in the possession of Betty Keane Rossbaum.

53   John Francis Keane, Sr., to Paul A. and Joseph A. Keane, 4 November
      1921. Original in the possession of Betty Keane Rossbaum.

54   Susan Elizabeth (Sheahan) Keane to Paul A. and Joseph A. Keane,
      18 November 19[20]. Original in the possession of Betty Keane
      Rossbaum.

55 Susan Elizabeth (Sheahan) Keane to Paul A. and Joseph A. Keane, 9 February 19[21]. Original in the possession of Betty Keane Rossbaum.

56 John T. Bethell, Richard M. Hunt, and Robert Shenton, *Harvard A to Z* (Cambridge, Mass.: Harvard University Press, 2004).

57 Harvard Alumni Association and Associated Harvard Clubs, *Harvard Alumni Bulletin*, vol. 20 (reprint, Charleston, S.C.: Nabu Press, 2011), p. 140.

58 *Harvard College Class of 1921: Decennial Report* (Cambridge, Mass.: Harvard University, 1931), p. 142.

59 *Harvard Class of 1921: Twenty-fifth Anniversary Report* (Cambridge, Mass.: Harvard University, 1946), pp. 381–382.

60 The children recalled memories of these years in a conversation that was recorded in November 2011; a transcript is reprinted as Appendix II.

61 "Keane, Inc. Chairman and CEO Receives Harvard Business School Alumni Achievement Award," *The Free Library* 07 June 1999, online at *www.thefreelibrary.com/Keane, Inc. Chairman and CEO Receives Harvard Business School Alumni...-a054806853,* accessed November 2011.

Additional References

Diana C. Schwerdtle, *Newtown, Connecticut: Past and Present* (Newtown, Conn.: League of Women Voters of Newtown, 1975).

Lynn Winfield Wilson, *History of Fairfield County, Connecticut* (Chicago: S. J. Clark Publishing Co., 1929).

PART III

1 Daniel Kane [Keane] household, 1870 U.S. Census, Fairfield County, Conn., town of Newtown, National Archives and Records Administration (NARA) Microfilm Publication M593, roll 98, p. 68, dwelling 582, family 614.

2 Newtown, Fairfield County, Conn.: Deaths, 1886, p. 532.

3 Calculated from the birth of Mary Keane.

4 Newtown, Fairfield County, Conn.: Deaths, 1906, p. 276.

5 Ibid.; Charles R. Hale Collection, Headstone Inscriptions town of Newtown, Connecticut: St. Rose's Cemetery (413–415) (Hartford: Connecticut State Library, 1935), p. 166.

6 April 1857 Revision, Kilclogher Townland, Kilballyowen Parish, Rahona Electoral Division. *General Valuation Revision Lists, Kilrush*

Rural District (Clare), 1856–1945, Family History Library (FHL) Microfilm 819463.

7   Based on the January 1865 birth of Michael Joseph Keane in New-town, Conn.

8   Daniel Kane [Keane] household, 1870 U.S. Census, Fairfield County, Conn., town of Newtown, NARA Microfilm Publication M593, roll 98, p. 68, dwelling 582, family 614.

9   Daniel Keane household, 1880 U.S. Census, Fairfield County, town of Newtown, NARA Microfilm Publication T9-0094, roll 94, p. 197C, dwelling 315, family 350.

10   Anna Keating household, 1900 U.S. Census, Fairfield County, town of Newtown, FHL microfilm 1240134, roll 134, p. 19A, dwelling 365, family 375. Almost all records from the 1890 census were destroyed by fire in 1921.

11   Charles R. Hale Collection, Headstone Inscriptions town of New-town, Connecticut: St. Rose's Cemetery (413–415) (Hartford: Connecticut State Library, 1935), p. 166.

12   According to the 1900 U.S. Census, Margaret was the mother of ten children, five of whom were living in 1900. As the early Irish parish registers were often incomplete, it is possible that she gave birth to at least two additional children while in Ireland who died before the family left for America.

13   Carrigaholt (County Clare) Catholic Parish Registers. Microfilmed by the National Library of Ireland, 1973, FHL Microfilm 926099.

14   Her death has not been found in the Carrigaholt Catholic Parish Registers, and it is possible that she is the Mary Keane listed on the SS *Kangaroo* in 1863, which would mean she traveled with her parents and younger brother John to America. It is also possible that she died soon after the family's arrival in the United States, as no record of her has been located in the records of Newtown or the federal census records. Records of the Immigration and Naturalization Service; National Archives, *Passenger Lists of Vessels Arriving at New York, New York, 1820–1897,* NARA Microfilm Publication M237, roll 231, line 39, list number 707.

15   Carrigaholt (County Clare) Catholic Parish Registers, microfilmed by the National Library of Ireland, 1973, FHL Microfilm 926099 and Anna Keating household, 1900 U.S. Census, Fairfield County, Conn., town of Newtown, NARA Microfilm Publication T623, roll 134, enumeration district 82, sheet 19A, dwelling 365, family 375.

16   Newtown, Conn. Vital Records: Marriages, book 1, 1883, pp. 322–323.

17 Daniel G. Keane household, 1900 U.S. Census, Fairfield County, Conn., town of Newtown, NARA Microfilm Publication T623, roll 132, enumeration district 82, p. 9A, dwelling 159, family 166.

18 Newtown, Fairfield County, Conn.: Marriages, 1889, pp. 334–335.

19 Carrigaholt (County Clare) Catholic Parish Registers. Microfilmed by the National Library of Ireland, 1973. FHL Microfilm 926099.

20 St. Thomas Church, Red Creek, Wayne County, New York: Marriages, 1891, p. [1].

21 Joseph M. Keane household, 1900 U.S. Census, New Haven County, Conn., city of New Haven, NARA Microfilm Publication T623, roll 145, enumeration district 360, p. 15B, dwelling 185, family 308.

22 New Haven, New Haven County, Conn.: Marriages, 1893, pp. 234–235.

23 Newtown, Fairfield County, Conn.: Births, 1867, p.106.

24 Newtown, Fairfield County, Conn.: Marriages, 1905, p. 22.

25 Newtown, Fairfield County, Conn.: Births, 1870, pp. 4–5.

26 Newtown, Fairfield County, Conn.: Deaths, 1870, pp. 448–449.

27 Newtown, Fairfield County, Conn.: Births, 1872, pp. 16–17.

28 Newtown, Fairfield County, Conn.: Deaths, 1876, pp. 476–477.

29 Carrigaholt (County Clare) Catholic Parish Registers. Microfilmed by the National Library of Ireland, 1973. FHL Microfilm 926099; Anna Keating household, 1900 U.S. Census, Fairfield County, Conn., town of Newtown, NARA Microfilm Publication T623, roll 134, enumeration district 82, sheet 19A, dwelling 365, family 375. She was baptized as Hannah, but records indicate that she went by "Anna" or "Annie" for most of her life.

30 "Mrs. Anna A. K. Keating," *Bridgeport Telegram,* 4 March 1927, p. 2.

31 Newtown, Conn. Vital Records: Marriages, book 1, 1883, pp. 322–323.

32 Calculated from births of children and the 1900 U.S. Census.

33 Newtown, Conn., Vital Records: Births, book 2, pp. 96–97.

34 "Miss Mary M. Keating," *Bridgeport Post,* 12 April 1967, p. 61.

35 Ibid.

36 *Connecticut Death Index.*

37 Ibid.

38 "George Burns, Jr. Epidemic Victim Father also Sick," *Bridgeport Telegram,* 31 October 1918, p. 1.

39 *Commemorative Biographical Record of Fairfield County, Connecticut . . .* (Chicago: J. H. Beers and Company, 1889), p. 913; U.S. Selective

Service System, *World War I Selective Service System Draft Registration Cards, 1917–1918* (Washington, D.C.: NARA), State of Connecticut, George Patrick Burns, no. 715; George Burns household, 1900 U.S. Census, Fairfield County, Conn., town of Bridgeport, NARA Microfilm Publication T623, roll 32, enumeration district 32, sheet 5B, dwelling 93, family 110; "George Burns, Jr. Epidemic Victim Father also Sick," *Bridgeport Telegram,* 31 October 1918, p. 1.

40 Newtown, Fairfield County, Conn.: Births, 1889, book 2, pp. 124–125.

41 Based on the couple's appearance in the 1920 U.S. Census.

42 Newtown, Fairfield County, Connecticut: Births, 1889, book 2, pp. 132–133.

43 *Connecticut Death Index.*

44 Based on their enumerations in the 1920 and 1930 U.S. Censuses.

45 Social Security Death Index; *Connecticut Death Index.*

46 Ibid.

47 "Mrs. Frank M. Davey," *Bridgeport Post,* 8 April 1964, p. 55.

48 Social Security Death Index.

49 "Personal Mentions," *Bridgeport Telegram,* 5 April 1923, p. 20.

50 Daniel G. Keane household, 1900 U.S. Census, Fairfield County, Conn., town of Newtown, NARA Microfilm Publication T623, roll 132, enumeration district 82, p. 9A, dwelling 159, family 166.

51 "Daniel G. Cane" is noted as a widower in the 1910 U.S. Census, Essex County, N.J., town of East Orange, NARA Microfilm Publication T624, roll 885, enumeration district 153, sheet 6A, dwelling 92, family 106.

52 Newtown, Fairfield County, Conn.: Marriages, 1889, pp. 334–335.

53 Daniel G. Keane household, 1900 U.S. Census, Fairfield County, Conn., town of Newtown, NARA Microfilm Publication T623, roll 132, enumeration district 82, p. 9A, dwelling 159, family 166.

54 The last record found for Daniel G. Keane is his appearance in the 1910 U.S. Census in New Jersey though it is likely he died by 1920, when his son was living with relatives in Connecticut.

55 Daniel "Cane" household, 1910 U.S. Census, Essex County, N.J., town of East Orange, NARA Microfilm Publication T624, roll 885, enumeration district 153, sheet 6A, dwelling 92, family 106.

56 Daniel G. Keane household, 1900 U.S. Census, Fairfield County, Conn., town of Newtown, NARA Microfilm Publication T623, roll 132, enumeration district 82, p. 9A, dwelling 159, family 166.

57   Daniel Keane household, 1910 U.S. Census, Essex County, New Jersey, town of East Orange, NARA Microfilm Publication T624, roll 885, enumeration district 153, sheet 6A, dwelling 92, family 106.

58   Newtown, Conn., Vital Records: Births, 1891, book 2, pp. 140–141.

59   "Miss Martina M. Keane," *Bridgeport Post,* 17 October 1961, p. 29.

60   Interview with Dorothy Keane Achtmeyer, 29 Nov. 2011.

61   Records of the Immigration and Naturalization Service; National Archives, *Passenger and Crew Lists of Vessels Arriving at New York, New York, 1897–1957,* NARA Microfilm Publication T715, roll 3377, p. 62.

62   "Many Priests in Sanctuary for Wedding Mass," *Bridgeport Telegram,* 21 October 1926, p. 16.

63   "Miss Martina M. Keane," *Bridgeport Post,* 17 October 1961, p. 29.

64   Newtown, Fairfield County, Conn.: Births, 1894, book 2, pp. 154–155.

65   Newtown, Fairfield County, Conn.: Deaths, 1897, book 2, pp. 232–233.

66   Newtown Fairfield County, Conn.: Births, 1896, book 2, pp. 78–79.

67   "Dr. Vincent Keane Ex-Optician Dies," *Bridgeport Sunday Post,* 9 December 1973, p. G5.

68   Ibid.

69   Social Security Death Index.

70   Ibid.

71   U.S. Selective Service System, *World War I Selective Service System Draft Registration Cards, 1917–1918* (Washington, D.C.: NARA), State of Connecticut, Vincent Keane, no. 158.

72   Anna Keating household, 1920 U.S. Census, Fairfield County, Conn., city of Bridgeport, NARA Microfilm Publication T625, roll 175, enumeration district 56, p. 5B, dwelling 73, family 127.

73   D. Vincent Keane household, 1930 U.S. Census, Fairfield County, Conn., city of Bridgeport, NARA Microfilm Publication T626, roll 254, enumeration district 87, sheet 15B, dwelling 165, family 306.

74   *Selective Service Registration Cards, World War II: Fourth Registration* (Washington, D.C.: NARA), D. Vincent Keane, number 2283622.

75   "Dr. Vincent Keane Ex-Optician Dies," *Bridgeport Sunday Post,* 9 December 1973, p. G5.

76   "Keane Heads Draft Bd. 14, Succeeding Dr. Williams," *Bridgeport Sunday Post,* 22 October 1967, p. 2.

77   "Caseria Named to Draft Board," *Bridgeport Sunday Post,* 4 January 1972, p. 23.

78   "Dr. Vincent Keane Ex-Optician Dies," *Bridgeport Sunday Post*, 9 December 1973, p. G5.

79   *Connecticut Death Index.*

80   Carrigaholt (County Clare) Catholic Parish Registers, microfilmed by the National Library of Ireland, 1973; FHL Microfilm 926099.

81   "John F. Keane Dies Following Brief Illness," *Bridgeport Telegram*, 30 September 1922, p. 21.

82   St. Thomas Church, Red Creek, Wayne County, N.Y.: Marriages, 1891, p. [1].

83   John F. Keane household, 1900 U.S. Census, Fairfield County, Conn., city of Bridgeport, NARA Microfilm Publication T623, roll 131, enumeration district 8, p. 8A, dwelling 122, family 152.

84   "Susan E. Keane Dead; Funeral to be Saturday," *Bridgeport Telegram*, 16 June 1921, p. 3.

85   Bridgeport, Fairfield County, Conn.: Births, 1892, p. 110.

86   "Many Priests in Sanctuary for Mass," *Bridgeport Telegram*, 21 October 1926, p. 16.

87   Bridgeport, Fairfield County, Conn.: Births, 1894, p. 156.

88   Bridgeport, Fairfield County, Conn.: Deaths, 1894, pp. 59–60.

89   Bridgeport, Fairfield County, Conn.: Births, 1895, p. 217.

90   Newtown, Fairfield County, Conn.: Deaths, 1898, pp. 234–235.

91   Bridgeport, Fairfield County, Conn.: Births, 1896, p. 503.

92   Bridgeport, Fairfield County, Conn.: Deaths, 1898, pp. 278–279.

93   Bridgeport, Fairfield County, Conn.: Births, 1898, pp. 150–151.

94   Information supplied by John F. Keane III.

95   Bridgeport, Fairfield County, Conn.: Births, 1899, p. 287.

96   *Connecticut Death Index.*

97   Connecticut Vital Records, obtained through from Angela Kasek, April 2012.

98   Connecticut Vital Records, obtained from Angela Kasek, April 2012.

99   Information supplied by Robert Medlin.

100   Connecticut Vital Records, obtained from Angela Kasek, April 2012.

101   "Obituaries—Francis B. Keane," *Bridgeport Post*, 25 July 1967, p. 32.

102   Social Security Death Index.

103   Connecticut Vital Records, obtained from Angela Kasek, April 2012.

104   "Obituaries—Francis B. Keane," *Bridgeport Post*, 25 July 1967, p. 32.

105   Connecticut Vital Records, obtained from Angela Kasek, April 2012.

106   Joseph M. Keane [*sic*] household, 1900 U.S. Census, New Haven County, Conn., city of New Haven, NARA Microfilm Publication T623, roll 145, enumeration district 360, p. 15B, dwelling 185, family 308.

107   The last appearance of M. Joseph Keane in the New Haven City Directories is in 1926, after which his wife is listed at the family address.

108   New Haven, New Haven County, Conn.: Marriages, 1893, pp. 234–235.

109   Joseph M. Keane [*sic*] household, 1900 U.S. Census, New Haven County, Conn., city of New Haven, NARA Microfilm Publication T623, roll 145, enumeration district 360, p. 15B, dwelling 185, family 308; *Connecticut Death Index*.

110   *Connecticut Death Index*.

111   1892 Bridgeport, Conn., City Directory, p. 184.

112   1919 New Haven, Conn., City Directory, p. 631.

113   1927 New Haven, Conn., City Directory, p. 773.

114   New Haven, New Haven County, Conn.: Births, 1894, volume 40, p. 47.

115   Calculated from enumerations in the 1920 and 1930 U.S. Census and the birth of their son John (b. 1928).

116   Bridgeport, Fairfield County, Conn.: Births, 1896, p. 348.

117   Calculated from enumerations in the 1920 and 1930 U.S. Censuses.

118   Joseph M. Keane [*sic*] household, 1900 U.S. Census, New Haven County, Conn., city of New Haven, NARA Microfilm Publication T623, roll 145, enumeration district 360, p. 15B, dwelling 185, family 308.

119   *Connecticut Death Index*.

120   John Caruson, "I Say, Start 'em Young," *Hampden Daily News*, 12 July 2006.

121   Margaret Keane household, 1930 U.S. Census, New Haven County, Conn., town of Hamden, NARA Microfilm Publication T626, roll 273, enumeration district 5-140, sheet 7B, dwelling 120, family 178.

122   "Reunion at AB Will Feature 88th Arnold College Banquet," *Bridgeport Post,* 3 May 1974, p. 3.

123   Social Security Death Index; Texas Death Index, 1964–1998, online at *FamilySearch.org,* accessed October 2010.

124   Edwin Moore Pomeroy, *History and Genealogy of the Pomeroy Family and Collateral Lines, England, Ireland, America; Comprising the Ancestors and Descendants of George Pomeroy of Pennsylvania* ([Penn.]: J. N. Pomeroy, 1959], pp. 871–872 [hereafter *Pomeroy Genealogy*].

125   Michael J. Keane household, 1910 U.S. Census, New Haven County,
        Conn., town of New Haven, NARA Microfilm Publication T623, roll
        145, enumeration district 389, p. 27B, dwelling 185, family 308.

126   Ibid.

127   Margaret Keane household, 1930 U.S. Census, New Haven County,
        Conn., town of Hamden, NARA Microfilm Publication T626, roll
        273, enumeration district 5-140, sheet 7B, dwelling 120, family 178.

128   Newtown, Fairfield County, Conn.: Births, 1867, p. 106.

129   No record of Daniel has been found after this appearance in the 1940
        city directory.

130   Newtown, Fairfield County, Conn.: Marriages, 1905, p. 22.

131   Daniel P. Keane household, 1910 U.S. Census, Fairfield County,
        Conn., city of Bridgeport, NARA Microfilm Publication T625, roll
        128, enumeration district 32, sheet 20A, dwelling 164, family 421.

132   "The Kearney Family Tree," on *Ancestry.com*, accessed October 2011;
        Charles R. Hale Collection, Cemetery Inscriptions of St. Rose
        Cemetery, Sandy Hook (Newtown), Fairfield County, Conn.

133   1900 Bridgeport, Conn., City Directory, p. 225.

134   1902 Bridgeport, Conn., City Directory, p. 232.

135   1904 Bridgeport, Conn., City Directory, p. 256.

136   1906 Bridgeport, Conn., City Directory, p. 273.

137   Daniel P. Keane household, 1910 U.S. Census, Fairfield County,
        Conn., city of Bridgeport, NARA Microfilm Publication T625, roll
        128, enumeration district 32, sheet 20A, dwelling 164, family 421.

138   1912 Bridgeport, Conn., City Directory, p. 292.

139   1940 Bridgeport, Conn., City Directory, online at *Ancestry.com,*
        accessed October 2011.

140   Newtown, Fairfield County, Conn.: Births, 1889, book 2, pp. 124–125.

141   *Connecticut Death Index.*

142   Based on the couple's appearance in the 1920 U.S. Census.

143   William J. Casey household, 1920 U.S. Census, Fairfield County,
        Conn., town of Stamford, NARA Microfilm Publication T625, roll
        178, enumeration district 159, sheet 1B, dwelling 4, family 17.

144   *Connecticut Death Index; Social Security Death Index.*

145   1916 Bridgeport, Conn., City Directory, p. 561.

146   William J. Casey household, 1920 U.S. Census, Fairfield County,
        Conn., town of Stamford, NARA Microfilm Publication T625, roll
        178, enumeration district 159, sheet 1B, dwelling 4, family 17.

147 William J. Casey household, 1930 U.S. Census, Fairfield County, Conn., town of Stamford, NARA Microfilm Publication T626, roll 260, enumeration district 204, sheet 31B, dwelling 575, family 795.

148 *Connecticut Death Index.*

149 Ibid.

150 Ibid.

151 U.S. Public Records Index, Volume 1 online at *Ancestry.com,* accessed May 2011.

152 Ibid.

153 Records of NARA, Record Group 64; National Archives at College Park, Md., Electronic Army Serial Number Merged File, 1938–1946 [archival database]; World War II Army Enlistment Records.

154 *Connecticut Death Index.*

155 Ibid.

156 "Personal Mentions," *Bridgeport Telegram,* 5 April 1923, p. 20.

157 U.S. Selective Service System, *World War I Selective Service System Draft Registration Cards, 1917–1918* (Washington, D.C.: NARA), State of Connecticut, Otto William Heise, no. 1009.

158 Social Security Death Index.

159 U.S. Selective Service System, *World War I Selective Service System Draft Registration Cards, 1917–1918* (Washington, D.C.: NARA), State of Connecticut, Otto William Heise, no. 1009.

160 "Otto W. Heise Dies at Age 77," *Bridgeport Post,* 17 May 1972, p. 4.

161 "Rival of No. 1 Wife Asks Out," *Sunday Herald,* 19 February 1950, p. 1.

162 "Otto W. Heise is sued for divorce by wife," *Bridgeport Sunday Post,* 24 January 1959, p. A10.

163 "Obituaries—Mrs. Susan K. Heise," *Bridgeport Post,* 6 June 1973, p. 62.

164 U.S. Public Records Index, Volume 1 online at *Ancestry.com,* accessed May 2011.

165 "Obituaries—Mrs. Susan K. Heise," *Bridgeport Post,* 6 June 1973, p. 62; "Thomas Cummings," obituary in *Daytona Beach News-Journal,* 15 May 2012, viewed via *United States Obituary Collection*, online database at Ancestry.com.

166 Thomas Cummings obituary (see note 165); Connecticut Department of Public Health, Connecticut Marriage File, 1981–2001.

167 Bridgeport, Fairfield County, Conn.: Births, 1892, p. 110.

168 *Connecticut Death Index.*

169   "Many Priests in Sanctuary for Mass," *Bridgeport Telegram,* 21 October 1926, p. 16.

170   U.S. Selective Service System, *World War I Selective Service System Draft Registration Cards, 1917–1918* (Washington, D.C.: NARA), M1509, Fairfield County, Conn., "Edward E. Bray," Draft Board 3.

171   "Obituaries," *Bridgeport Post,* 31 July 1973, p. 30.

172   National Archives and Records Administration (NARA), *Passport Applications, January 2, 1906–March 31, 1925; ARC Identifier 583830 / MLR Number A1 534*; NARA Microfilm Publication M1490, roll 2009, no. 185043; information supplied by Susan Bray Walker.

173   Information supplied by Susan Bray Walker.

174   "Obituaries," *Bridgeport Post,* 31 July 1973, p. 30.

175   Information supplied by Susan Bray Walker.

176   Information supplied by David E. Bray.

177   Bridgeport, Fairfield County, Conn.: Births, 1898, pp. 150–151.

178   Information supplied by John F. Keane III.

179   Victoire Le Caron, Certificate and Record of Birth, State of New York (1903), Certificate no. 23915; information supplied by John F. Keane III.

180   Charles Kelly and Victoire Le Caron, Certificate and Record of Marriage, State of New York (1922), no. 14143.

181   U.S. Selective Service System, *World War I Selective Service System Draft Registration Cards, 1917–1918* (Washington, D.C.: NARA), State of Connecticut, John F. Keane, no. 1834.

182   *Harvard Class of 1921 Twenty-fifth Anniversary Report* (Cambridge, Mass.: Harvard University Press, 1946), pp. 381–382.

183   National Archives and Records Administration (NARA), *Passport Applications, January 2, 1906–March 31, 1925; ARC Identifier 583830 / MLR Number A1 534*; NARA Microfilm Publication M1490, roll 2027, no. 191535.

184   Records of the Immigration and Naturalization Service; National Archives, *Passenger and Crew Lists of Vessels Arriving at New York, New York, 1897–1957,* NARA Microfilm Publication T715, roll 3988, p. 80.

185   Records of the Immigration and Naturalization Service; National Archives, *Passenger and Crew Lists of Vessels Arriving at New York, New York, 1897–1957,* NARA Microfilm Publication T715, roll 4259, p. 25.

186   Social Security Death Index.

187   Application for membership, Empire State Society of the National Society Sons of the American Revolution, 1952, membership no. 75628; information supplied by Linda Keane Smith.

188 Information supplied by Kathy Aird, daughter of Victoire Keane Barth.

189 Information supplied by John Francis Keane III.

190 Information supplied by Kevin Thomas Keane.

191 "Elizabeth Ann Rice of JC is Bride of Kevin T. Keane," *Sunday Press,* 28 June 1953, p. 6B.

192 Information supplied by Susan Keane Trivison.

193 Information supplied by Andrée Keane Shields.

194 Bridgeport, Fairfield County, Conn.: Births, 1899, p. 287.

195 "Rev. D. A. Keane Services Slated," *Bridgeport Post,* 16 October 1961, p. 26.

196 "Fr. Keane, S.J., Made Rector of Cranwell," *Springfield Union*, 22 June 1951, p. 1.

197 *Boston Daily Globe,* 16 October 1961; *Springfield Union*, 22 June 1951.

198 Ibid.

199 *Springfield Union*, 22 June 1951; "Other 30," *Boston Daily Globe,* 21 May 1945, p. 6.

200 "Fr. Maxwell Named President of Boston College," *Boston Daily Globe,* 22 June 1951, p. 1.

201 "Home News," *Botolphian*, Christmas 1925, p. 69.

202 *Boston Daily Globe,* 16 October 1961; *Springfield Union,* 22 June 1951.

203 "Changes in Boston College Faculty: New Instructors in High School Also Announced," *Boston Daily Globe,* 11 July 1936.

204 "B.C. High Cornerstone Laid by Archbishop," *Boston Daily Globe,* 30 May 1950, p. 48.

205 *Boston Daily Globe,* 30 May 1950.

206 "Pleads for Religion in Educating Child; B.C. High Principal Gives Last of Five Sermons," *Boston Daily Globe,* 4 April 1938, p. 20; "Fr. Keane Cites Popes' Burden in Lenten Talk," *Boston Daily Globe,* 19 February 1940, p. 11; "Bishop Cushing Warns of Pagan Trend at Gathering of B.C. High Students, Alumni," *Boston Daily Globe,* 28 April 1941, p. 11.

207 "Sophomores at Tufts Elect Officers," *Boston Daily Globe,* 10 December 1938, p. 5; "B.C. High School Has Flag Raising Service at New Pole," *Boston Daily Globe,* 17 October 1942, p. 11.

208 *Springfield Union*, 22 June 1951; *Boston Daily Globe,* 22 June 1951.

209 *Springfield Union*, 22 June 1951.

210 "Cranwell Prep Celebrates Best Fall Sports Campaign," *Springfield Union,* 16 December 1956, p. 4B.

211   "Cranwell Expands Athletic Facilities," *Springfield Union*, 17 November
       1956, p. 34; "Cranwell to Have Baseball Diamond," *Springfield Union*,
       22 November 1956, p. 31.

212   *Springfield Union*, 16 December 1956.

213   "Fr. Geary Named Superior of Jesuit School in Haverhill," *Boston Daily
       Globe*, 1 August 1958, p. 18; *Boston Daily Globe*, 16 October 1961.

214   *Boston Daily Globe*, 16 October 1961; James J. Regan, "What Do These
       Men Have in Common?" Boston College High School Annual Fund
       publication (1976); Rev. Thomas P. O'Malley, SJ, "Remembering BC
       High" (homily, Mass, BC High, Boston, Mass., 20 February 2006);
       New England Jesuit Oral History Program, ed. Richard W. Rousseau, vol.
       62, *Fr. Gerard L. McLaughlin, S.J.* (Weston, Mass.: Society of Jesus of
       New England, 2008); vol. 109, *Fr. Charles J. Dunn, S.J.* (2010); and vol.
       49, *Fr. Robert G. Doherty, S.J.* (2008).

215   Email from Susan Bray Walker, 8 Dec. 2012.

216   *Boston Daily Globe,* 16 October 1961 and obituary of Rev. D. A. Keane
       (1961); "Rev. D. A. Keane Services Slated," *Bridgeport Post,* 16 October
       1961, p. 26.

217   "Funeral Tomorrow of Father Keane," *Boston Daily Globe,* 17 October
       1961, p. 24.

218   *Connecticut Death Index.*

219   Ibid.

220   Social Security Death Index; information supplied by Herbert C.
       Achtmeyer.

221   Information about Paul Keane supplied by Herbert C. Achtmeyer.

222   Email from Herbert C. Achtmeyer, 2 Aug. 2012.

223   "Paul A. Keane Dies . . ." *Bridgeport Post,* 16 Nov. 1975, p. B7; email
       from Herbert C. Achtmeyer, 2 Aug. 2012.

224   Email from Herbert C. Achtmeyer, 2 Aug. 2012.

225   Information supplied by Betty Keane Rossbaum.

226   Information supplied by Dorothy Keane Achtmeyer.

227   Connecticut Vital Records, obtained from Angela Kasek, April 2012.

228   Information supplied by Robert Medlin.

229   Ibid.

230   Interview with Dorothy Keane Achtmeyer.

231   Interview with Susan Keane Trivison.

232   Information supplied by Robert Medlin.

233   Connecticut Vital Records, obtained from Angela Kasek, April 2012.

234   *Connecticut Death Index.*

235   Information supplied by Patricia Keane Sparkman.

236   Interview with Susan Keane Trivison.

237   Information supplied by Patricia Keane Sparkman.

238   New Haven, New Haven County, Conn.: Births, 1894, volume 40, p. 47.

239   *Connecticut Death Index.*

240   Calculated from enumerations in the 1920 and 1930 U.S. Censuses and the birth of their son, John (b. 1928); "Obituaries—Mrs. Corina McCoy," *Brownsville Herald,* 25 February 1974, p. 2.

241   Alberta Young household, 1930 U.S. Census, Cameron County, Texas, city of Brownsville, NARA Microfilm Publication T626, roll 2305, enumeration district 31-6, sheet 11B, dwelling 89, family 746.

242   *Reunion in Print, Yale 1916 Twenty-Five Year Book,* ed. Fairfax Downey and William A. James (New Haven, Conn.: Yale University Press, 1942), p. 174 [hereafter *Reunion in Print*].

243   "City Briefs," *Brownsville Herald,* 26 April 1934, p. 2.

244   *Reunion in Print.*

245   Ibid., p. 174.

246   Daniel J. Keane, 1920 U.S. Census, Luna County, N.M., division of Camp Furlong, NARA Microfilm Publication T625, roll 1076, enumeration district 72, sheet 41B, family 110, dwelling 65.

247   *Reunion in Print*, p. 174.

248   *Selective Service Registration Cards, World War II: Fourth Registration.* NARA, Daniel Joseph Keane, no. U4153.

249   Texas Department of Health, Bureau of Vital Statistics, Birth Index.

250   Texas Department of Health, Bureau of Vital Statistics, Marriage Index.

251   "Record is Set in Graduation," *Brownsville Herald,* 26 May 1946, p. 9.

252   "Completes Course," *Brownsville Herald,* 22 April 1951, p. 23.

253   "People and Events," *Brownsville Herald,* 26 May 1965, p. 14.

254   U.S. Public Records Index, Volume 1 online at *Ancestry.com,* accessed May 2011.

255   Bridgeport, Fairfield County, Conn.: Births, 1896, p. 348.

256   *Connecticut Death Index.*

257   Calculated from enumerations in the 1920 and 1930 U.S. Censuses.

258   Bridgeport, Fairfield County, Conn.: Births, 1896, p. 348.

259   *Connecticut Death Index.*

260   Connecticut Council of Defense, *History of Hamden Men in the World War* (New Haven, Conn.: Tuttle, Morehouse, and Taylor Co., 1920), p. 167.

261   Records of the Immigration and Naturalization Service; National Archives, *Passenger and Crew Lists of Vessels Arriving at New York, New York, 1897–1957,* NARA Microfilm Publication T715, roll 2813, p. 181.

262   Records of the Immigration and Naturalization Service; National Archives, *Passenger Lists of Vessels Arriving at San Francisco, 1893–1953,* NARA Microfilm Publication M1410, roll 214, p. 108.

263   James L. Keane, 1930 U.S. Census, Hartford County, Conn., city of Hartford, NARA Microfilm Publication T626, roll 265, enumeration district 2-76, sheet 8A, dwelling 26, family 53.

264   Records of the Immigration and Naturalization Service; National Archives, *Passenger and Crew Lists of Vessels Arriving at New York, New York, 1897–1957,* NARA Microfilm Publication T715, roll 5066, p. 73.

265   *Selective Service Registration Cards, World War II: Fourth Registration* (Washington, D.C.: NARA), James L., number U1944.

266   James Keane Household, 1940 U.S. Census, Hartford County, Conn., City of Newington, NARA Microfilm Publication M627, roll 506, enumeration district 2-190, p. 12B.

267   Social Security Death Index; Texas Death Index, 1964–1998, online at *FamilySearch.org,* accessed October 2010.

268   Social Security Death Index.

269   *Pomeroy Genealogy,* pp. 871–872.

270   Ibid.

271   Social Security Death Index.

272   NARA, *Passport Applications, January 2, 1906–March 31, 1925*; *ARC Identifier 583830 / MLR Number A1 534*; NARA Microfilm Publication M1490, roll 1652, #51028.

273   *Army and Navy Journal,* vol. 76 (1938); "Keanes Return From Ceremony," *San Antonio Express,* 4 July 1940, p. 4.

274   *Pomeroy Genealogy,* pp. 871–872.

275   "Keanes Attend Wedding in Holland," *San Antonio Express,* 30 August 1963, p. 1D.

276   Wesleyan University: Mathematics and Science Faculty, online at *www.wesleyan.edu,* accessed June 2011.

277   *Pomeroy Genealogy,* pp. 871–872.

278   Texas Department of State Health Services. *Texas Divorce Index, 1968–2002.*

279   "Engagements," *San Antonio Express/News,* 29 March 1964, p. 2F.

280   Texas Department of State Health Services., *Texas Divorce Index, 1968–2002;* U.S. Public Records Index, Volume 1 online at *Ancestry.com,* accessed May 2011.

281   *Pomeroy Genealogy,* pp. 871–872.

282   Texas Department of State Health Services, *Texas Marriage Index, 1966–2002.*

283   Texas Department of Health, Bureau of Vital Statistics, *Texas Birth Index,* 1939, p. 369.

284   Information about this family group supplied by Susan Bray Walker.

285   Social Security Death Index.

286   Application for membership, Empire State Society of the National Society Sons of the American Revolution, 1952, membership no. 75628.

287   Social Security Death Index.

288   Information about this family group supplied by Linda Keane Smith.

289   Letter from Linda Keane Smith, 29 Aug. 2012.

290   Ibid.

291   Information supplied by Dolly Keane Dugan.

292   Scott Campbell Steward and Newbold Le Roy, 3rd, *The Le Roy Family in America: 1753–2003* (Boston, Mass., and Laconia, N.H., 2003), pp. 179, 284.

293   Information about this family group supplied by Kathy Aird and Andrée Aird Primrose.

294   Information about this family group supplied by John Francis Keane III.

295   Information about this family group supplied by Kevin Thomas Keane.

296   Information about this family group supplied by Susan Keane Trivison.

297   Information about this family group supplied by Andrée Keane Shields.

298   Information about this family group supplied by Betty Keane Rossbaum.

299   Information about this family group supplied by Herbert and Dorothy Keane Achtmeyer.

300   Information about this family group supplied by Robert Medlin.

301   Information about this family group supplied by Patricia Keane Sparkman.

302 Information about this family group supplied by Justy Carlo Keane and Patricia Keane Sparkman.

303 Information about this family group supplied by Susan Bray Walker.

304 Ibid.

305 Information about this family group supplied by Clare Logan Guydish.

306 Information about this family group supplied by Andrée Aird Primrose.

307 Ibid.

308 Information about this family group supplied by John Francis Keane III and Elizabeth Furnivall Keane.

309 Ibid.

310 Ibid.

311 Information about this family group supplied by Kevin Thomas Keane.

312 Ibid.

313 Ibid.

314 Ibid.

315 Information about this family group supplied by Susan Keane Trivison.

316 Information about this family group supplied by Andrée Keane Shields.

317 Ibid.

318 Information about this family group supplied by Betty Keane Rossbaum.

319 Ibid.

320 Information about this family group supplied by Herbert and Dorothy Keane Achtmeyer.

321 Ibid.

322 Information about this family group supplied by Patricia Keane Sparkman and John Sparkman, Jr.

323 Information about this family group supplied by Justy Carlo Keane.

324 Ibid.

APPENDIX I

1 Based upon information gathered from State of New York, Department of Health of the City of New York, Bureau of Records, Standard Certificate of Death, "Susan F. P. Thomas" (1911), Reg. No. 17778.

2 Based on the birth of Margaret's first child, Jeremiah, who was born in Connecticut in 1856, and Spencer C. Platt's appearance in the 1861 Civil War Draft Registration of New York City.

3   Calculated from Herbert [*sic*] Lynch household, 1870 U.S. Census, New Haven County, Conn., town of Orange, NARA Microfilm Publication M593, roll 112, p. 597 [stamped], dwelling 134, family 144.

4   Calculated from the birth of their presumed first child, Jeremiah, born in 1856 in Connecticut.

5   Based on the probable death of Daniel Sheahan (before 1867) and the birth of Mary, the probable first child of Hubert and Margaret (Geary) Lynch, in 1867/1868.

6   Snowden Thomas household, 1900 U.S. Census, Monmouth County, N.J., Neptune township, NARA Microfilm Publication T623, roll 987, enumeration district 137 sheet 7A, dwelling 154, family 158.

7   They were likely married by 1861, when Spencer C. Platt reported his status as "married" on the 1861 Civil War Draft Registration in New York City.

8   Herbert [*sic*] Lynch household, 1870 U.S. Census, New Haven County, Conn., town of Orange, NARA Microfilm Publication M593, roll 112, p. 597 [stamped], dwelling 134, family 144.

9   The last known record of Margaret is an entry in the 1894 Bridgeport City Directory, which notes she had removed to Port Byron, N.Y.

10   Based on the birth of their presumed first child, Jeremiah, born in Connecticut in 1856. Some members of the Sheahan family spelled the name *Sheehan*. For each person with that surname, we have used the spelling that we have found most prevalent in the records.

11   Based on the estimated birthdate of Margaret Geary and her second marriage to Hubert Lynch.

12   Based on the probable death of Daniel Sheahan (before 1867) and the birth of Mary, the probable first child of Hubert and Margaret (Geary) Lynch, in 1867/1868.

13   Calculated from Herbert [*sic*] Lynch household, 1870 U.S. Census, New Haven County, Conn., town of Orange, NARA Microfilm Publication M593, roll 112, p. 597 [stamped], dwelling 134, family 144. No further definitive record of Hubert Lynch has been located after 1880.

14   Bridgeport, Conn., Vital Records: Births, 1856, p. 24.

15   Jeremiah and Susan Sheahan, Bridgeport [Conn.] Probate District, 1867, no. 2538.

16   Ibid.

17   Harry D. Benson household, 1870 U.S. Census, New Haven County, Conn., town of Orange, NARA Microfilm Publication M593, roll 112, p. 597 [stamped], dwelling 111, family 119.

18   Daniel Sheahan, Bridgeport [Conn.] Probate District, 1867, no. 2539.
      The guardianship records are filed under the name *Sheahan,* but the
      records themselves spell the surname both ways.

19   *Official Letter Book of Gov. Richard D. Hubbard, October 1877–January
      1879* (Hartford: Connecticut State Library, 1934), various pages.

20   Based upon the letters written to the governor of Connecticut and
      other documents regarding her daughter's treatment.

21   John G. Pete household, 1880 U.S. Census, Fairfield County, Conn.,
      town of Huntington, NARA Microfilm Publication T9, roll 85,
      enumeration district 124, p. 29, dwelling 171, family 305.

22   Trumbull [Fairfield County], Connecticut Land Records, vol. 14, p.
      330; Trumbull [Fairfield County], Connecticut Land Records, vol. 15,
      p. 152; Trumbull [Fairfield County], Connecticut Land Records, vol.
      14, p. 93.

23   1882 Waterbury, Conn., City Directory, p. 182.

24   1883 Waterbury, Conn., City Directory, p. 206; 1884 Waterbury, Conn.,
      City Directory, p. 209.

25   1886 Waterbury, Conn., City Directory, p. 217.

26   1887 Waterbury, Conn., City Directory, p. 241.

27   1888 Waterbury, Conn., City Directory, p. 254.

28   1893 Bridgeport, Conn., City Directory, p. 305; 1894 Bridgeport,
      Conn., City Directory, pp. 205 and 304.

29   No record of Margaret has been found in the 1900 U.S. Census in the
      New England states, or in Virginia, Maryland, Washington, D.C., or
      New York.

30   Bridgeport, Conn., Vital Records: Births, 1856, book 1, p. 24.

31   Waterbury, Conn., Vital Records: Marriages, 1884, book 2, pp. 82–83.

32   Massachusetts Vital Records: Births, town of Waltham, 1858, p. 204.

33   Waterbury, Conn., Vital Records: Marriages, book 2, pp. 310–311.

34   John F. Keane household, 1900 U.S. Census, Fairfield County, Conn.,
      city of Bridgeport, NARA Microfilm Publication T623, roll 131,
      enumeration district 8, p. 8A, dwelling 122, family 152.

35   St. Thomas Church, Red Creek, Wayne County, New York: Marriages,
      1891, p. [1].

36   Hubert Lynch household, 1870 U.S. Census, New Haven County,
      Conn., town of Orange, NARA Microfilm Publication M593, roll
      112, p. 600 [stamped], dwelling 134, family 144.

37   *Headstone Inscriptions — Town of Milford, Connecticut,* comp. Charles R.
      Hale. FHL Microfilm 3347.

38 Snowden Thomas household, 1900 U.S. Census, Monmouth County, N.J., Neptune Township, NARA Microfilm Publication T623, roll 987, enumeration district 137, sheet 7A, dwelling 154, family 158.

39 State of New York, Department of Health of the City of New York, Bureau of Records, Standard Certificate of Death, "Susan F. P. Thomas" (1911), Reg. No. 17778.

40 Neither Spencer nor Susan has been located in the 1860 U.S. Census, though they were likely married by 1861, when Spencer C. Platt noted he was married on New York City's Civil War Draft Registration.

41 Index Register of Deaths in Monmouth County [N.J.], 1892–1893, p. 80, line 57.

42 *The Thomas Book,* pp. 43 and 597.

43 Philadelphia, Philadelphia County, Penn.: Death Certificates, 1902, no. 24902.

44 Cited in G. Lewis Platt, *The Platt Lineage: A Genealogical Research and Record* (New York: Thomas Whitaker, 1891), p. 366.

45 *Consolidated Lists of Civil War Draft Registrations, 1863–1865,* NM-65, entry 172; Records of the Provost Marshal General's Bureau (Civil War), Record Group 110. National Archives, Washington D.C.: New York City, 6th Congressional District, no. 208.

46 *U.S. IRS Tax Assessment Lists, 1862–1918,* NARA Microfilm Publication M603, roll 49.

47 Sylvain Cazalet, *History of the New York Medical College and Hospital for Women,* online at *homeoint.org/cazalet/histo/newyork.htm,* accessed September 2011.

48 Arthur Wayne Hafner, ed., *Directory of Deceased American Physicians* (Chicago: American Medical Association, 1993).

49 Spencer Platt household, 1870 U.S. Census, Kings County, N.Y., Brooklyn 3rd Ward. NARA Microfilm Publication M593, roll 946, pg. 246, lines 19–20.

50 *Auburn First United Methodist Church Membership List Summary Circa 1872–1885,* Cayuga County, N.Y., USGenWeb, online at *www.rootsweb.ancestry.com/~nycayuga/church/aub1ume/2mem1875_85.html,* accessed January 2010.

51 Bradley O. Banks household, 1880 U.S. Census, Fairfield County, Conn., borough of Norwalk, NARA Microfilm Publication T9, roll 96, enumeration district 146, sheet 131 [stamped], dwelling 61, family 104.

52 Information about these events is from Isaac Grant Thompson and Robely D. Cook, eds, *The New York Supreme Court Reports: Cases*

Determined in the Supreme Court of New York from November 1873 to March 1874, vol. 2 (Albany, N.Y.: John D. Parsons, Jr., 1874), pp. 25–52.

53 Thompson and Cook, *The New York Supreme Court Reports*, pp. 25–52.

54 "Contempt of Court. The Last Move in the Litigation over the Platt Estate," *New York Times,* 29 June 1880, p. 3.

55 Cayuga County, N.Y.: Deed Records, vol. 154, pp. 484–486.

56 Ibid., vol. 163, pp. 103–105.

57 Ibid., vol. 163, pp. 105–108.

58 Ibid., vol. 170, pp. 105–107.

59 "Long Litigation Ended," *New York Times,* 1 September 1886, p. 8.

60 Edmund H. Smith, ed. *Central Reporter: All Cases Determined in the Courts of Last Resort*, vol. 9 (Rochester, N.Y.: The Lawyer's Co-Operative Publishing Company, 1887), pp. 61–66.

61 Cayuga County, N.Y.: Deed Records, vol. 171, pp. 344–346.

62 Ibid., vol. 173, pp. 47–49.

63 Ibid., vol. 177, pp. 8–9.

64 Index Register of Deaths in Monmouth County [N.J.], 1892–1893, p. 80, line 57.

65 "For Sale," *Fair Haven Register*, 1890–1894.

66 Cayuga County, N.Y.: Deed Records, vol. 177, pp. 93–94.

67 *The Thomas Book,* pp. 43 and 597.

68 Snowden Thomas household, 1900 U.S. Census, Monmouth County, N.J., Neptune Township, NARA Microfilm Publication T623, roll 987, enumeration district 137, sheet 7A, dwelling 154, family 158.

69 Philadelphia, Philadelphia County, Penn.: Death Certificate, 1902, no. 24902.

70 "Funeral of Rev. Dr. T. S. Thomas," *Philadelphia Inquirer*, 5 October 1907, vol. 157, issue 97, p. 9.

71 Sarah Whorton household, 1910 U.S. Census, New York County, N.Y., borough of Manhattan, NARA Microfilm Publication T624, roll 1023, enumeration district 588, sheet 1B.

72 State of New York, Department of Health of the City of New York, Bureau of Records, Standard Certificate of Death, "Susan F. P. Thomas" (1911), Reg. No. 17778.

73 Bridgeport, Conn., Vital Records: Births, 1856, book 1, p. 24.

74 As of April 1930 Jeremiah was living in the St. Andrews Home for the Aged in New Haven, Conn.

75   Waterbury, Conn., Vital Records: Marriages, 1884, book 2, pp. 82–83.

76   Jeremiah Sheahan household, 1900 U.S. Census, Fairfield County, Conn., town of Bridgeport, NARA Microfilm Publication T623, roll 131, enumeration district 10, sheet 10B.

77   The last record of Mary (Ryan) Sheahan is found in the 1919 Bridgeport City Directory.

78   Jeremiah and Susan Sheahan, Bridgeport [Conn.] Probate District, 1867, no. 2538.

79   1883 Waterbury, Conn., City Directory, p. 206.

80   1884 Waterbury, Conn., City Directory, p. 209.

81   Cayuga County, New York, Deed Records, vol. 173, pp. 47–49.

82   Ibid., vol. 177, pp. 8–9.

83   Ibid., vol. 176, pp. 628–629.

84   1894 Bridgeport, Conn., City Directory, p. 305.

85   1896 Bridgeport, Conn., City Directory, p. 336.

86   1898 Bridgeport, Conn., City Directory, p. [360].

87   Jeremiah Sheahan household, 1900 U.S. Census, Fairfield County, Conn., town of Bridgeport, NARA Microfilm Publication T623, roll 131, enumeration district 10, sheet 10B.

88   1907 Bridgeport, Conn., City Directory, p. 507.

89   1922 New Haven, Conn., City Directory, p. [900]; John F. Keene [*sic*] household, 1910 U.S. Census, Fairfield County, Conn., city of Bridgeport, NARA Microfilm Publication T624, roll 128, enumeration district 8, sheet 5A, family 78, dwelling 99.

90   1925 New Haven, Conn., City Directory, p. 921; 1927 New Haven, Conn., City Directory, p. 1079.

91   St. Andrew's Home for the Aged enumeration, 1930 U.S. Census, New Haven County, Conn., city of New Haven, NARA Microfilm Publication T626, roll 274, enumeration district 5-7, supervisor's district 5, sheet 1B, line 79.

92   Waterbury, Conn., Vital Records: Births, book 3, p. 2.

93   Ibid., pp. 338–339.

94   City of Chicago, Cook County [Illinois] Certificate of Death, 1937, no. 21643, "Edward Jerome Sheahan."

95   Waterbury, Conn., Vital Records: Births, book 4, pp. 45–46.

96   Bridgeport, Conn., Vital Records: Deaths, book 3, pp. 2–3.

97   Massachusetts Vital Records: Births, town of Waltham, 1858, p. 204. The
      spelling of Daniel's surname differs in different records. His children
      seem to have standardized the spelling of the name as *Sheehan*.

98   Connecticut State Department of Health, Medical Certificate of
      Death, "Daniel Sheehan" (1941), no. 267.

99   Waterbury, Conn., Vital Records: Marriages, book 2, pp. 310–311.

100   Daniel Sheahan household, 1920 U.S. Census, New Haven County,
      Conn., city of Waterbury, NARA Microfilm Publication T625, roll
      195, enumeration district 499, sheet 4A, dwelling 70, family 83.

101   Annie's last appearance in the U.S. Census is in 1920; her husband,
      Daniel J. Sheahan, is listed as a widower in 1930.

102   Daniel Sheahan, Bridgeport [Conn.] Probate District, 1867, no. 2539.

103   Bradley O. Banks household, 1880 U.S. Census, Fairfield County, Conn.,
      borough of Norwalk, NARA Microfilm Publication T9, roll 96,
      enumeration district 146, sheet 131 [stamped], dwelling 61, family 104.

104   1882 Waterbury, Conn., City Directory, p. 182; 1884 Waterbury, Conn.,
      City Directory, p. 209.

105   1885 Waterbury, Conn., City Directory, p. 208.

106   1887 Waterbury, Conn., City Directory, p. 241.

107   1888 Waterbury, Conn., City Directory, p. 254.

108   Cayuga County, New York Deed Records, vol. 171, pp. 344–346.

109   Daniel J. Sheehan household, 1892 New York State Census, Cayuga
      County, N.Y., town of Sterling, second election district, p. 12.

110   Cayuga County, New York Deed Records, vol. 177, pp. 191–192.

111   Ibid., vol. 177, pp. 287–288.

112   Daniel J. Sheehan household, 1900 U.S. Census, Cayuga County,
      N.Y., town of Throop, NARA Microfilm Publication T623, roll 1013,
      enumeration district 46, sheet 7B, dwelling 151, p. 159.

113   Daniel J. Sheehan household, 1905 New York State Census, Cayuga
      County, N.Y., town of Throop, first election district, p. 13, lines 9–14.

114   Daniel Sheehan household, 1910 U.S. Census, New Haven County,
      Conn., town of Fairfield, NARA Microfilm Publication T624, roll
      140, enumeration district 47, sheet 1B, dwelling 13, family 14.

115   Daniel Sheehan household, 1920 U.S. Census, New Haven County,
      Conn., city of Waterbury, NARA Microfilm Publication T625, roll
      195, enumeration district 499, sheet 4A, dwelling 70, family 83.

116   Connecticut State Department of Health, Medical Certificate of
      Death, "Daniel Sheehan" (1941), no. 267.

117   U.S. Selective Service System, *World War I Selective Service System Draft Registration Cards, 1917–1918* (Washington, D.C.: NARA), State of Connecticut, Spencer Alfred Sheehan, no. 1642.

118   Spencer Sheehan household, 1920 U.S. Census, New Haven County, Conn., city of Waterbury, NARA Publication T625, roll 195, enumeration district 449, sheet 4A, family 40, line 38.

119   Social Security Death Index; "Walter J. Sheehan Dies in Florida," Auburn, N.Y., *Citizen-Advertiser*, 4 February 1964, p. 2.

120   Walter J. Sheehan Dies in Florida," Auburn, N.Y., *Citizen-Advertiser*, 4 February 1964, p. 2.

121   Social Security Death Index.

122   Ibid.

123   Ibid.

124   Daniel J. Sheehan household, 1900 U.S. Census, Cayuga County, N.Y., town of Throop, NARA Microfilm Publication T623, roll 1013, enumeration district 46, sheet 7B, dwelling 151, p. 159.

125   John F. Keane household, 1900 U.S. Census, Fairfield County, Conn., city of Bridgeport, NARA Microfilm Publication T623, roll 131, enumeration district 8, p. 8A, dwelling 122, family 152.

126   "Susan E. Keane Dead; Funeral to be Saturday," *Bridgeport Telegram*, 16 June 1921, p. 3.

127   St. Thomas Church, Red Creek, Wayne County, N.Y.: Marriages, 1891, p. [1].

128   Waterbury, Conn., Vital Records: Births, book 3, pp. 338–339.

129   City of Chicago, Cook County [Illinois] Certificate of Death, 1937, no. 21643, "Edward Jerome Sheehan."

130   Passenger Lists of Vessels Arriving at San Francisco, 1893–1953, NARA Microfilm Publication M1410, roll 425, ship SS *Virginia*, arrived 18 March 1929.

131   Ibid.

132   City of Chicago, Cook County [Illinois] Certificate of Death, 1937, no. 6014420, "Amelia Sheehan."

133   NARA, *Passport Applications, January 2, 1906–March 31, 1925*; *ARC Identifier 583830 / MLR Number A1 534*; NARA Microfilm Publication M1490, roll 193.

134   U.S. Selective Service System, *World War I Selective Service System Draft Registration Cards, 1917–1918* (Washington, D.C.: NARA), State of New York, no. 2214.

135   Edward J. Sheehan household, 1920 U.S. Census, Kings County, N.Y., city of Brooklyn. NARA Microfilm Publication T625, roll 1157, enumeration district, sheet 6B, dwelling 64, family 152.

136   1929 Chicago, Illinois, City Directory.

137   Passenger Lists of Vessels Arriving at San Francisco, 1893–1953, NARA Microfilm Publication M1410, roll 425, ship SS *Virginia,* arrived 18 March 1929.

138   Edward J. Sheehan household, 1930 U.S. Census, Cook County, Ill., city of Chicago, NARA Microfilm Publication T626, roll 422, enumeration district 16-181, sheet 211B, dwelling 84, family 223.

139   City of Chicago, Cook County [Ill.] Certificate of Death, 1937, no. 21643, "Edward Jerome Sheehan."

140   Records of the Immigration and Naturalization Service; National Archives, *Passenger and Crew Lists of Vessels Arriving at New York, New York, 1897–1957,* NARA Microfilm Publication T715, roll 4818, p. 86.

141   City of Chicago, Cook County [Ill.] Certificate of Marriage, 1930, no. 1282941, "Thomas Francis Gallagher and Beatrice Marie Sheehan."

142   U.S. Selective Service System, *World War I Selective Service System Draft Registration Cards, 1917–1918* (Washington, D.C.: NARA), State of Connecticut, Spencer Alfred Sheehan, no. 1642.

143   Social Security Death Index.

144   Spencer Sheehan household, 1920 U.S. Census, New Haven County, Conn., city of Waterbury, NARA Publication T625, roll 195, enumeration district 449, sheet 4A, family 40, line 38.

145   Helen G. Sheehan household, 1930 U.S. Census, New Haven County, Conn., city of Waterbury, NARA Publication T626, roll 279, enumeration district 5-229, sheet 4A, p. 211 [printed], family 34, line 6.

146   U.S. Selective Service System, *World War I Selective Service System Draft Registration Cards, 1917–1918* (Washington, D.C.: NARA), State of Connecticut, Spencer Alfred Sheehan, no. 1642.

147   Spencer Sheehan household, 1920 U.S. Census, New Haven County, Conn., city of Waterbury, NARA Publication T625, roll 195, enumeration district 449, sheet 4A, family 40, line 38.

148   Helen G. Sheehan household, 1930 U.S. Census, New Haven County, Conn., city of Waterbury, NARA Publication T626, roll 279, enumeration district 5-229, sheet 4A, p. 211 [printed], family 34, line 6.

149   "Bill Sheehan," *Hot Springs Village Voice,* 10 March 2004, online at *www.hsvvoice.com*, accessed May 2011.

150   Ibid.

151   Texas State Department of Health Services, *Texas Marriage Index, 1966–2002.*

152   "Bill Sheehan," *Hot Springs Village Voice,* 10 March 2004, online at *www.hsvvoice.com,* accessed May 2011.

153   U.S. Public Records Index, Volume 1, online at *Ancestry.com,* accessed May 2011.

154   Ibid.

155   *Muster Rolls of U.S. Navy Ships, Stations, and Other Naval Activities, 01/01/1939–01/01/1949,* Record Group 24, *Records of the Bureau of Naval Personnel, 1798–2007;* NARA Series ARC *594996;* MLR *A1 135* and U.S. Public Records Index, Volume 1 online at *Ancestry.com,* accessed May 2011.

156   Social Security Death Index.

157   "Walter J. Sheehan Dies in Florida," Auburn, N.Y., *Citizen-Advertiser,* 4 February 1964, p. 2.

158   Ibid.

159   Social Security Death Index.

160   "Walter J. Sheehan Dies in Florida," Auburn, N.Y., *Citizen-Advertiser,* 4 February 1964, p. 2.

161   State of Florida, *Florida Death Index, 1877–1998* (Jacksonville: Florida Department of Health, Office of Vital Records, 1998).

162   Ibid.

163   Florida Department of Health, *Florida Divorce Index, 1927–2001* (Jacksonville: Florida Department of Health, certificate no. 040026).

164   Ibid.

165   National Cemetery Administration, *Nationwide Gravesite Locator,* online at *http://gravelocator.cem.va.gov.*

166   Social Security Death Index.

167   Ibid.

168   Pinellas County, Fla., Probate Division: Estate of William Daniel Sheehan, Sr., file no. 99-205.

169   Ibid.

170   Pinellas County, Fla., 6th Judicial Circuit Court, case no. 77-4764-99.

171   Records of the Immigration and Naturalization Service; National Archives, *Passenger and Crew Lists of Vessels Arriving at New York, New York, 1897–1957,* NARA Microfilm Publication T715, roll 4818, p. 86.

172   "Beatrice Sheehan Gallagher," *Augusta Chronicle,* 2 March 1988, p. 3B.

173   City of Chicago, Cook County [Ill.] Certificate of Marriage, 1930, no. 1282941, "Thomas Francis Gallagher and Beatrice Marie Sheehan."

174   Social Security Death Index.

175   "Thomas Gallagher," *Augusta Chronicle* 22 June 1984, p. 3C.

176   Records of the Immigration and Naturalization Service; National Archives, *Passenger and Crew Lists of Vessels Arriving at New York, New York, 1897–1957*, NARA Microfilm Publication T715, roll 4818, p. 86.

177   Beatrice Marie Sheehan, "A Study of the Biuret Reaction of an Amino Alcohol, Epichloramine" (Chicago: University of Chicago, 1931).

178   "Thomas Gallagher," *Augusta Chronicle,* 22 June 1984, p. 3C.

179   "Beatrice Sheehan Gallagher," *Augusta Chronicle*, 2 March 1988, p. 3B.

180   Ibid.

181   Pinellas County, Fla. 6th Judicial Circuit Court, case no. 77-4764-99.

182   Ibid.

183   Ibid.

ILLUSTRATION CREDITS

Grateful acknowledgment is made to the individuals and institutions who provided images for inclusion in this Keane family history. Keane family members have been particularly generous with their photographs and documents.

Main text:

18 Excerpted from *Primary Valuation of Tenements* for the Townland of Kilcloher, Parish of Kilballyowen, Barony of Moyarta, printed 20 August 1855.

19 Detail of Ordnance Survey Map of Kilcloher.

21 Kilcloher Townland, Kilballyowen Parish, Rahona Electoral Division, *General Valuation Revision Lists, Kilrush Rural District (Clare), 1856–1945,* Family History Library (FHL) Microfilm 819463.

37 Courtesy of David Bray.

46 Courtesy of Susan Bray Walker.

50 Courtesy of Susan Bray Walker.

Photo pages:

1 From *Colton's General Atlas* (1859), in the holdings of the New England Historic Genealogical Society.

2 Both images courtesy Clare County Library, Ireland. Photo of the Little Ark today: Sonia Schorman.

3 Top: From *Illustrated London News,* obtained via Clare County Library, Ireland. Bottom: Photo of Loop Head: Roger & Sue Diel. Courtesy Clare County Library.

4 Top: Library of Congress Prints and Photographs Division, LC-DIG-pga-01468. Bottom: Birds-eye view created by O. H. Bailey & Co. (Milwaukee: American Oleograph Co., 1875), Library of Congress, call no. G3784.B7A3 1875 .B3.

5 Top: Courtesy of Perkins School for the Blind, Watertown, Mass. Bottom: Courtesy of David Bray.

6 Top left: Courtesy of Betty Keane Rossbaum. Top right: Courtesy of Susan Bray Walker. Bottom: Courtesy of David Bray.

7 Top: Courtesy of Susan Bray Walker. Middle row: Courtesy of Betty Keane Rossbaum. Bottom left: Courtesy of David Bray. Bottom right: Courtesy of Herbert and Dorothy Keane Achtmeyer.

8   Top: Courtesy of Kevin Thomas Keane. Bottom: Courtesy of Susan Bray Walker.

9   Top left: Courtesy of John Francis Keane III. Top right: Courtesy of Andrée Keane Shields. Bottom left: Courtesy of Susan Bray Walker. Bottom right: National Archives and Records Administration (NARA), Washington D.C., *Passport Applications, January 2, 1906–March 31, 1925*; ARC Identifier 583830 / MLR Number A1 534; NARA Series: M1490; Roll # 2009.

10   Courtesy of David Bray.

11   Top: Courtesy of Susan Bray Walker. Bottom left and center: Courtesy of Herbert and Dorothy Achtmeyer. Bottom right: Courtesy of Patricia Keane Sparkman.

12   Top left and bottom: Courtesy of John Francis Keane III. Top right: Courtesy of Linda Keane Smith.

13   Courtesy of Andrée Keane Shields.

14   Top: Courtesy of Kevin Thomas Keane. Bottom left and right: Courtesy of Patricia Keane Sparkman.

15   Courtesy of Susan Bray Walker.

16   Courtesy of Patricia Keane Sparkman.

17   Top: Courtesy of David Bray. Bottom: Courtesy of Susan Bray Walker.

18   Top: Courtesy of Susan Bray Walker. Bottom: Courtesy of William Walker.

19   Courtesy of Christina "Justy" Keane.

20   Courtesy of Kevin Robert Keane.

21   Top row: Courtesy of Robert Medlin. Middle and bottom rows: Courtesy of Betty Keane Rossbaum and family.

22   Courtesy of Herbert and Dorothy Achtmeyer and family.

23   Top and middle: Courtesy of Patricia Keane Sparkman. Bottom: Courtesy of John C. Sparkman, Jr.

24   Top: Courtesy of Kevin Thomas Keane. Bottom row: Courtesy of Andrée Aird Primrose.

25   Top row: Courtesy of Clare Guydish. Bottom: Courtesy of Andrée Aird Primrose.

26   Courtesy of John Francis Keane III and family.

27   Courtesy of John Francis Keane III and family. Top photo by Caroline Bolick.

28   Top: Courtesy of Kevin Thomas Keane. Bottom: Courtesy of Susan Keane Trivison.

29   Courtesy of Andrée Keane Shields and family.

30   Top, middle left, bottom: Courtesy of Linda Keane Smith. Middle right: Courtesy of Glynn Keane Dugan.

31   Top: Courtesy of Glynn Keane Dugan. Middle and bottom: Courtesy of Linda Keane Smith.

32   Courtesy of David Bray.

INDEX

Blank lines indicate unknown names. Superscript numbers indicate generations. Page numbers precede by the letter p *refer to the photo inserts. Boldface page references correlate to an individual's primary listing.*